MW00776286

ECLIPSES

The Power Points of Astrology

by

Derek Appleby
and Maurice McCann

THE AQUARIAN PRESS

First published 1989

© DEREK APPLEBY and MAURICE McCANN 1989

*All rights reserved. No part of this book may be reproduced or
utilized in any form or by any means, electronic or mechanical,
including photocopying, recording or by any information storage and
retrieval system, without permission in writing from the Publisher.*

British Library Cataloguing in Publication Data

Appleby, Derek
Eclipses: the power-points of astrology.
1. Solar System. Eclipses. Astrological
aspects
I. Title   II. McCann, Maurice
133.5'85232

ISBN 0-85030-481-4

*The Aquarian Press is part of the Thorsons Publishing Group,
Wellingborough, Northamptonshire, NN8 2RQ, England*

Phototypeset by Harper Phototypesetters Limited, Northampton
Printed in Great Britain by Biddles Limited, Guildford, Surrey

1 3 5 7 9 10 8 6 4 2

ACKNOWLEDGEMENTS

We would like to express our appreciation to Pat Harding of Ridlington, Norfolk, Joyclyn Appleby of Torquay, Devon, and George Taylor of Durban, South Africa. Our thanks to Mike Harding and Nick Evans for technical assistance, and to Ananda Bagley of Electric Ephemeris, 214 Finchley Road, London NW3 for generously supplying the ephemeris used for all our calculations.

CONTENTS

INTRODUCTION

It became apparent, early in our astrological careers, that eclipses of the Sun and Moon have an important part to play in all branches of astrological study, but we were disappointed and somewhat frustrated to find a paucity of literature on the subject.

Eclipses, particularly total eclipses, demand universal attention because they cannot be ignored. Naturally they are of special interest to astrologers and astronomers, but also biologists, anthropologists and other scientists find them worthy of study because of the observable effects they have upon the human, animal and vegetable kingdoms. At a total eclipse, as the light of the Sun is obscured by the Moon and darkness falls, flowers which normally close up by night and open by day react by closing their petals; birds go to roost and animals begin to bed-down. As totality ends, the cock stretches his neck and begins to crow, to welcome the 'new day'.

On 30 June 1973, one of the three exceptionally long eclipses of this century occurred. It offered scientists a unique opportunity to record the event with the aid of the most modern equipment. This eclipse lasted 7 minutes 4 seconds and will not recur until 25 June 2150 when the period of totality will last 7 minutes 14 seconds. British, French and American scientists aboard Concorde, the most advanced aeroplane of our age, were able to follow the track of the eclipse from Las Palmas in the Canary Islands and witness the obscuration of the Sun for 70 minutes. The eclipse tracked over regions of Africa, giving anthropologists the opportunity to record the reactions of the El Molo tribe who live by the shores of Lake Rudolph. However, the natives thought the scientists with all their paraphernalia had come to take away the Sun. Fortunately for the scientists, the tribesmen were reassured when the Sun appeared again.

Most countries of the world have their myths concerning eclipses. In many religions, drum-beating would be carried out and shouting

and other noises made to frighten off the heavenly monsters and
beasts that were thought to threaten the Sun or the Moon. Since
the Sun's rays always returned, such ceremonies were inevitably
successful in chasing the enemy away.

Responsibility for destroying the light of the Sun was attributed
to the dragon in China and Thailand. The North American Indians
believed it was the fault of the dogs and coyotes, while the Indians
of South America put it down to the jaguar. Throughout Africa and
Indonesia snakes were given the blame, but in India, more accurately,
it was Rahu and Ketu (the Indian names for the north and south
nodes). The most romantic and attractive explanation was given by
the Tahitians. The light of heaven was obscured as the Sun and Moon
came together to make love, and so beget the stars.

The rules laid down by Ptolemy in his *Tetrabiblos* have been
generally accepted by astrologers since they were formulated. They
do not appear to have been seriously tested, at least in modern times.
We have not set out to test the rules exhaustively but to demonstrate
that there is good reason to take them seriously.

We offer for your consideration the results of specific studies
concerning various aspects of the application of eclipses to mundane
and natal astrology. We hope that you will accept that eclipses are
worthy of respect, and take our studies as a starting point for your
own investigations. Make a start by listing all the eclipses which have
occurred during your lifetime, and see how they apply in your own
chart.

Regiomontanus cusps have been used throughout this book as
it is the preferred system of the authors. All secondary progressions
are based on the day-for-a-year method and the angles have been
progressed using solar arc in longitude unless otherwise stated.

The many charts in this book contain the planetary symbols
familiar to anyone with a knowledge of astrology, but for ease of
recognition we show here the symbols we have employed to represent
New Moons, Full Moons and solar and lunar eclipses:

New Moon: ☽
Full Moon: ○
Solar Eclipse: ◑
Lunar Eclipse: ●

1.

'BLACK MUNDAY'

In modern Europe, eclipses of the Sun and Moon come and go with little comment outside astrological and astronomical circles, yet in other days the appearance of a solar eclipse, especially one that was visible, was enough to cause a considerable stir among all classes and conditions of people. As astrologers, we are primarily concerned with the astrological judgement of solar and lunar eclipses, as that is what fascinates and excites us, and we are impatient to share our investigations with you. Before we begin at the beginning and attempt to describe what an eclipse actually is, and how it differs from a run-of-the-mill New or Full Moon, let us dip into history and see what our astrological forefathers made of 'Black Munday!'

On 'Black Munday', 29 March 1652 (O.S.), at 10.30 a.m. the Sun was eclipsed in the 19th degree of Aries (see Fig. 1.1), and this phenomenon provoked something akin to panic throughout the country. The rich loaded up their coaches and fled from London, while mountebanks did a thriving trade in cordials which purported to allay the effects of the eclipse. At Dalkeith, the poor were said to have thrown away their possessions, 'casting themselves on their backs, and their eyes towards heaven and praying most passionately that Christ would let them see the Sun again, and save them'. Panic and terror was not universal, however; the contemporary diarist John Evelyn, who seems to have spent much of his time listening to sermons, made the following entry for that day: 'Was that celebrated Eclipse of the Sun, so much threatened by the Astrologers, & had so exceedingly alarm'd the whole Nation, so as hardly any would worke, none stir out of their houses; so ridiculously were they abused by knavish and ignorant star-gazers'.

Certainly this eclipse was the subject of much comment by leading astrologers of the time. Astrologically the eclipse chart is rather strenuous, with Saturn on the Ascendant at London, and the eclipse

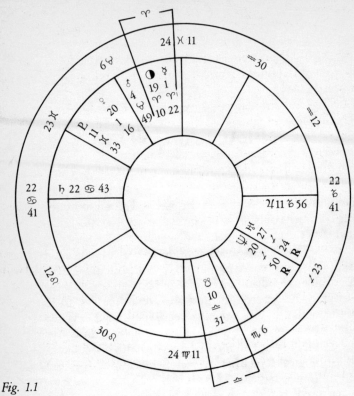

Fig. 1.1

BLACK MUNDAY
8 APRIL 1652 (N.S.)
10.30 A.M., LONDON

degree applying by square aspect to it from the tenth house. John
Booker called it 'the greatest Eclipse that we have had in England
these many Centuryes of years'. He predicted great problems for
all kinds of honourable personages, such as emperors, kings, princes,
lords, governors, magistrates, and those holding high office — in
particular those who had the nineteenth degree of cardinal signs
in prominent places in their nativities, or any direction to those
degrees.

   The evil configurations of the eclipse, with the Moon applying
to the most hateful and unfortunate square of Saturn weak by sign
in the Ascendant, ruler of the seventh, eighth, and ninth houses,
in opposition to his own house, in square to the Sun, and in partile
opposition to an ill-dignified Jupiter, made the astronomer Andreas
Argolus set the figure for Rome in his ephemeris for 1652. 'Three

words say it all', wrote Booker, '*perniciem offeres magnam*', (which freely translated means 'God help the Pope!'). Nine hundred days would the effects of this eclipse afflict all the places under the dominion of the cardinal signs, beginning at Michaelmas, reaching their height about St Jamestide 1653, and ending in the middle of March 1655.

George Wharton agreed that the eclipse was bad news for men in high places, and predicted the exile, captivity or slaughter of some famous king or prince. He also thought that there would be trouble between the common people and magistrates, resulting in ruin to both. He listed all the towns and cities ruled by cardinal signs, and 29 different kinds of disaster. He calculated that the duration of the eclipse would be 2 hours 28 minutes 48 seconds, and that its effect would manifest between 4 August 1652 and 26 January 1654.

Nicholas Culpepper really went to town: 'All the evils the sword, sedition, famine, pestilence can do to Europe, may be expected from this Eclipse.' According to him, few princes in Europe would escape the fury of God's vengeance to be visited on them through this eclipse, indeed every place in the world where the eclipse was visible and angular was in for a hard time, 'together with HOGHENS MOGHENS, ILLUSTRISSIMO's and TITTILLADO's'. He quoted a number of biblical texts of a doomladen and threatening nature, and warmed to his theme with:

> The Lord of the Eclipse is Mars, who, according to Origanus, threatens that the fruits of the earth shall be consumed by fire, heat, and the dryness of ayr, extorted to violence, or consumed by soldiery; he threatens sickness of heat and dryness, war and bloodshed, rapine and extortion; he sets Europe together by the ears, one Nation against another, divides Kingdoms against themselves; he raiseth sedition and tumults, Kings are mad, and subjects stubborn, violent diseases of choler, young men perish by the sword and by the pestilence, Cities are consumed by fire, and ruined, Countries are spoyled by injuries, murther, rapine and theeving, and the ayr is hot, pestilential and mortal.

Culpepper absolved Rome from the effects of the eclipse, and for that reason could not see the second coming of Christ happening during its potency, but this eclipse would make way for it. He concluded with a few exhortations of a biblical nature to princes, to the saints, to England, and 'the poor dejected Jew'.

A most interesting exposition of the effects of this eclipse came from the pen of William Lilly, in his book *Annus Tenebrosus*, specially written on the eclipse, and we feel it is worth repeating it in some detail. He said that with 11 digits (out of a possible 12) of the Sun's surface obscured, the eclipse was as near to total as made no difference. '. . . two years and one quarter shall all Europe be sensible of this prodigious eclipse its effects.'

It would be disastrous, he said, for all cities which had the sign of the eclipse (Aries) upon their Ascendant at their first foundation, and it would be felt by the greatest persons of Europe. England would be affected very powerfully: 'God of all the world what wilt thou do with us English? If thou deprive us of our lights, of our worthies, of our Members of Parliament, of our Nobles, of our Gentry, as such as have commanded, such as have governed, such as have not obeyed.' He predicted 'new rule or dominion' in Italy, but not in England, a great misfortune to or the death of the King of Spain, and warned

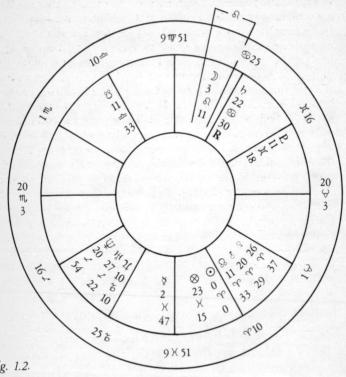

Fig. 1.2.

ARIES INGRESS
19 MARCH 1652 (N.S.)
22.53.45 HRS, LONDON

the French that war was at their gates. Lilly agreed with his colleagues about the general misfortune that this eclipse would bring to those in high office and positions, although he also included fishermen and those who lived close to the sea, but in the light of the contemporary political scene and subsequent developments, it is his observations on the fortunes of the Dutch and Scots that we find particularly interesting: '. . . but give me leave to say, that according to the best of my understanding, it designs or predicts an absolute falling out or breach of friendship betwixt us and the Dutch.' After mentioning that the Aries ingress of that year (*see* Fig. 1.2) indicated the same thing, he then went on to compare the two races astrologically:

> The English have Aries, a fiery, dry, manly and warlike sign the Ascendant of England; the Hollanders have Cancer, a moist, waterish and feminine, phlegmatic sign for their Ascendant. Aries has the representation of cattle, on which we feed; Cancer pressents Fish, Herbs and Trash, on which the Hollander feeds: England is dry, mountainous: Holland is moist and waterish, low and moorish: The English love War and to fight at Land; the Hollander is totally for the Sea. We have a commanding regal sign for England, they a weak and effeminate one; Aries beholds Cancer with a Quadrate; neither Nation love each other. In regard Mars doth signify England, and the Moon both Scotland and the Hollander, and the two planets natures are so contrary as fire and water, therefore though we have done both Dutch and Scots so many civilities, and enriched both those unthankful people, and thereby have deserved so much at both their hands, yet they never did, nor will they ever effect us, yet will they ever be acting cruelties upon our People wheresoever they can find advantage against them: besides, the two signs viz. Aries and Cancer do behold each other with square aspect, or an aspect of malice. This eclipse doth promise us many rich prizes from the Dutch, both in the Levant Sea, on the coasts of Turkey in the Straights and upon our own coasts, if they do not comply with our present authority, yea many within our own harbours.

He did make many references to 'Commonwealth' (which England then was, having decapitated its king in 1649), and indicated that the eclipse was very powerful for England with some benefits for the country:

> . . . the raising up of some one man or men, or state or commonwealth unto a greater height of sovereignty, rule or command, than either he hath at present (if this befall a particular man) or that

commonwealth or state, if Providence dispose of his greatness there we English are not excluded from this dominion. Nothing will impede us from being great and terrible to all Europe but our own Divisions.

Lilly concluded his discourse by bringing down the wrath of the eclipse upon all manner of four-footed beasts, sheep, oxen and cows, horses, rabbits and hogs. He predicted piracy on the high seas, and much damage from high tides, sea floods, and land floods. His final warning reads:

This eclipse is the portent of Famine in Ireland, mortality and poverty in Scotland, a general misfortune unto the Dutch in all their sea services; of corruption and self-ends amongst them; of a plague, a death of men both in England, Ireland, and Scotland.

At the time of the eclipse, the English Civil War was coming to an end, Charles II had fled to France, and the last Royalist stronghold was to fall with the capitulation of Dunettar Castle in May of that year. Lilly was probably quite close to the political situation. He had been consulted by both King Charles I and prominent Parliamentarians at various times and was doubtless able to make some shrewd political judgements about the likely course events might take. Nevertheless it is remarkable, in view of his predictions about the Dutch, that the first Anglo-Dutch War effectively began on 19 May 1652 when Admiral Blake engaged a Dutch fleet off the Goodwin Sands, causing them to withdraw with the loss of two vessels. A declaration of war followed in July. There were a number of sea battles of significance over the next two years, culminating in the Battle of Texel on 31 July 1653, when the combined Dutch fleet of about a hundred ships, in an attempt to shatter the English blockade, engaged the English fleet (which was of equal strength) and was forced to withdraw after a bitter 12-hour contest and the loss of 30 men-of-war, the death of 1,600 sailors and their Admiral Maarten Tromp. The war ended with the signing of the Treaty of Westminster on 5 April 1654.

As for the Commonwealth, one man did rise up to greater heights of power and sovereignty in England, for within the potency of the eclipse, on 20 April 1653, Oliver Cromwell dissolved the Rump Parliament, and when the Barebones or Little Parliament failed, he was solemnly installed as Lord Protector on 16 December 1653.

Whether there was famine in Ireland we cannot say, but there was certainly suffering, with the final suppression of the 1641

Rebellion by Cromwellian forces at Galway in May 1652. Even in France, which was ruled by a minor, Louis XIV, and Cardinal Mazarin, a civil war which had its roots in a revolt against absolutism, known as the Fronde, lasted from 1648 until 1653. There was a battle on 5 July 1652 which resulted in the collapse of the Fronde in Paris, although it held out for a further year in Bordeaux.

Lilly's predictions for this eclipse were really most impressive, and while the sceptic might be forgiven for dismissing them as inspired guesswork, it must be said that he did carefully explain his astrological reasoning in his exposition. Indeed, far from abusing his readers (as alleged by John Evelyn), Lilly went to great pains to reassure them in his book *Annus Tenebrosus*:

> Whereas I find a general fear possessing mens spirits concerning the darkness which the eclipse portends, and some queries whether it threaten not danger unto these people who are either in the fields about their labouring occasions, or otherwise occupied without doors on their domestic affairs, I say it threatens no man or cattle with danger in that consideration . . . there is no danger at all to any that shall be the spectators of it.

It is doubtful whether we can ever fully appreciate his judgements in retrospect, for the flavour of the times has evaporated with the passage of the centuries.

2.

THE ASTRONOMY OF ECLIPSES

The Ecliptic

The ecliptic, or Sun-Earth plane, is the path described by the apparent motion of the Sun as seen from the Earth. The ecliptic is a great circle of 360° celestial longitude. It is divided into 12 signs of 30°

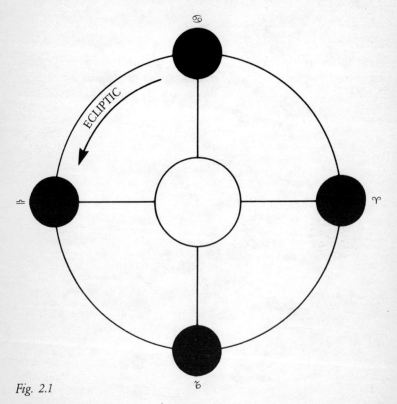

Fig. 2.1

each, and the positions of the planets can be measured in relation to its arc in degrees, minutes, and seconds of longitude, beginning at 0° Aries, and moving through the zodiac sign by sign to the end of Pisces. The positons of the planets can also be measured in celestial latitude noth or south of the Sun-Earth plane.

Figure 2.1 demonstrates the situation. The Earth is taken to be static. The Sun appears to move along the ecliptic, and its position can be fixed at any time in longitude, e.g. 0° Aries, 0° Cancer, 0° Libra, 0° Capricorn. Since the Sun and the Earth together create the Sun-Earth plane, they cannot be north or south of each other, so the Sun never has any latitude.

Celestial longitude and latitude should not be confused with terrestrial longitude and latitude. Longitude on Earth is the distance of any place east or west of the Greenwich Meridian and latitude on Earth is the distance of any place north or south of the equator.

Syzygies

A lunation, or New Moon, is the phenomenon which occurs when the Moon, during her orbit of the Earth, arrives at the same zodiacal

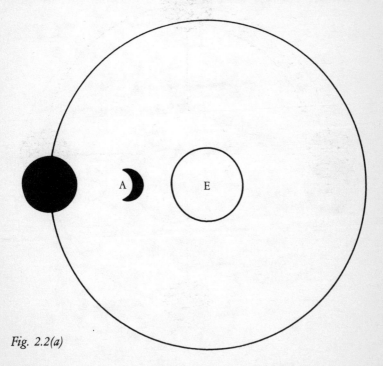

Fig. 2.2(a)

position as the Sun. As she passes that conjunction, the Moon begins to wax, or increase in light, until she arrives at the opposite point to the Sun, at which point she becomes a Full Moon. As she passes that opposition to the Sun, the Moon begins to wane, or decrease in light, until she makes the conjunction with the Sun once more. New and Full Moons are known collectively as *syzygies*.

Figure 2.2(a) shows the Moon, at **A**, in the same zodiacal position as the Sun, say at 0° Aries. She thus interposes herself between the Sun and the Earth, and she will be visible in the night sky as a thin crescent, the New Moon. Figure 2.2(b) shows the Moon, at **B**, in the opposite zodiacal position to the Sun, say at 0° Libra. The Earth thus interposes itself between the Sun and the Moon; the Moon will then be visible in the night sky as a bright disc, the Full Moon.

An astronomical (synodic) 'lunation' is the period between identical phases of the Moon. Since the Earth moves around the Sun, the astronomical lunation is slightly longer than the orbital period of the Moon. It is in fact 29.53059 Earth days.

Eclipses

One heavenly body is said to be eclipsed by another when the latter

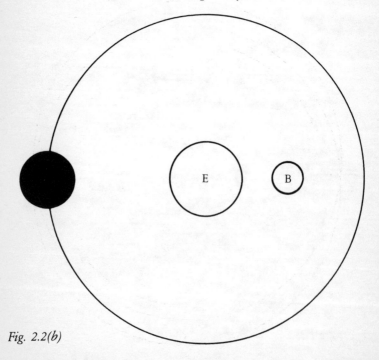

Fig. 2.2(b)

passes between the observer and the first body so as to obscure all or part of it. When, at a New Moon, the light of the Sun is totally or partially obscured by the body of the Moon, a solar eclipse occurs. When, at a Full Moon, the shadow of the Earth totally or partially obscures the disc of the Moon, a lunar eclipse occurs.

Why isn't *every* syzygy an eclipse? What is it that makes a New Moon different from a solar eclipse and a Full Moon different from a lunar eclipse?

The Nodes

If the Moon revolved around the Earth in the plane of the ecliptic, every syzygy would be an eclipse, but since the orbit of the Moon is inclined to the ecliptic by 5 degrees, so that she is sometimes above the Sun-Earth plane and sometimes below it and therefore has latitude, only about 16 per cent of syzygies actually turn out to be eclipses.

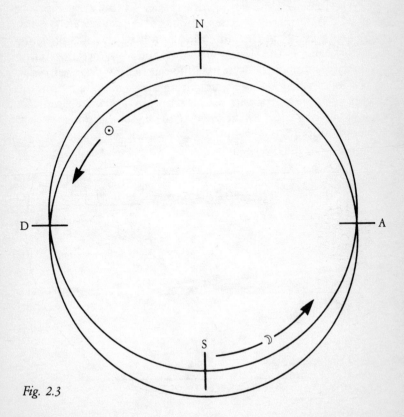

Fig. 2.3

Figure 2.3 demonstrates the monthly movement of the Moon, and gives an idea of how her orbit is inclined to the ecliptic. Imagine the Earth static and the Sun and Moon moving along the ecliptic. Now see how at point **A**, the ascending node, the Moon cuts the ecliptic and thus has no latitude. She then begins to rise until she reaches her greatest northern latitude at **N**. She cuts the ecliptic again at the descending node **D**, and reaches her greatest southern latitude at **S**, before moving towards the ascending node once more. The maximum latitude of the Moon is a little over 5°.

Twelve times and a bit, or 12.368266 times, in the course of a year the Moon follows this pattern, and twice a month she cuts the ecliptic, once at each nodal point. Figure 2.4 illustrates the movement of the Moon for February 1986. She began the month having just cut the ecliptic at the descending node and rapidly descended to 5° of south latitude. She cut the ecliptic at the ascending node on the 14 February, rose to 5° of north latitude and, as the month ended, she was approaching the descending node again. The Moon, moving at approximately 13° a day, completes her orbit of the ecliptic in a synodic month, but the Sun, trundling along at a stately 1° a day, only manages 30° in the same time. It follows that at some time during the month the Moon will pass the Sun (conjunction). At that point they will enjoy the same longitude and a New Moon will occur. It also follows that at some time during the course of a month the Moon will pass the opposite point to the Sun (opposition). At that point their longitudes will be opposed to one another and there will be a Full Moon. More often than not she will conjunct or oppose the Sun when she has latitude and is nowhere near the ecliptic, as

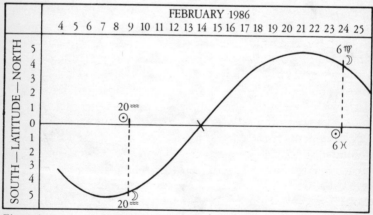

Fig. 2.4

she did on 9 February 1986 when there was a New Moon and on 24 February 1986 when there was a Full Moon. More often than not the Moon will cross the ecliptic when she is not in conjunction with or in opposition to the Sun, as she did on 14 February 1986, so then there cannot be a New or Full Moon let alone an eclipse. If at the same time as the Moon is in conjunction with or in opposition to the Sun she is also upon or close to the ecliptic and thus has little or no latitude, the New Moon will be a solar eclipse and the Full Moon a lunar eclipse, as on 10 April 1986, and 17 October 1986 (see Fig. 2.5).

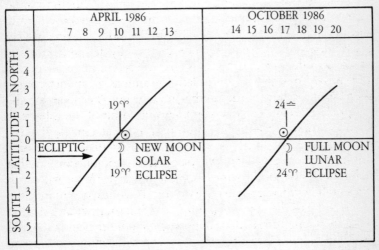

Fig. 2.5

Now because the Moon moves about 12 times faster than the Sun, she intersects the ecliptic 24 times a year, but the Sun only manages to be in the area of intersection on two occasions during the year, once at the ascending node and once at the descending node. So twice a year there is a time when the line of the nodes is pointing towards the Sun; this is the moment of node alignment. If the Moon arrives at a node at the same moment as node alignment, there will be an exactly central eclipse of Sun or Moon, but this coincidence rarely happens. There is a two-week period on either side of the exact moment of node alignment when the line of the nodes is almost in line with the Sun. A New or Full Moon falling during these periods will usually be close enough to the nodes to cause an eclipse. The closer a syzygy is to the exact moment of node alignment, the more central is the eclipse; the further away the syzygy is from the moment

of node alignment, the more marginal the eclipse becomes so that
eventually it ceases to be an eclipse at all. When the Moon is within
18° of the node an eclipse may occur. When she gets to within 11°
of the node, eclipses will begin to be central, which means that there
is a line on the surface of the Earth from any point of which the
centres of Sun and Moon appear coincident.

In essence, the requirements of an eclipse are a New or Full Moon
occurring on or very near the ecliptic, with the Moon having little
or no latitude, and an imaginary straight line that could be drawn
from the Earth linking the centres of Sun and Moon.

Eclipse seasons

The first so-called eclipse season occurs as the Moon comes close to
the ascending node, and for about a month there is the likelihood
of syzygies turning out to be eclipses. About six months later the
Moon arrives at the opposite point of her greater orbit and thus close
to the descending node, and syzygies falling close to this point will
again cause eclipses. So there are two eclipse seasons within the year,
the first linked with the ascending node and the second with the
descending node.

If the time between one node alignment and the next node
alignment happened to be exactly six months, eclipses would always
occur at the same season of the year, but the actual time is 173.3
days, so eclipse seasons regress, and eclipses will therefore eventually
occur in every season.

The Moon's nodes revolve in the ecliptic from east to west once
in every 18.5995 years. For example, on 1 January 1986 the ascending
node was at 5° 47′ Taurus, while 19 years earlier, on 1 January 1967,
it was at 13° 19′ Taurus. The actual annual change is in the order
of 19° 20′ 28″.

Eclipse intensity

The orbit of the Moon around the Earth is elliptical, so at certain
times she is closer to the Earth than at others and thus appears larger
in the sky. For example, on 8 January 1986 the Moon was in perigee
(her nearest point to the Earth), on 20 January she was in apogee
(her greatest distance from the Earth), and on 4 February she was
in perigee again. The Moon's revolution from perigee to perigee is
known as an *anomalistic month*. Obviously the closer the Moon is
to the Earth, the greater the degree of obscuration, either by the body
of the Moon to the disc of the Sun in the case of a solar eclipse,

or by the shadow of the Earth on the disc of the Moon in the case of a lunar eclipse. (See Fig. 2.6.)

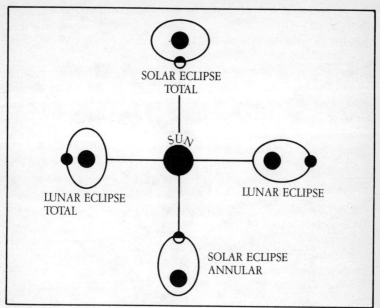

Fig. 2.6

It is an interesting fact that even when at her brightest the Moon only reflects 7 per cent of the Sun's light.

Visibility
A solar eclipse is total when the disc of the Sun is completely obscured, it is annular when the disc of the Sun is visible all around the Moon,

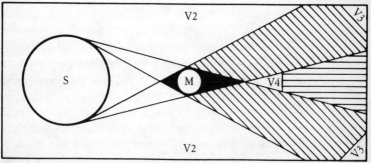

Fig. 2.7

and it is partial when only a part of the Sun's disc is obscured. A lunar eclipse may be total, partial or penumbral (when astronomically it barely qualifies as an eclipse). Astrologers take no account of penumbral lunar eclipses.

Figure 2.7 shows how a solar eclipse is formed. It will be seen that the Moon (**M**) casts shadows represented by the shaded areas in the space surrounding the Sun (**S**). The intensity of the eclipse to the viewer (**V**) will vary according to his position. At **V1**, in the heavily shaded areas, the eclipse will be *total*; at **V2**, outside the shaded areas, the eclipse will not be visible; at **V3**, within the diagonally shaded areas, the eclipse will be *partial*; at **V4**, within the horizontally shaded areas, the Sun will be visible all around the Moon — this is an *annular* eclipse. The degree to which the eclipse will be experienced, whether total, partial or annular, will depend upon the relationship of the Earth to the Sun and Moon as explained above, and the location of the viewer upon the surface of the Earth at the time of the eclipse.

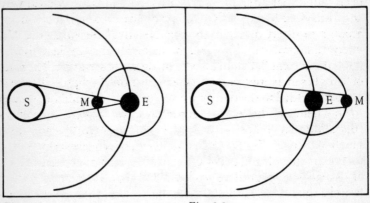

Fig. 2.8   *Fig. 2.9*

Figure 2.8 represents a solar eclipse, with part of the Earth's surface within a shadow cone (over this area the eclipse will be total).

Figure 2.9 represents a lunar eclipse, with the whole of the Moon within the cone, and demonstrates how the eclipse would be visible over a complete hemisphere of the Earth.

Duration
The duration of an eclipse, from first to last contact, of the Moon with the Sun, depends upon the anomalies of Sun and Moon, i.e., their distances from apogee. This length of time varies between two

hours and five hours, and the period of totality between one and
seven minutes.

It is important for the astrologer to know the duration of an eclipse,
and this and other relevant information does appear in some
almanacs. For the mathematically inclined, Sepharial explains how
to work it out in his *Eclipses in Theory and Practice*.

Frequency

Solar eclipses occur more often than lunar eclipses, with a miminum
of two in a year to a maximum of five. There are usually two lunar
eclipses a year, but sometimes only one and sometimes none that
are total or partial.

The Saros Cycle

The Sun's passage through one of the nodes is 18.6 days less than
a tropical year, and thus an *eclipse year* is about 346.4 days. It has
been found that after 19 eclipse years, equalling 18 tropical years
and 11 days, or 10 days if five leap years have occurred, the Sun and
Moon return very nearly to the same relative position again. This
interval is known as the *saros* and was named by the Greeks, although
it was the ancient Babylonians who made the observation. The value
of Saros lies in its application to the prediction of eclipses. If 18 years
11 days is added to the date of a given eclipse, it should be possible
to anticipate another eclipse. For interest, we took the date of the
'Black Munday' eclipse — 8 April 1652 (Gregorian) — and using
Hugh MacCraig's *The 200 Year Ephemeris*, which gives eclipse dates
for the nineteenth and twentieth centuries, added successive blocks
of 18 years 11 days until we arrived at 17 July 1814. Sure enough we
found a solar eclipse listed for that date. Then, through the magic
of the computer, we checked out the ones in between. In each case
an eclipse fell within a day of the dates we had calculated. The first
column below gives the date of the eclipse. The second column gives
the degree of the eclipse, the third the degree of the node (ascending
node in every case), the fourth the distance between the eclipse degree
and the node degree, and the fifth the celestial latitude of the Moon:

Eclipse date	Moon		Node		Sun/Node	Lat. Moon
08.4.1652	19°10′	Aries	10°31′	Aries	8°39′	0°47′N
19.4.1670	29°52′	Aries	21°48′	Aries	8° 4′	0°44′N
30.4.1688	10°31′	Taurus	03°05′	Taurus	7°26′	0°41′N
12.5.1706	21°06′	Taurus	14°22′	Taurus	6°44′	0°37′N

Eclipse date	Moon		Node		Sun/Node	Lat. Moon
22.5.1724	01°39′	Gemini	25°38′	Taurus	6° 1′	0°33′N
03.6.1742	12°09′	Gemini	06°55′	Gemini	5°14′	0°28′N
13.6.1760	22°37′	Gemini	18°12′	Gemini	4°25′	0°24′N
24.6.1778	03°04′	Cancer	29°29′	Gemini	3°35′	0°19′N
04.7.1796	13°31′	Cancer	10°46′	Cancer	2°45′	0°14′N
17.7.1814	23°58′	Cancer	22°03′	Cancer	1°55′	0°10′N

Although there is an eclipse again after a Saros, and although the situation is very similar, there are differences. If the nodical month was the same as the synodic month, the Moon would be at the same distance from the node after a Saros, but it is not; she is slightly further back, because a Saros consists of 223 synodic months (6585.321 days) and 242 nodical months (6585.357 days). Another measure which almost coincides is 239 anomalistic months (6585.538 days). Thus, after a Saros, the Moon returns not only very close to its previous position with respect to the node, but also with respect to its distance from the Earth. The Moon therefore appears practically the same size from the Earth and the duration of the eclipse is very similar. The fraction .321 days from the synodic months measure has the effect of making each successive eclipse in a Saros series occur about 116° of terrestial longitude further west, so that after three Saros cycles it will have returned almost to its original position, but farther north or south.

It will be seen from the above list that after each Saros the eclipse degree is a little nearer the node, so the eclipse will be visible a little further south each time. It will also be apparent that eventually the series will pass the point where an eclipse is possible, within 18° of the node, or 11° for a central eclipse, so it must have a beginning and an end. There are some 70 eclipses in a series spanning 1,260 years.

With the knowledge of Saros, a computer and a good programme, it is arguably possible to examine the astrological detail of any eclipse in history or the future.

3.

THE GENERAL EFFECTS OF ECLIPSES

Judgement

It is important to distinguish between mundane and natal astrology when judging the effects of eclipses, lunations and plenilunia. Although these branches of the art frequently intertwine, there are definite differences of application. We shall deal specificially with natal astrology in the last chapters of this book; in this first part we are mainly but not exclusively concerned with mundane matters.

We are firmly convinced that the technique of judging mundane charts is, in the final analysis, a matter of individual art. It is just not possible to lay down a set of rules which, if followed carefully, will allow any astrologer to predict the effects of an eclipse. The condition of each planet, each house, and each aspect must be carefully weighed in the mind of an artist, and assessed against the background of contemporary affairs. After much consideration, not a little inspiration, and a dash of luck, the astrologer may arrive at a judgement which is later vindicated by events.

There is no infallible formula, but nearly two thousand years ago Claudius Ptolemy set out in the *Tetrabiblos* a system of judgement which has survived the passage of time and has been employed by astrologers ever since. Ptolemy's method was described by William Lilly in *An Easie and Familiar Method Whereby to Judge the Effects Depending upon Eclipses Either of the Sun or Moon.* The essence of Ptolemy's method is incorporated into this chapter, for it provides a convenient base upon which the astrologer can build according to his or her experience. (Lilly's pamphlet is reproduced in its entirety in Appendix 1.)

Mundane Charts

When attempting judgement of eclipses, or any mundane figure, the chart should be timed for the moment the particular phenomenon occurred and located for the city one is interested in, or the capital city of the nation under consideration. We will shortly deal with the traditional method for arriving at the most likely time when the effects of an eclipse may be expected to manifest, and, while we intend to concentrate upon eclipses, lunations and plenilunia, it will be necessary from time to time to refer to the following mundane charts for the purposes of comparison.

Cardinal Ingress Figures — Figures erected for the Sun's ingress into each of the cardinal signs (Aries, Cancer, Libra, Capricorn) are thought to give general indications of events which will affect the nation during the period of the figure's potency. The beginning of the astrological year is taken from the moment of the Sun's ingress into Aries (the vernal equinox), and it is this chart which is usually regarded as the most important of the ingresses. However, the traditional rule states that it is potent for the whole of the year only if a fixed sign rises, for six months if a common sign rises, and for three months only if a cardinal sign is upon the Ascendant. It follows that at the expiry of the potency of one chart, the chief consideration is transferred to the next one in line, taking Aries as the starting point.

Neomenium — *the New Moon of the Year* — The New Moon of the Year is generally reckoned to be the lunation preceding the Aries ingress, but some say it is the lunation nearest the ingress and we concur with that view. Its value and the likely span of its influence is uncertain.

Great conjunctions and other phenomena — Conjunctions occurring between Jupiter, Saturn, Uranus, Neptune or Pluto are liable to be most significant in the judgement of future developments, most probably on a long-term basis, and this field is wide open for investigation by aspiring astrologers. Charts may be erected for other phenomena such as the ingress into the signs of the outer planets, comets, etc.

When judging mundane charts, one must relate the houses, signs and planets in the scheme to national affairs, and a broad description of their influence and areas of dominion follows.

The rulerships suggested in the following lists provide a starting point. Later we will attempt to demonstrate their validity or otherwise by investigating, from an astrological standpoint, certain important events in the experience of nations, cities, great men and humble citizens.

The Influence of the Houses and Signs

The first house — Aries   **National identity**
The condition of a nation and its population; the collective national character.

The second house — Taurus   **The economy**
National finance and resources; financial institutions; trade.

The third house — Gemini   **Communications**
All forms of national communications; schools; language; neighbouring countries.

The fourth house — Cancer   **Heritage**
National roots, tradition, the collective experience of the race; agriculture and land; property; weather; opposition to the government; the common people and women in particular. *This house should refelect the stability of a nation, or lack of it.*

The fifth house — Leo   **Culture and leisure**
The creative expression of a nation; all art forms; sport and entertainment; speculation and gambling; children and the birth-rate; national celebrations; ambassadors; the House of Lords.

The sixth house — Virgo   **Health and service**
The medical profession and the health of the people (it is probable that the National Health Service is a twelfth house matter); the armed forces; the workers (some say Trades Unions, but there is a case for giving them to the eleventh house); servants of the nation — the Civil Service.

The seventh house — Libra   **Diplomacy**
International relations; treaties and alliances; wars and disputes; marriage and divorce.

The eighth house — Scorpio   **Mortality and Regeneration**
By tradition this house is concerned with public mortality and the death of national figures, but we have given it the description *regeneration* because we feel it shows the ability of a nation to recover

from devastation and disaster, the things that result from the seventh house of war. International finance; death duties; mortgages, insurance and taxation.

The ninth house — Sagittarius   Aspiration
Religion, law, philosophy and science; higher education; international communications, shipping and aviation; colonial affairs; books and publishing.

The tenth house — Capricorn   Government
Monarchs, dictators, presidents; national power and prestige; the 'Establishment'. This is the house of power and those who wield it are found here. The House of Commons, which actually advises those in power, is of the eleventh house.

The eleventh house — Aquarius   Associations
The House of Commons; local authorities; associations, societies, fraternal groups (possibly Trades Unions). Friends of the nation (this house holds sway over countries with which a nation has a special relationship, and in Britain's case it might be appropriate to include Australia, Canada and New Zealand, and perhaps even the USA). We have found this house important in respect of child adoption.

The twelfth house — Pisces   Care and crime
The sick, hospitals and asylums; charitable organizations and institutions; The National Health Service. Enclosed orders; occult societies; prisons, criminals and crime; spies and subversives; the secret service; scandal; public sorrow and distress.

The Dominion of the Planets

(Tradition gives a certain area of influence to each planet, we believe that many of these associations may need revising in the light of modern experience, so the planetary rulerships given below should be taken as a general guide.)

The Sun — The king; president; and those in control of the nation.
The Moon — The people; women in general; crops and weather.
Mercury — National communications; the media; education
Venus — Festivities; finance; arts: peace.
Mars — The armed forces; war and violence; pestilence.
Jupiter — Prosperity; the Law; the Church.

Saturn —   Land and buildings; administration and government; restrictive legislation.

Uranus —   The administrators of power; democracy; radical forces; electrical power; aviation; television.

Neptune —   Charitable institutions and hospitals; the sea and shipping; crime and scandal; oil and drugs.

Pluto —   Mines; criminal underworld; war; police; nuclear power.

While accepting these rulerships as a guide, it is always necessary to be flexible in one's approach to a mundane chart. For example: the Sun is the planet of the king, but a monarch is of the tenth house, so Saturn, ruler of the tenth sign, might also signify the king.

Time of Potency

Opinions vary as to the length of time an eclipse will remain potent. If there is validity in the claim that it will remain potent until the next eclipse, one may assume that it has an *immediate* effect. However, Ptolemy said that the effects of a solar eclipse endure for as many years as the obscuration, from first to last contact, lasts in hours; and a lunar eclipse for as many months as hours of obscuration. By this measurement a solar eclipse may remain potent for between two and five years. Ptolemy also suggested that, after calculating the length of time in years that a solar eclipse should remain effective, that period is then divided into equal parts and applied as follows:

(a) When the eclipse falls nearest to the *Eastern Horizon*, its first effects will manifest within the first four-month period after the date of the eclipse, and the height of its general influence will operate during the first third-part of the whole period of potency.

(b) If the eclipse falls nearest to the *Midheaven*, its first effects will manifest within the second four-month period after the date of the eclipse, and the height of its general influence will operate during the second third-part of the whole period of potency.

(c) When an eclipse falls nearest to the *Western Horizon*, the first effects will manifest during the third four-month period from the date of the eclipse, and the height of its general influence will operate during the final third-part of the whole period of potency.

The formula for a lunar eclipse is almost the same, but since we must deal in months instead of years, the first effects are reckoned in periods of ten days instead of four months.

Most authorities state that the effects of eclipses are felt mainly in those areas of the world where the eclipse itself is visible.

To summarize, we understand that a solar eclipse has a total span of potency extending over as many years as the eclipse itself lasted hours. It has an immediate effect which will manifest within the first, second, or final four-month period from the date of its occurrence. It has a general effect which will manifest within the first, second, or final third-part of its total span of potency.

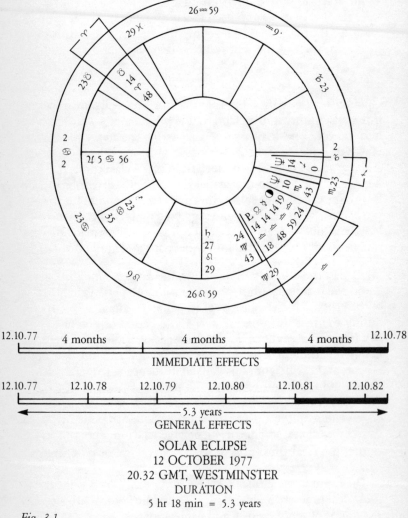

SOLAR ECLIPSE
12 OCTOBER 1977
20.32 GMT, WESTMINSTER
DURATION
5 hr 18 min = 5.3 years

Fig. 3.1

A lunar eclipse has a total span of potency which ranges over as many months as the eclipse lasted hours. It has an immediate effect which will manifest within the first, second, or third period of 10 days from the date of its occurrence. It has a general effect which will manifest within the first, second, or final third-part of its total span of potency.

The likely period during which the immediate and general effects of an eclipse may be expected to manifest is determined from the

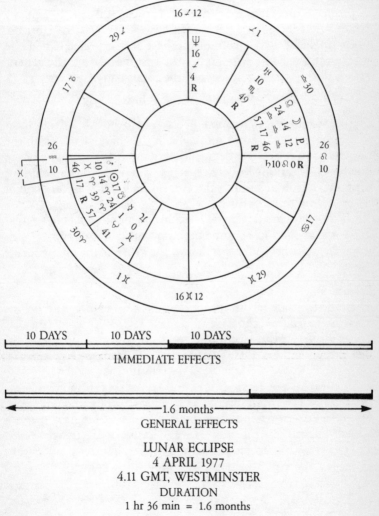

LUNAR ECLIPSE
4 APRIL 1977
4.11 GMT, WESTMINSTER
DURATION
1 hr 36 min = 1.6 months

Fig. 3.2

angle nearest which the eclipse falls in the mundane chart.

Figure 3.1 is a chart for the solar eclipse of 12 October 1977. It will be seen that the eclipse degree fell nearest the Western Horizon (tradition seems to ignore the IC), so the immediate effects may have been expected to manifest within the third four-month period. The duration of the eclipse was 5 hours 18 minutes, which approximates to 5 years 4 months and therefore the general effects of this eclipse may have been expected to manifest in the final 19-month period of its total span of potency.

Figure 3.2 is a chart for the lunar eclipse of 4 April 1977. It will be seen that the eclipse degree fell nearest the Western Horizon. The immediate effects may therefore have been expected to manifest within the final 10-day period of the first month and the general effects during the last 16 days of the total span of potency.

The Lord of the Eclipse

The old astrologers always appointed as Lord of the Eclipse, the planet which they judged most prominent in the chart. It was often the one closest to the eclipse degree itself, powerful at an angle, or the one which was most heavily aspected. The Lord of the Eclipse is supposed to colour strongly the events which follow it, for good or ill, according to its nature.

They knew of seven planets. The Sun and Moon could not be used as they were considered to be the principal causes of events, with the ability to either confirm or destroy the virtues of the predominant planets.

Saturn

The evil effects of Saturn spring from his cold nature, and he was thought to cause sickness and disease related to cold, such as rheumatism. He is also connected with poverty, misery, sorrow, and deaths among the old. He stirs up very cold, frosty and icy weather, with much snow. At sea, he is responsible for violent storms, shipwrecks and dangerous voyages, and a dearth of fish and waterfowl. In rivers he causes overflowings, violent inundations, and pollution. On the land, Saturn indicates the destruction of crops by plagues of pests, such as caterpillars, worms and locusts, and damage to corn and hay from hailstorms and tempests. Cattle suffer from disease or lack of proper provisions. All produce becomes scarce and expensive.

Jupiter

Jupiter produces increase in all things and signifies fertility, tranquility and prosperity. Government is generous, Law is just, churchmen rise and prosper. All living creatures useful to man breed well, and crops are good. Weather is windy, warm and moist, inclining to showers. Sailors sail without danger and rivers do not flood immoderately.

Mars

Mars causes violence of all kinds. Under his influence lawlessness increases; there are murders, thefts, robberies, many contentious lawsuits and duels. Government is tyrannical and there is danger of war. Mars, particularly in a fiery sign, causes dryness, drought, great heat, thunder, lightning, hurricanes, and whirlwinds. At sea, he causes sudden and violent storms and many shipwrecks, and he dries up rivers and fountains. Crops suffer because of drought and provisions therefore become scarce. The minds of men are provoked to rashness, children are difficult, and many young men die. Mars often brings to light an inventive genius.

Venus

Venus acts very like Jupiter but with added grace. She gives peace and plenty, happy marriages and excellent alliances and treaties.

Mercury

Mercury does not act alone, but is strongly influenced by the planet with whom he has closest aspect. His own nature creates much movement, industry, craft and sublety. There is much disputation and controversy. Mercury influences the weather by producing high winds, sudden storms, thunder, lightning and earthquakes, and for this reason he is generally destructive to crops. When west of the Sun, he increases the water of rivers; when east, he lessens them.

The influences of the planets are varied and modified by their aspects one with the other, by the signs they occupy, and their power in the chart. The interpretation of the many possible combinations is a matter of art, and in modern times we cannot ignore the influence of Uranus, Neptune and Pluto.

Countries and Regions

All ancient authorities appear to agree that the effects of an eclipse are powerful only in those countries where it is visible, and particularly when the degree of the eclipse falls close to an important position in the chart of the nation or its ruler, or in the sign which is traditionally associated with the region of the Earth governed by the sign the eclipse is in.

For ages past, certain countries and parts of the world have been associated with certain signs, and astrologers have generally repeated correlations given by Ptolemy. World conditions have changed considerably since Ptolemy's day, and there would seem to be little point in repeating his oft repeated rulerships. However, traditional connections between countries and signs of the zodiac often seem to make astrological sense. We rest content with Aries for England, Cancer for Scotland, Taurus for Ireland, and Gemini for Wales. Yet, the stubborn pride of France seems well symbolized by Leo; noisy, voluble, bustling America can be nought but Geminian; suspicious Scorpio fits Russia like a glove, and what better description of Chinese art and courtesy than Libra?

Astrologers are ever searching for correspondences, and there are a number of systems of astro-geography which divide up the Earth according to degrees of the zodiac. Charles Harvey, writing in *Mundane Astrology*, reviews 11 of these propositions and points out some remarkable correlations. Yet, at the end of the day, unless one is prepared to devote a lifetime to that one area of research, one must move on and work with what is available.

So set your chart for the time of an eclipse, note its duration, and the parts of the world in which it is visible. Calculate when its main effects are likely to manifest, and make your interpretation as best you can. Look at eclipses past and see what happened then. Make your interpretation of new eclipses and see if you are right, and eventually study future eclipses and speculate what will happen. There are many charts available for study, such as those of nations, cities, monarchs and great leaders. Relate your observations to those charts; you might stumble on something important and add to the great store of astrological knowledge.

Propositions

There is a logical case for accepting that the effects of a solar eclipse will manifest at some time during the year following its occurrence, even if two solar eclipses overlap to some extent. However, when considering a series of eclipses of varying duration, the general effects could well conflict to such an extent that the astrologer becomes totally lost in the resulting mish-mash. So questions then arise. If one accepts the theory that an eclipse chart may be judged of itself as a valid mundane chart and that the promise of experience symbolized within it will manifest at some time during the year following, must one also accept that other promises of experience contained within the chart will manifest after a delay of some three years or more? If so, which experiences will be *immediate* and which *delayed*?

We are doubtful whether the quality of the chart persists beyond the range of a year, but we do believe that the *eclipse degree* itself may remain potent for much longer, and we will present evidence to illustrate this point. We certainly believe there is a case for suggesting that an eclipse chart may be judged of itself as a mundane chart, but whether judgements based on it may be made with confidence, given the wide range of interpretive possibilities applicable to modern life, remains to be seen. The full importance of an eclipse becomes apparent when taken together with various national and inception charts, and also when applied to the nativities of monarchs, dictators, presidents and other important people in the life of a nation. With these points in mind, we make the following propositions which we will later explore:

1 An eclipse chart is valid and gives indications of forthcoming events and experiences which will befall a nation within the possible range of a year.
2 Independently of the quality of the eclipse chart itself, the eclipse degree may remain potent in the cosmos, as a powerful source of energy, for a period of as many years as hours of eclipse duration.
3 When important transits and/or progressions in a national or inception chart configure with potent eclipse degrees, it can have the effect of bringing the influences suggested by those progressions and/or transits into experience within a given time.
4 The potency of a lunar eclipse degree persists in the cosmos in the same way as a solar eclipse.

We shall embark upon the examination of several critical situations in the life of a nation, in an attempt to discover whether the relevant eclipse charts convincingly described the events, hinted at them, or gave no indication at all.

The Decanates

According to old astrologers, solar and lunar eclipses have specific effects according to the decanate of the sign in which they fall. We can find little evidence to support this ancient theory, and it is doubtful if Ptolemy or the seventeenth-century English astrologers expected that the wide ranging descriptions given below were supposed to be taken literally. It is noticeable that under the decanates ruled by the Sun misfortune is predicted to monarchs, nobles and important people. Apart from this, the descriptions of the likely effects have little relevance to modern life. Also, it will be noticed that all the descriptions given below suggest misfortune and evil experience, and we cannot say that eclipses are invariably of such a nature. Finally, it is completely unrealistic to suggest that merely because an eclipse falls in a certain decanate the far-reaching effects indicated will occur, irrespective of the other indications in the chart.

Eclipses cannot be taken on their own, independently of other planetary influences accompanying the eclipse, and without reference to natal, national, or other mundane figures.

Despite these reservations we feel it right to give the list below, as a matter of record and for the interest of the reader, but in so doing we urge great caution in its acceptance.

The Effects of Eclipses in the Decanates of the Signs According to Ancient Astrology

Aries first decanate — ruler Mars
Solar: Much military activity, war; sedition and controversy; intemperate weather, tendency for dryness of the air.
Lunar: Fevers; incendiarism; forest fires; dryness of air; many caterpillers and vermin.

Aries second decanate — ruler the Sun
Solar: The death, imprisonment or restraint of a king, prince, or eminent person; destruction of fruit trees, and the rotting of agricultural and garden produce with ill effects upon men and beasts.
Lunar: Pestilence and fatality in most diseases, few that are sick escape.

Aries third decanate — ruler Venus
Solar: Sorrow and lamentation among all people; the death of a great woman; destruction of smaller live-stock, such as sheep, goats, rabbits and hares.
Lunar: Abortive births and dangers to women; death of many great ladies.

Taurus first decanate — ruler Mercury
Solar: Affliction to the professional classes who will be involved in

much business activity to little effect; harmful to corn.

Lunar: Death and disease among cattle and horses.

Taurus second decanate — ruler the Moon

Solar: Travellers are particularly at risk; many aborted and unnatural or defective births.

Lunar: Death of a queen; dearth of seed and barrenness of the earth.

Taurus third decanate — ruler Saturn

Solar: Plague and famine; high death rate among cattle and horses.

Lunar: Snakes and creeping things suffer a plague, also rats, mice and other vermin.

Gemini first decanate — ruler Jupiter

Solar: Dissension and strife among priests, merchants and mechanics; general lawlessness and neglect of religious duties; breach of covenants.

Lunar: Incursions and rapines by enemies; fraudulent negotiations; many petitions, treaties and missives; much employment for scribes and secretaries.

Gemini second decanate — ruler Mars

Solar: Piracy at sea; murder and general discontent among the people; fruitless treaties.

Lunar: Sudden military activity; judges careful of executing justice.

Gemini third decante — ruler the Sun

Solar: Death of a king or eminent person; difficulties for the government with finance, legislation, etc.

Lunar: Death of a famous man, usually a scholar.

Cancer first decanate — ruler Venus

Solar: Strange and varied weather; men take up arms on the pretence of religion.

Lunar: Excites men's minds to war and treachery.

Cancer second decanate — ruler Mercury

Solar: Deceit and treachery among men; rivers and fountains dry up.

Lunar: The people suffer intolerable financial burdens; much harm at sea.

Cancer third decanate — ruler the Moon

Solar: Sickness amongst men and spread of venereal disease; sedition and rebelliousness.

Lunar: Death, disease and misfortune to common women.

Leo first decanate — ruler Saturn

Solar: Death of a famous prince; scarcity of corn and grain; national financial crisis.

Lunar: Unexpected sickness or death of a great prince or notable person, usually of royal blood.

Leo second decanate — ruler Jupiter

Solar: Many trials and tribulations for kings, princes, great men and magistrates.

Lunar: Journey of a king; changes and catastrophe in world affairs.

Leo third decanate — ruler Mars

Solar: Sacrilege, violence in towns, theft; scarcity of horses and disease amongst them.

Lunar: The military and the common people are agitated; they pursue new ideas, and seek new laws and change of rulers.

Virgo first decanate — ruler the Sun

Solar: The much lamented death of a prince or great man, and general ruin and slaughter among men; scarcity of corn and all foodstuffs.

Lunar: Sickness of kings; general discord and dissension among men.

Virgo second decanate — ruler Venus

Solar: Famine, plague, sedition; great drought causing poor crops of summer corn.

Lunar: Scandals affecting professional men, and great criticism of their oppression, bribery and indirect dealings.

Virgo third decanate — ruler Mercury

Solar: Trouble, adversity, poverty and persecution of poets, painters, and mercurial men; murders and banishments.

Lunar: Sickness and disease among the people; scarcity of bread and grain.

Libra first decanate — ruler the Moon

Solar: Corruption of the air; plague; much wantonness among youth; scarcity of provisions.

Lunar: Hail storms, bad weather, high winds, great storms.

Libra second decanate — ruler Saturn

Solar: Death of a king, prince or eminent man; breach of customs; famine.

Lunar: Misfortune to and punishment of corrupt lawyers and informers.

Libra third decanate — ruler Jupiter

Solar: Afflicts the rich and their possessions.

Lunar: Death of an illustrious person; religious bigots cause trouble in high places.

Scorpio first decanate — ruler Mars

Solar: Much public disorder and violence; murders, dissensions, captivities; underhand practices and treasons.

Lunar: Thunder, lightning and earthquakes.

Scorpio second decanate — ruler the Sun

Solar: Destruction of a peaceful king or person of worth.

Lunar: Fever and pestilence, destroys olives and infects the air.

Scorpio third decanate — ruler Venus

Solar: The rise of a tyrant; the discontent with or deposition of a king or governor.

Lunar: Sedition, murder, success of evil purposes; general disease and sickness.

Sagittarius first decanate — ruler Mercury

Solar: Dissensions, hatred and mistrust among men.

Lunar: Many thefts and rapines.

Sagittarius second decanate — ruler the Moon

Solar: Death of asses and mules, and all large animals useful to man.

Lunar: Disease afflicts horses and mules; piracy at sea.

Sagittarius third decanate — ruler Saturn

Solar: Affects horses; prejudices armies on foot; afflicts the affairs of the nobility.

Lunar: Plague; great evils afflict mankind.

Capricorn first decanate — ruler Jupiter

Solar: Unhappy accidents to great men; transmigration or constant movement of the king or eminent persons; rebellion among the nobility and the common people.

Lunar: Slander and conspiracy rampant; untimely death of a worthy person.

Capricorn second decanate — ruler Mars

Solar: Riots and mutinies among soldiers; presages scarcity of corn and famine.

Lunar: Military disorder, incursions, robberies and captivities.

Capricorn third decanate — ruler the Sun

Solar: Turbulent motion of a king; famine, bad crops, little hay and grass.

Lunar: Death of a king; conspiracies or mutinies among the people.

Aquarius first decanate — ruler Venus

Solar: Public sorrow and mourning; comfort to the countryman.

Lunar: Sickness of a king.

Aquarius second decanate — ruler Mercury

Solar: Robberies, rapines, famine, earthquakes, much public discontent.

Lunar: Hinders the seed-time.

Aquarius third decanate — ruler the Moon

Solar: The death of field cattle; great inundations succeed the eclipse.

Lunar: Causes change in all things.

Pisces first decanate — ruler Saturn

Solar: Dries up rivers; coasts made dangerous; scarcity of fish.

Lunar: Sorrow to priest and religious houses.

Pisces second decanate — ruler Jupiter

Solar: Death of a famous and good man; destruction of fish; threatens an earthquake; scandal affecting a great churchman.

Lunar: Death of a great person.

Pisces third decanate — ruler Mars

Solar: Sedition, cruelty, bitterness, inhumanity of soldiers; controversy among divines and lawyers.

Lunar: Robberies, promiscuous assaults and rapines on land and sea.

4.

Three Kings

Can the astrological symbolism within an eclipse chart be related to actual happenings? In this chapter we shall consider three monarchs, isolate some important moments in the life of a nation, and see if events which gripped the attention of the whole population could have reasonably been prejudged from an eclipse chart. Let us home in on Great Britain in 1936.

17 January — It was announced from Sandringham that the King (George V) was suffering from bronchial catarrh and that signs of cardiac weakness were regarded with some disquiet.

18 January — Although the King had some hours of restful sleep, the cardiac weakness and embarrassment of the circulation increased and gave cause for anxiety.

10 January — His Majesty, it was announced, maintained strength and passed a quiet day. The Archbishop of Canterbury went to Sandringham. Crowds gathered at Buckingham Palace to read bulletins, and prayers were said in churches of all denominations throughout the Empire.

20 January — At 9.25 p.m. a bulletin announced: 'The King's life is moving peacefully towards its close.' At five minutes before midnight the King died, in the 71st year of his life and the 26th year of his reign.

21 January — At St James's Palace, Privy Councillors took the oath to the new monarch, Edward VIII, who made a declaration during which he said: 'I am determined to follow in my father's footsteps, and work as he did throughout his life for the happiness and welfare of all classes of my subjects.'

At the age of 42, Edward was not married, but in 1931 he had met Mrs Wallis Simpson, a twice-married American socialite. By 1934 he had been determined to marry her and fully intended to bring the affair into the open, but the failing health of the King delayed matters, so the situation did not become public knowledge until he himself was King. The question then arose; how could the King, the head of the Church of England, marry a divorced woman. The nation split into two camps. There was much sympathy for Edward among ordinary people, and Winston Churchill and Lord Beaverbrook (proprietor of the *Daily Express*) were strong in his support, but the Establishment was generally against him, in particular Cosmo Gordon Lang, the Archbishop of Canterbury. Several possible solutions were advanced, but in discussions with the Prime Minister, Stanley Baldwin, Edward could find no compromise. He was, in fact, obliged to choose between Mrs Simpson and the Throne — he chose his lady! There was no alternative then

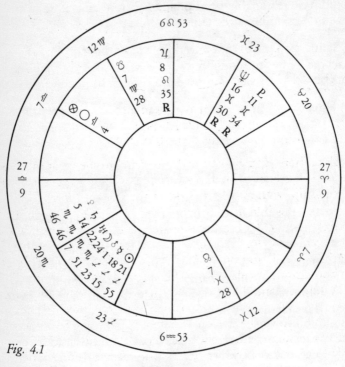

Fig. 4.1

GEORGE VI,
14 DECEMBER 1895
03.5 GMT, SANDRINGHAM

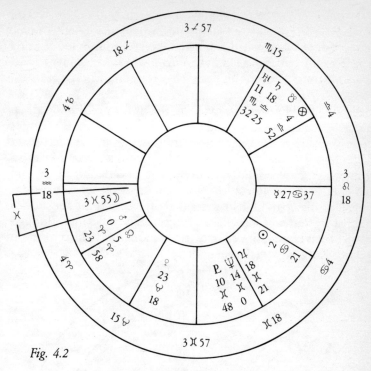

Fig. 4.2

EDWARD VIII,
23 JUNE 1894,
22.00 GMT, LONDON

to abdication. Edward VIII had succeeded to the greatest empire the world had known, but he found it impossble to accept the burden of kingship 'without the support of the woman I love'.

'It isn't possible, it isn't happening,' exclaimed George, Duke of York, as his elder brother prepared to abdicate. Thus it was on 10 December 1936, George VI became the King-Emperor in his brother's stead, and on 24 May 1937, at Westminster Abbey, St Edward's crown was placed upon his head. Edward became the Duke of Windsor, married his love, and spent the rest of his life in exile.

George VI, a reluctant monarch, was not prepared for the responsibility which was thrust upon him, yet he was to preside over one of the most challenging periods of British history. He reigned only 15 years, five of which were spent in the Second World War. He inherited a vast Empire, but before he died he was to witness the beginning of its dissolution.

Astrologically it was right that George VI (see Fig. 4.1), rather than

Edward VIII (see Fig. 4.2), should have been King throughout those strenuous years, for his nativity fits nicely into the jig-saw of events. It was as if Lady Fate, seizing upon the abdication crisis, took George firmly by the hand and led him willynilly to his appointed place, so that he might act out his destined role upon the stage of British history.

In *Raphael's Ephermeris* for 1924, the nativity of Edward (then Prince of Wales) was discussed. The author's comments are most interesting: 'The position of Jupiter, ruler of the tenth, in detriment in the fourth house conjoined with Neptune, is not a promising position as far as kingship is concerned . . . it cannot really be said that the figure is one which would be expected for a successful monarch.' George VI had a regal chart, Jupiter in Leo at the Midheaven and a Moon-Uranus conjunction in Scorpio, through which he was directly linked across the centuries with the coronation chart of King Edgar (see Chapter 5).

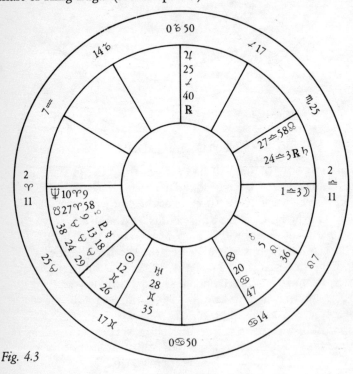

Fig. 4.3

GEORGE V,
3 JUNE 1865,
01.8 GMT, LONDON

In a little less than 12 months, Britain experienced the death
of George V, the abdication of Edward VIII, and the succession of
George VI. The astrologer is entitled to expect that these dramatic
events would be refelected in the heavens, and such a momentous
year affords us an ideal opportunity of testing the validity of several
mundane charts.

The Death of George V

We will begin our investigations by studying several charts but
concentrating upon one matter in particular, the death of George
V whose nativity is given in Fig. 4.3. Although our main purpose
is to discover whether an eclipse chart can be read of itself as a
mundane chart, on this occasion we will also consider an ingress and
a neomenium, for the purposes of comparison.

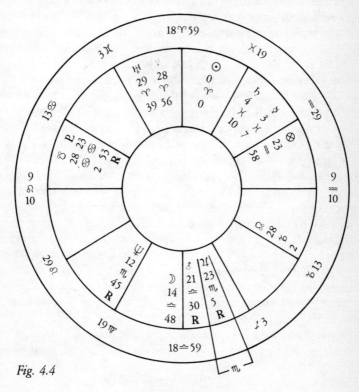

Fig. 4.4

ARIES INGRESS,
21 MARCH 1935,
13.18 GMT, LONDON

The Aries ingress — The King died during the potency of this chart (see Fig. 4.4). A fixed sign rises, so it is valid for the whole year according to ancient rule. At the moment of the Sun's entry into Aries, the prevalent planetary pattern was a heavy T-square linking Mars and Pluto with the Venus—Uranus conjunction, and the Moon moving towards aspects to all of them. The Sun itself falls in the ninth house, and this would normally be seen as placing an emphasis upon foreign and colonial affairs, and other matters connected with that house, but the Sun has no strong aspects, and the main emphasis of the chart falls upon the fourth cusp and the tenth house. Mars is ruler of the tenth house, and the tenth house controls the monarch; the significator of George V is therefore Mars. If the condition of Mars may be seen as reflecting the condition of the King, then the King is not in very good shape because Mars is weak by sign, retrograde, and involved in a heavy cardinal T-square. We should also view with some concern the presence of the Venus—Uranus conjunction, another arm of the T-square, in the house of the King. Dramatic events involving the monarchy might be expected from this chart. Venus in the tenth can indicate great public functions and regal ceremonies, but when she is badly aspected she may also presage a royal death. This was Jubilee Year, so there was certainly ceremonial — indeed, the King expressed himself astonished by the warmth of the reception he received from the ordinary people. This was a time of high unemployment and great poverty, but the relationship between the monarch and his subjects can be seen from the mutual reception between Mars, ruler of the tenth, and Venus, ruler of the fourth, for although they completely oppose each other, the harmony of the mutual reception shows the bond of affection that linked the King and the people. The nation had a big party and thus justified the presence of Venus in the tenth house and her mutual reception with Mars. Yet at the time of the ingress, Mars, representing the King, is shown weak and retrograde, and we would suggest that the eventual square with Pluto and opposition with Uranus, which must form when Mars turns direct, is sufficient to arouse fear for the life of the King.

We are concentrating upon the King, but it is worth noting that there was also drama in Government circles. The Prime Minister, Ramsay MacDonald, resigned, there was a General Election in November, and Stanley Baldwin took over as head of a National Government. This is an ingress chart and the house in which the ingress point falls is supposed to be significant. We should therefore mention important events of a ninth house nature, forming part

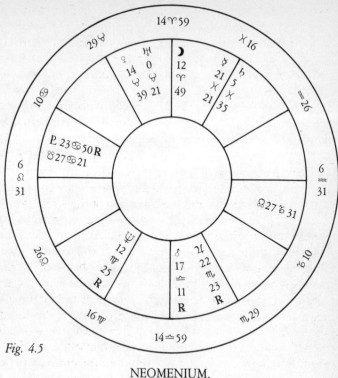

Fig. 4.5

NEOMENIUM,
3 APRIL 1935,
12.12 GMT, LONDON

of the build-up to the Second World War, which did engage the serious attention of the nation during 1935. Conscription was introduced in Germany, Italy invaded Abyssinia, and the Anglo-German Naval Agreement was signed which, among other things, allowed the construction of U-Boats.

The New Moon of the Year — Of the two charts with a claim to the designation New Moon of the Year, it is probably the lunation *nearest* the Aries ingress (see Fig. 4.5) which makes most sense in the light of known facts. The actual lunation falls very close to the Midheaven, thereby focusing attention upon tenth house affairs. It falls opposed to the tenth ruler, Mars, and he is still weak and retrograde, but angular. Mars again describes the King well, and the square with Pluto is still in force. Venus, strong in the tenth, maintains her reception with Mars; it is clear that the neomenium expresses a similar message to the ingress.

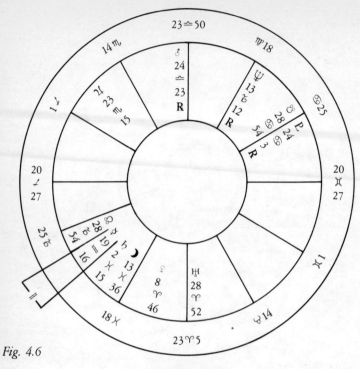

Fig. 4.6

NEOMENIUM,
5 MARCH 1935,
2.41 GMT, LONDON

We cannot escape the fact that the chart for the New Moon *preceding* the Aries ingress (see Fig. 4.6) also shows a strenuous pattern closely involving the MC–IC, and the retrograde Mars right upon the Midheaven looks particularly threatening. However, if we stick strictly to traditional rulerships, the King is symbolized by Venus, whereas in the previous chart he is shown by Mars, ruler of the tenth. We suggest that the former chart is more appropriate.

When these mundane figures are set against the nativities of all three monarchs, George V, Edward VIII and George VI, (see Fig. 4.7), several telling contacts emerge:

George V — The ingress degree itself falls upon the King's Ascendant, but since this connection occurred at every Aries ingress it is relatively unimportant. It is Saturn, ruler of his Midheaven, which is mainly affected by the ingress; ingress Pluto is square to it, and ingress Mars (significator of the King in the ingress chart) is very

GEORGE V NATAL		A 2 ♈ 8	♂ 5 ♌ 35		♆ 10 ♈ 9					♄ 24 ♎ 3
ARIES INGRESS	☉ 0 ♈ 0							♂ 21 ♎ 30		♇ 23 ♋ 53
NEOMENIUM			A 6 ♌ 31		☽ 12 ♈ 49	♂ 17 ♎ 11				♇ 23 ♋ 50
EDWARD VIII NATAL	♂ 0 ♈ 23	☽ 3 ♓ 55				♃ 18 ♊ 21	♄ 18 ♎ 25			
ARIES INGRESS	☉ 0 ♈ 0	♄ 4 ♓ 10						♂ 21 ♎ 30		
NEOMENIUM			♄ 5 ♓ 35			♂ 17 ♎ 11				
GEORGE VI			M 6 ☊ 58	♃ 8 ☊ 33				♅ 22 ♏ 7		☽ 24 ♏ 51
ARIES INGRESS					A 9 ♌ 9				♃ 23 ♏ 3	
NEOMENIUM			A 6 ♌ 31					♃ 22 ♏ 23		

Fig. 4.7

close to it. It can clearly be seen how, once Mars had turned direct, he would move to activate the square between Pluto and Saturn.

The neomenium produces contacts with the King's nativity very similar to the ingress, but the ingress is sharper. The main difference is the place of the lunation itself which falls very close to the King's rising Neptune in Aries; bronchial catarrh was a feature of his final illness.

Edward VIII — When George V died, Edward VIII became King. The ruler of Edward's Midheaven is Jupiter, and there are no direct sharp contacts between the ingress or the neomenium and the natal Jupiter. However, Jupiter is radically trine Saturn, and Saturn is struck by the retrograde Mars of both ingress and Neomenium. Also, the Saturn of both mundane charts is conjunct Edward's intercepted first house Moon, and she is ruler of his sixth house of duty. The actual ingress degree falls upon Edward's radical Mars, but again this is a contact which occurred at every Aries ingress.

For those astrologers who take the fourth house of a nativity as signifying the native's father, it will be satisfying to note that the ingress Venus–Uranus conjunction fell square to Edward's Mercury, ruler of his fourth house.

George VI — It is of some interest that the ascending degrees of both the ingress and the neomenium are conjunct George's Midheaven–Jupiter conjunction, but the most outstanding contact is the link between the Jupiter of both charts and the King's Uranus–Moon conjunction. As will be seen later, in Chapter 5, this aspect relates intimately to the coronation chart of Edgar.

The Solar Eclipses

You will remember that the traditional rule states that a solar eclipse remains potent in the cosmos for as many years as the eclipse persisted in hours, and that its first effects are felt within the first, second, or third period of four months from the date of its occurrence, according to the angle nearest to which it fell. This implies an immediate potency range of one year. Other authorities hold that the effects of eclipses will be delayed by up to six months. It is all most confusing, and to some extent contradictory, but for the purposes of this example we will work on the basis which follows.

1 Solar eclipses may give indications of forthcoming events in the

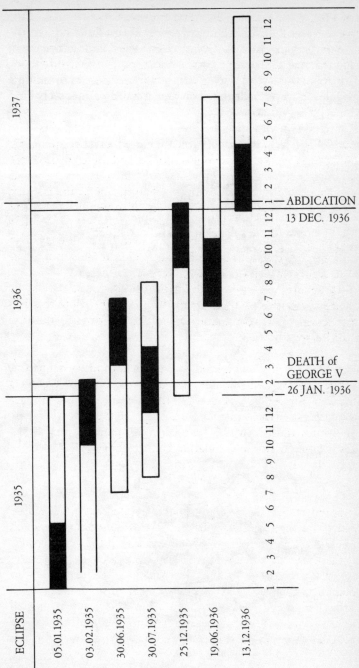

Fig. 4.8

life of a nation. The chart should be drawn for the moment of the eclipse and set for the capital city of the nation under consideration.
2 The immediate effect of a solar eclipse will manifest some time during the year following its occurrence.
3 The delayed effect of a solar eclipse will manifest at some time following the eclipse, calculated on the basis of a year for every hour of the eclipse's duration.
4 The rapidity with which the immediate or delayed effects of an eclipse will be felt depends upon which angle of the chart it fell nearest to.

We have in mind the death of George V, the succession and abdication of Edward VIII, and the succession and coronation of George VI. In 1935 there were five solar eclipses and two lunar eclipses; in 1936 there were two solar eclipses and two lunar eclipses; and in 1937 there were two solar eclipses and two lunar eclipses. However,

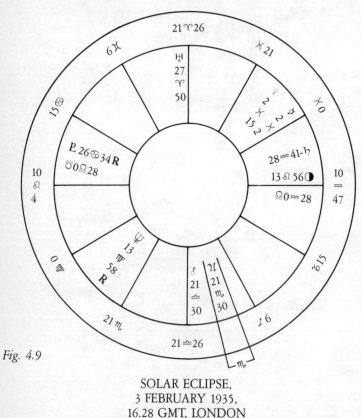

Fig. 4.9

SOLAR ECLIPSE,
3 FEBRUARY 1935,
16.28 GMT, LONDON

in 1937, all the eclipses fell after the coronation in May, so we will concern ourselves only with the eclipses of 1935 and 1936.

Accepting the theory that the timing of the immediate effects of a solar eclipse is determined from the angle nearest to which it fell, Fig. 4.8 shows how the seven solar eclipses of 1935 and 1936 spread their influence over a three-year period. George V died on 20 January 1936, and we can see how two solar eclipses cast their ray over that critical date; these were on 3 February 1935 and 30 July 1935.

The first eclipse — The chart for the eclipse of 3 February 1935 (see Fig. 4.9) shows Uranus at the Midheaven and Mars, ruler of the tenth house, at the fourth cusp, and these two are closely opposed to one another. The tenth house of a mundane chart is the house of the monarch, and this opposition could be said to indicate disruptive events in tenth house affairs leading to a change of sovereign. It is

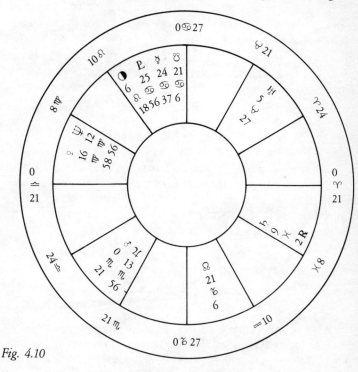

Fig. 4.10

SOLAR ECLIPSE,
30 JULY 1935,
9.34 GMT, LONDON

a powerful opposition, both angular and cardinal, and links in T-square with Pluto in the twelfth house of national sorrow. Mars is the significator of the King, and just 25 days after this eclipse he turned retrograde at 25° Libra, but it is fascinating to observe that Mars completed his opposition with Uranus and square to Pluto before turning retrograde. One really could not get a clearer indication of the event than the one symbolized here.

The second eclipse — The chart for the eclipse of 30 July 1935 (see Fig. 4.10) has the eclipse degree closest to the Midheaven, so the immediate effects should manifest during the second four-month period from the date of its occurrence. This chart shows the Moon as significator of the King through her rulership of the tenth house. The eclipse degree is closely square to Uranus in the eighth house of the chart, and square with Mars in the second house, creating a T-square in fixed signs. We cannot say that this chart is quite as clear as the previous one, but it definitely speaks of dramatic change in tenth house affairs. Indeed, the eclipse itself signifies the monarch through the Moon as ruler of the tenth, and the Sun as natural significator in the royal sign of Leo.

Leave aside for the moment all the detail of the eclipse charts save the actual eclipse degrees. Remember that there were five solar eclipses in the year leading up to the death of George V, and these and their degrees were as follows: 5 January, 14° Capricorn; 3 February, 14° Aquarius; 30 June, 8° Cancer; 30 July, 6° Leo; 25 December, 3° Capricorn. Now do any of these degrees relate to the nativity of George V? It will be noticed at once that 6° Leo falls right upon the King's Mars, and Mars is the ruler of his Ascendant and eighth house. It fell just under six months before the event and it will be seen later how, as far as nativities are concerned, the effects of an eclipse may be delayed for up to six months.

Abdication
On Thursday, 10 December 1936, the Prime Minister, Stanley Baldwin, handed to the Speaker of the House of Commons 'a message from His Majesty the King, signed by His Majesty's own hand'.

> After long and anxious consideration, I have determined to renounce the throne to which I succeeded on the death of my father, and am now communicating this, My final and irrevocable decision. Realizing as I do the gravity of this step, I can only hope that I shall have the understanding of My peoples in the decision I have taken and the reasons which have led Me to take it. I will not now enter into My private feelings, but I would beg that it should be remembered that

the burden which constantly rests upon the shoulders of a Sovereign is so heavy that it can only be borne in circumstances different from those in which I now find Myself. I conceive that I am not overlooking the duty that rests on Me to place in the forefront of the public interest, when I declare that I am conscious that I can no longer discharge this heavy task with efficiency or with satisfaction to Myself.

I have accordingly this morning executed an Instrument of Abdication in the terms following:

I, Edward VIII, of Great Britain, Ireland, and the British Dominions beyond the Seas, King, Emperor of India, do hereby declare My irrevocable determination to renounce the Throne for Myself and My descendants, and My desire that effect should be given to this Instrument of Abdication immediately.

In token whereof I have hereunto set my Hand this tenth day of December, nineteen hundred and thirty-six, in the presence of the witnesses whose signatures are subscribed.

(Signed) EDWARD R.I.

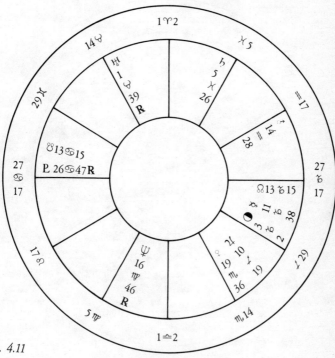

Fig. 4.11

SOLAR ECLIPSE,
25 DECEMBER 1935,
17.51 GMT, LONDON

On Thursday, 10 December 1936, the Prime Minister introduced a bill, described as 'a measure to give effect to His Majesty's declaration of abdication and for purposes connected therewith'. The bill was read for the first time on 10 December. On the following day it was passed by both Houses of Parliament and received the Royal Assent. The enactment of the bill was agreed by the Dominion of Canada, the Commonwealth of Australia, the Dominion of New Zealand, and the Union of South Africa. At the moment the bill received the Royal Assent, Edward VIII ceased to be King. On Saturday 12 December 1936, His Majesty King George VI was proclaimed.

The eclipse which, according to Ptolemy's rules, cast its ray over the abdication occurred on 25 December 1935 (see Fig. 4.11), but although that eclipse fell closest to the Western Angle, it was below the Earth at London and therefore not visible. Pluto occurs right

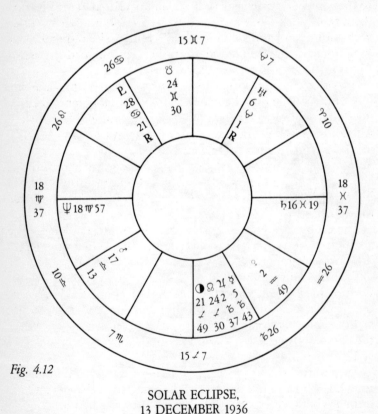

Fig. 4.12

SOLAR ECLIPSE,
13 DECEMBER 1936
23.26 GMT, LONDON

on the Ascendant trine the Midheaven but has no strong aspects with any other body. Mars, significator of the King, is in Aquarius, separating from a good aspect of Jupiter in Sagittarius, while Venus, in Scorpio, separates from him by square, but there is little to indicate the enormity of the event.

The eclipse which occurred on 13 December 1936 (see Fig. 4.12), one day after the proclamation of George VI, seems more appropriate. In this chart, Saturn, from the Western Angle, is closing in to oppose Neptune at the Ascendant, with the Midheaven poised to square both planets. Saturn by nature has connection with the tenth sign of Capricorn, and enjoys a mutual reception with Jupiter. The eclipse degree is almost conjunct the IC, with Mercury, ruler of the tenth house, just separating from a conjunction of Jupiter in the fourth house and the tenth sign. It might be reasoned that a head of state (Saturn) could resign (Neptune); that the very foundations of the country received a severe jolt (eclipse conjunct IC); that the potential damage is limited and mitigated by Jupiter, in mutual reception with Saturn, and as dispositor of the eclipse itself; and that a new king (Mercury in Capricorn) has just been proclaimed (Jupiter in Capricorn).

This eclipse chart has more to commend it than the previous one, but it is a rogue in that the manifestation of its apparent potential does not conform to the traditional rules of timing. Nevertheless, when it is set against the nativities of Edward VIII and George VI, it produces many interesting contacts.

Jupiter at 3° Capricorn justifies designation as Lord of the Eclipse, and he is opposed to Edward's Sun at 2° Cancer, which is ruler of his seventh house. It was Edward's intended marriage that provoked the abdication.

The eclipse degree at 22° Sagittarius is conjunct George's Sun at 22° Sagittarius, ruler of his tenth house. The abdication brought him to the Throne.

Edward's fourth house Pluto–Neptune conjunction at 11°–14° Gemini suggests exile; the eclipse MC is 15° Gemini. Edward's weak tenth house ruler Jupite at 18° Gemini is squared by eclipse Saturn at 16° Pisces, Neptune at 19° Virgo, the Ascendant at 19° Virgo, the part of fortune at 19° Virgo, and opposed by the eclipse degree at 22° Sagittarius.

The fact that the eclipse degree is conjunct George's tenth house ruler and opposed to Edward's tenth house ruler shows a striking intimacy between events, eclipse and the royal nativities.

We have been considering a set of related events connected with

the monarchy, but it is important to remember that an eclipse chart
can be judged just like a normal mundane chart, so that the astrologer
may divine indications of a whole range of happenings which flavour
national life during the potency period of an eclipse.

This first glance seems to suggest that there is evidence that an
eclipse chart can faithfully reflect events, and that there is some
validity in the old theory that the timing should be determined from
the angle nearest the eclipse degree. Yet we have also seen an example
of a rogue chart which does not conform to traditional rules of timing,
where the eclipse degree fell at the Northern Angle. This angle was
not mentioned by Ptolemy, probably because an eclipse at this point
is below the Earth and therefore not visible at the place for which
the chart is set.

When we leave aside all the details of an eclipse chart apart from
the degrees of the planets, we see how strong contacts emerge with
the nativities of those involved in the events suggested by the eclipse.

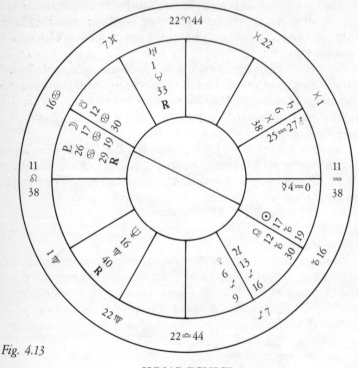

Fig. 4.13

LUNAR ECLIPSE
8 JANUARY 1936
18.16 GMT, LONDON

There is, however, no suggestion that the timing of the manifestation of an eclipse in *natal* astrology depends upon the angle nearest to the eclipse degree, and we have found no evidence to suggest that this mundane rule should be extended to nativities.

The Lunar Eclipses

Lunar eclipses do not have the same range as solar eclipses, according to ancient authorities, their immediate effects being only discernible within the month following their occurrence. Also, they are supposed mainly to affect the common people, while solar eclipses concern rulers and great men. There was only one lunar eclipse falling close to the momentous events we are considering, and that was on 8 January 1936, about 13 days before the death of King George V. Let's see whether or not the chart of this eclipse (Fig. 4.13) reflects the King's death.

Here we see the Moon hastening to a conjunction of Pluto in the sign of Cancer and the twelfth house of national sorrow; so the public is about to undergo a deeply emotional and disturbing experience. The significator of the King, Mars, is struggling towards a change of sign into Pisces where he will make a conjunction with Saturn in the eighth house of the chart. Uranus is retrograding back towards a conjunction with the Midheaven degree, which suggests drama and disruption in tenth house affairs, but Uranus does turn direct three days later.

The King died 13 days after this eclipse, five days before the actual conjunction of Mars–Saturn at 8°20' Pisces. We do not recognize any powerful transits to the eclipse chart on the day of death, but the chart itself reasonably describes what happened.

We believe that the examples shown above illustrate quite well the power of eclipses in mundane charts. The ancient formulae appear to work in the case of the crisis related to the British monarchy in the thirties. We stay with the British Isles for another example which extends our study to the consideration of the delayed power of eclipses.

5.

THE BATTLE OF BRITAIN

We have demonstrated how an eclipse chart, set for the capital city of a nation, may be judged of itself as a valid mundane chart. We have also shown how the ancient rule concerning the timing of the manifestation of the first effects of an eclipse certainly holds good in some cases, so that the promise of the chart comes to pass within the first, second or third fourth-month period following the eclipse, according to the angle nearest the eclipse degree.

According to Ptolemy, eclipses have a further effect, a long-term delayed effect: *A solar eclipse will remain potent for as many years as the eclipse endured hours, and a lunar eclipse for as many months as hours of duration.* The effects of the eclipse will manifest during the first, second, or final third-part of the total span of potency, according to the angle nearest the eclipse degree.

It may be supposed from this formula that the promise of the eclipse chart will be delayed as described. Perhaps this is so, but we have yet to be convinced. It is our contention, however, that the potential of the chart itself may be confined to the appropriate four-month period, but that the *eclipse degree alone remains potent*, independently of other indications in the chart, and that the full power of the eclipse degree manifests when it relates to radical and/or progressed planetary patterns of other horoscopes to which it may be applied. Further, we think there is evidence to show that the potency of a lunar eclipse should not be confined to a number of months equal to hours of eclipse duration. We suggest that when considering the long-term delayed effects of eclipses the potency of the lunar eclipse degree should be calculated on the same basis as that of a solar eclipse. In his book *Mundane Astrology*, Manik Chand Jain made no distinction between solar and lunar eclipses in this connection and demonstrated how, when falling upon sensitive points of a national chart, their influence often manifested after a delay of two to three years.

Let us now set the scene for our first demonstration of the delayed effects of eclipses in respect of two British national charts.

On Christmas Day 1066, the Duke of Normandy was crowned King of England at Westminster. This ritual was the culmination of the last successful invasion of the British Isles; 'William the Bastard' had claimed the crown of England by conquest!

An astrological chart for the moment of this coronation is generally accepted as the birth map of the nation, and there is no doubt that it is important. Yet there is another moment, and we believe it to be a puissant moment — the coronation of Edgar I, King of all England, on 11 May 973, with 'great ceremony' at Bath. This chart may have some special relevance to the institution of the monarchy itself; indeed there is a case for suggesting that it is the birth chart of the British monarchy.

England sailed through a large part of her history represented by

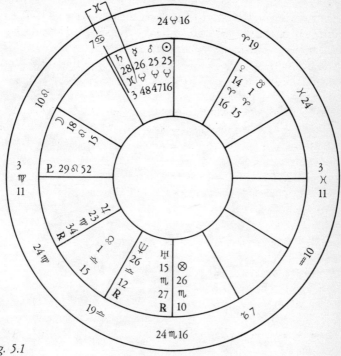

Fig. 5.1

CORONATION OF EDGAR,
11 MAY 973
NOON, BATH

these two charts until 1 May 1707, when the kingdoms of England
and Scotland united. Less than one hundred years later, on 1 January
1801, the Act of Union came into force, creating the United Kingdom
of Great Britain and Ireland. Finally, on 7 December 1922, a further
change produced the United Kingdom of Great Britain and Northern
Ireland. British astrologers thus have five national charts to play with,
all worthy of serious consideration.

Ten centuries have passed since the coronation of Edgar, each
marked with the colourful doings of our forefathers and impressed
with the characters of those who, for a few short years, played out
their destined roles upon the stage of British history. Any decade
within that thousand years might produce an intriguing story, but
for the purposes of this demonstration we wish to turn the spotlight
upon one event and the circumstances surrounding it — a three-
month period, just a trice within a millenium — the Battle of Britain.

This amazing contest was probably the first great battle of the

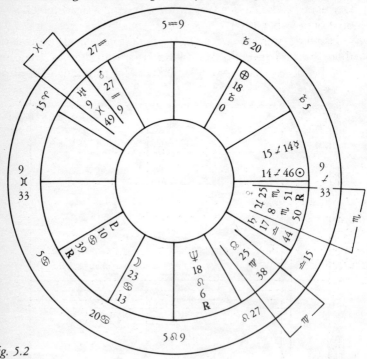

Fig. 5.2

UNITED KINGDOM,
7 DECEMBER 1922,
15.28 GMT, LONDON

air, and it occurred early in the Second World War. For this illustration we have selected two of the five national charts: the 973 chart, (see Fig. 5.1), because it is rarely discussed by modern astrologers, and we are anxious to show that it is at least worthy of consideration; and the 1922 chart (see Fig. 5.2), because it is the only one that may be conveniently progressed by computerless students of astrology.

Declaration of War

On 1 September 1939, Nazi Germany invaded Poland. Earlier that year Britain and France had given guarantees of assistance to Poland in the event of attack by a foreign power, so an ultimatum was issued to Germany requiring the withdrawal of her troops. The ultimatum expired at 11 a.m. on 3 September 1939; the Germans had not complied and we were at war. Forty minutes before the British ultimatum ran out a similarly worded ultimatum was delivered to Germany by the French Government, giving a deadline of 5 a.m. on 4 September 1939.

Hostilities were not immediate. After the expiry of the ultimatum there came a period dubbed by the American press as 'the phony war', because no battles were fought between the Franco-British and

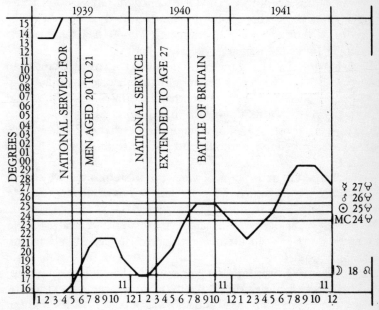

Fig. 5.3

the German forces from the collapse of Poland in September 1939 until the opening of Hitler's western offensive on 8 April 1940. This state of affairs seems vividly linked to the movement of the dramatic, disruptive and explosive Uranus!

Fig. 5.3 illustrates the movement of Uranus. The top half of the diagram represents the first 15° of any sign, and the bottom half the last 15° of any sign. The horizonal lines show highlighted degrees from the 973 chart:

27° = Mercury in Taurus
26° = the position of Mars in Taurus
25° = the position of the Sun in Taurus
24° = the Midheaven in Taurus
18° = the position of the Moon in Leo

The vertical lines pick out specific periods of time: May 1939, February 1940 and July/August/September 1940. Superimposed upon this scheme is the movement of Uranus in transit through Taurus. Obviously, during the transit, Uranus will square the Moon in Leo, and conjunct the Sun, Mars, Midheaven and Mercury in Taurus.

Throughout 1939, Uranus had been moving steadily towards that area of Taurus so emphasized in the 973 chart. On 29 August, five days before the outbreak of war, Uranus turned retrograde at 22° Taurus, 3° short of the conjunction with Sun–Mars. Uranus turned direct again on 27 January 1940 at 18° Taurus.

By 8 April, the date of the German western offensive, Uranus had reached 20° Taurus. During that month, British forces made landings on the continent, but two months later, by 7 June, they had withdrawn (the Dunkirk evacuation is another story). Uranus was at 23° Taurus, just 2° short of a conjunction with the 973 Sun–Mars. It would not be long before Britain felt the full might of Uranian power.

From the German point of view, the western offensive was an enormous success. Much of Europe was swallowed up by the Third Reich; Austria had been made part of the German state; Czechoslovakia had been declared a German protectorate; Poland was divided between Germany and Russia; Holland, Belgium, Luxembourg, Norway and Denmark had been overrun; and France had been cut in two; with the North under direct German control and the South under the puppet Vichy Government. Hungary, Rumania and the Balkans would also, in due course, suffer German invasion and domination.

Operation Sea Lion

In the summer of 1940, Hitler turned his attention to the British Isles. He knew that in order to pursue his ambitions in the east, he must neutralize these islands. The invasion was planned, code-named Sea Lion, and set for mid-August. The plan was to land 10 army divisions over four days along the South Coast and establish a wide bridge-head between Portsmouth and Ramsgate. After about a week, the main thrust inland would begin, the first objective being to secure the high ground between the Thames Estuary and Southampton and isolate London from the west. At the same time, a subsidiary operation with three divisions would sail from Cherbourg, land at Lyme Bay, and push northwards to the Severn Estuary. This initial force was to be followed by four more waves consisting of 26 divisions. It was a massive operation, one that would require an enormous number of transports. The first wave alone would require 3,500 sea-craft of various kinds, and this formidable armada had to be assembled along the opposite channel coast before setting off.

The problem for the Germans was the Royal Navy and the Royal Air Force. The idea of the wide bridge-head was to distract the British defence forces, but it would also prove difficult for the German Navy and Air Force to protect it, thus the German General Staff decided that air superiority was essential, and because of the sheer size of the operation it wanted the invasion deferred until the Spring of 1941. However, Marshall Goering, the flamboyant Chief of the Luftwaffe, assured all concerned that his Air Force would counter any interference from the Royal Navy, and 'drive the Royal Air Force from the skies'. So the invasion was set for mid-September, and Goering was given the go-ahead for a preliminary air offensive.

Britain stood alone; the great armada was assembling across the channel, a mere 20 miles away. Even to the most optimistic the position must have seemed dire. The British gritted their teeth, prepared to resist the invader, and lived for several months with the constant fear of German landings. Incredibly it didn't happen! The invasion barges did not sail, enemy soldiers did not leap upon the beaches or march through the streets of London. *The matter was determined in the air*!

Let us take a closer look at the 973 chart. Mars sits at the Midheaven conjunct Mercury and the Sun; this grouping is squared by a twelfth house Moon, and trined by Jupiter, ruler of the seventh house. When looking for the promise of war in a national chart, we must surely turn to Mars, the natural Lord of War, ruler of the military and of pestilence and violence. We must also consider the seventh house and its ruler, for this is the house of enemies, war, international disputes, and so on. From the radical pattern we may deduce that:

1 The people (Moon) are destined to suffer (twelfth house), through the experience of war (Mars).

2 The nation is likely to be successful in conflict and prevail over her enemies, because an elevated Mars trines Jupiter, ruler of the seventh house.

Here is the promise of experience enshrined in a foundation moment. If this chart is a valid one, we should expect this radical pattern to be highlighted in time of war.

The Battle

The actual battle fell into four phases. The first phase lasted from 3 July until 11 August, and consisted mainly of dive-bomb attacks upon British shipping in the Channel. The second phase was launched on 13 August — *Adlertag* (Eagle Day), when the Luftwaffe concentrated upon aircraft and ground stations in the South of England. Goering announced that he would obtain mastery of the air within four days.

Eleven days later, on 24 August, the Goering was obliged to launch a second attempt for mastery of the air. It was on this day that London was bombed. Ten German aircraft, having lost their way en route to their targets, dropped their bombs on central London and thus provoked an immediate reprisal raid upon Berlin by the RAF. This third phase lasted until 6 September. On 31 August, the RAF suffered its heaviest losses of the whole battle. At this stage Fighter Command was in a bad way; it had lost a large number of aircraft and many ground stations were completely destroyed. Had Goering pressed on with his attack upon the RAF, he might well have succeeded in completely destroying it, but he changed his tactics and concentrated upon the destruction of London.

The final phase of the battle began on 7 September. A thousand enemy aircraft bombed London by day and by night, and the invasion fleet across the Channel began to build-up. The Government issued a precautionary invasion warning, and church bells tolled. But this was the last major effort that the Germans were able to make. The RAF had developed and perfected its defence tactics and, on 15

September (remembered annually as the greatest day of the Battle of Britain), when the Germans dispatched their massive Air Armada against London, they were crushingly defeated. On that day every available British aircraft was in the air; all resources were totally committed. The Germans were surprised; this was supposed to be the death blow, and Hitler was forced to admit that the RAF was by no means defeated. The invasion was postponed until mid-October.

There was one more serious attempt. On 27 September, a desperate Goering hurled a final assault upon London, and once again the Germans suffered heavy losses and the RAF claimed a major victory. The next day, Prime Minister Winston Churchill signalled the Secretary of State for Air: 'Pray congratulate Fighter Command on the results of yesterday. The scale and intensity of the fighting and the heavy losses of the enemy . . . make 27 September rank with 15 September and 15 August as the third great and victorious day of the Fighter Command during the course of the Battle of Britain.'

From then on the German effort declined and on 12 October Hitler abandoned Sea Lion until 'the Spring of 1941'. The invasion fleet began to disperse. The Battle of Britain was over, and Britannia was still intact. During the battle the Germans lost 1,733 aircraft and the RAF 815 fighters.

It was Marshall Goering who unwittingly proved to be Britain's saviour. He persuaded the reluctant German High Command to attack in the summer of 1940 rather than in the spring of 1941, and then made the mistake at the most critical time, of lifting the pressure from the RAF and switching the main German effort to London, which gave the RAF a vital breathing space.

See how the transiting Uranus lacked just 3° of conjunction with the 973 chart Sun–Mars at the outbreak of war. It then turned retrograde and made no contacts within the period known as the 'Phoney War'. Just before the war began in earnest. Uranus began to climb towards that critical degree area again. *Throughout the Battle of Britain we find it exactly conjunct that most sensitive part of the 973 chart.* As the German effort declined and the danger of invasion receded, Uranus turned retrograde again.

Uranus was to pass over these sensitive degrees once more before moving on into Gemini, but was not to linger as he did at the outbreak of war and during the Battle of Britain. After retrograding back from 26° Taurus in October 1940, Uranus arrived at 22° Taurus by February 1941; he turned direct at that point and made contacts with all the sensitive degrees again, clearing them by June 1941.

During these months, British forces had some success against the Italians in Africa, but the period ended with Rommel encircling Tobruk and pushing the British back to Egypt. Uranus then made a brief sortie into Gemini, but returned to make a final contact by February 1942. This coincided with Rommel halting the British advance in North Africa, his taking of Benghazi, and the fall of Singapore to the Japanese.

Is it not marvellous that Uranus by transit was in conjunction with the Sun–Mars of a chart drawn for a moment almost a thousand years before, at a time of war and attempted invasion? Mars is by tradition Lord of War, and Uranus is by nature disruptive and explosive, and the combination of these influences is highly malefic. Bombardment of the Earth (the aspect occurred in Taurus), from aeroplanes (aviation is associated with Uranus) is such a literal description of what happened that it is almost too good (astrologically speaking) to be true.

Furthermore, the radical square between the 973 chart Sun–Mars and the Moon in Leo in the twelfth house is also activated by the transiting Uranus; thus the people (Moon) are made to suffer (twelfth house). Now Uranus was exactly square the 973 chart Moon during May 1939 and January 1940. On 29 April 1939, Parliament agreed to the principle of National Service, so that men of 20 to 21 years were required to undergo six months' training. On 1 January 1940, the King signed a proclamation extending liability for military service for men up to the age of 27 years. *Two million men were affected*. Thus, the contacts made with the 973 chart Moon by transiting Uranus coincided with considerable disruption to the lives of millions of ordinary folk.

We find these examples most impressive, for it certainly seems that the transit of Uranus over a critical degree area of Britain's 973 chart linked up with definite danger points in the war experience. Of course, Uranus returns to any given degree every 84 years, and there is certainly no justification for concluding that every time Uranus makes contact with the 973 chart Mars events as dramatic as those we are now concerned with will befall the British Isles. What special features made this particular Uranus transit so malefic?

Interesting results may be obtained by combining eclipses with transits, both in political and natal astrology. Solar and lunar eclipse often seem to sensitize areas of a radical chart well in advance of actual events. The effects of eclipses are usually delayed, in human nativities by up to six months and in national charts for a number of years.

We are focusing on two critical points in British history: the Outbreak of the Second World War and the Battle of Britain. Let us see what eclipses, if any, falling during the period 1936–1938, were significant for the 973 chart.

Lunar Eclipses

Date	Degree	To War	To Battle
8 January 1936	17° Cancer	3.7 years	4.6 years
4 July 1936	12° Capricorn	3.2 years	4.3 years
18 November 1937	25° Taurus	1.8 years	2.7 years
14 May 1938	23° Scorpio	1.4 years	2.3 years
7 October 1938	15° Taurus	0.9 years	1.8 years

Solar Eclipses

19 June 1936	28° Gemini	3.3 years	4.2 years
13 December 1936	22° Sagittarius	2.8 years	3.7 years
8 June 1937	17° Gemini	2.3 years	3.2 years
2 December 1937	10° Sagittarius	1.8 years	2.8 years
29 May 1938	7° Gemini	1.4 years	2.3 years
22 November 1938	19° Scorpio	0.9 years	1.8 years

The eclipses that clearly relate to the 973 chart are the lunar eclipse of 18 November 1937 at 25° Taurus (1.8 years before the war, 2.7 years before Eagle Day); and the lunar eclipse of 14 May 1938 at 23° Scorpio (1.4 years before the war, 2.3 years before Eagle Day).

The lunar eclipse at 25° Taurus fell conjunct at the 973 chart Sun–Mars, and the lunar eclipse at 23° Scorpio opposed that conjunction. We may say that these eclipses sensitized the radical pattern (an eclipse has an orb of no more than 8°). At the time of their occurrence, Uranus was way back in the middle degrees of Taurus; by 3 September 1939 he had moved to arrive within 3° of the 973 chart Sun–Mars, and war was declared. As Hitler's western offensive was launched, Uranus opposed the eclipse degree at 23° Scorpio and began to close with the 973 chart Midheaven. It was only when Uranus struck the eclipse degree and the 973 chart Sun–Mars at 25° Taurus that the war came to Britain with a vengeance.

New and Full Moons

When a point in a radical chart is sensitized by an eclipse, well in

18	19	20	21	22	23	24	25	26	27	28	29	30
☽						MC	☉	☍	☿			♇
☊						♅	♅	♅	♅			☊

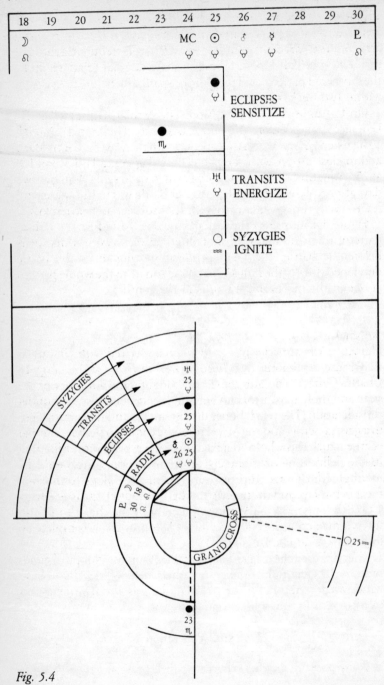

Fig. 5.4

advance of events, and then a transit arrives to agitate the sensitized area, *thus isolating a period of time during which the effects of the combination may be expected to manifest*, it is frequently the case that a New or Full Moon, falling in sharp angular relationship to the sensitized pattern, will provide the spark which unleashes events within two weeks or so.

On 15 August 1939, a New Moon (also a solar eclipse) fell at 21° Leo, just 19 days before the outbreak of war. Then, on 17 August 1940, when Uranus was in conjunction with the 973 chart Sun–Mars, and in close aspect with the two eclipse degrees, a Full Moon fell at 25° Aquarius, creating a Grand Cross in fixed signs. This was two days after Aldertag, when the great air battle was in full spate, and it was exactly two weeks later that the RAF suffered its heaviest losses.

Figure 5.4 illustrates the line of contacts. Note first the radical pattern: the two lunar eclipses falling between two to three years before the battle; the Uranus transit moving in as the battle developed; finally the Full Moon falling square to the whole pattern at one of the most critical points in the conflict.

Summary

Mars rules the armed forces, and when associated with Uranus 'it may cause explosions' (*An Introduction to Political Astrology* by Charles Carter). The Sun represents the supreme authority of the state and those in control of whatever department of state is under consideration. The tenth house denotes rulers and the government in a general sense, and the Moon rules the common people. A lunar eclipse struck this whole area by opposition aspect, promising that in the fullness of time these features of national life would be highlighted. Uranus, disruptive and alien, came along to threaten the government, and the people, through the radical square involving a twelfth house Moon. At the very height of the threat to British sovereignty and independence, a Full Moon struck to complete an impressive Grand Cross.

Why did the enemy fail? The radical tenth house grouping stands trine to Jupiter, ruler of the seventh house. While Uranus was wreaking devastation on the populace he was also in trine aspect to Jupiter, thus the attackers could not prevail and were forced to back off.

Through these examples we have tried to show how eclipses sensitize, transits energize, and syzygies ignite.

We should not make the mistake of overvaluing. Eclipses should be seen as fitting into an overall planetary pattern. Here we have seen a striking correspondence between a combination of eclipse and transit in a radical chart and events, which seem to coincide with the astrological nature of the combination. Impressive as these examples are, it is necessary to be cautious. Where possible, a radical chart should be *progressed*, and transits, eclipses, etc. superimposed upon the more important progressed aspects.

The 1922 Chart

Astrologers without sophisticated calculation aids may find it impossible to progress ancient charts. In such cases we must rely upon a combination of transit and eclipse. However, we do have one national chart which can be conveniently progressed, that of the United Kingdom of Great Britain and Northern Ireland. This map was presented in the *Astrological Journal* (June 1961), in an article by James Russell entitled: 'The Foundation Chart for the United Kingdom'. It is set for the moment when the Northern Ireland Parliament, meeting in Belfast on 7 December 1922, voted itself out of the Irish Free State and back into the United Kingdom.

There is no difficulty in obtaining an ephemeris for 1922, so it is a relatively simple matter to calculate the secondary progressions for any year. You will know that the measure of time — a-day-for-a-year — is valid in respect of human nativities, so why should it not work for national charts? Let us try it.

First of all we should examine the radix to discover whether the planetary patterns hold promise of war. It is, as we have said, the seventh house which has dominion over war. In this case the seventh house embodies a Sun–Mercury conjunction which is squared by an eleventh house Uranus; a seventh house experience could therefore be triggered by an eleventh house influence (friends of the nation, etc.). However, we have an even more positive indication in that Mars, the planet of war, is in the eleventh house and squaring Venus (ruler of the natural seventh sign) in the sixth house. We may expect either or both of these radical patterns to be highlighted in time of war.

Figure 5.5 shows the radical degrees of the 1922 chart, and listed below are the positions of the progressed planets and angles for the war years. See how, in *1939*, progressed Mars was square the radical Ascendant (and Descendant), and conjunct radical Uranus, thus invoking the square with Sun–Mercury. If the progress of Mars is followed down through the figure, it will be seen how he passes over the radical and progressed Uranus, and gradually begins to form

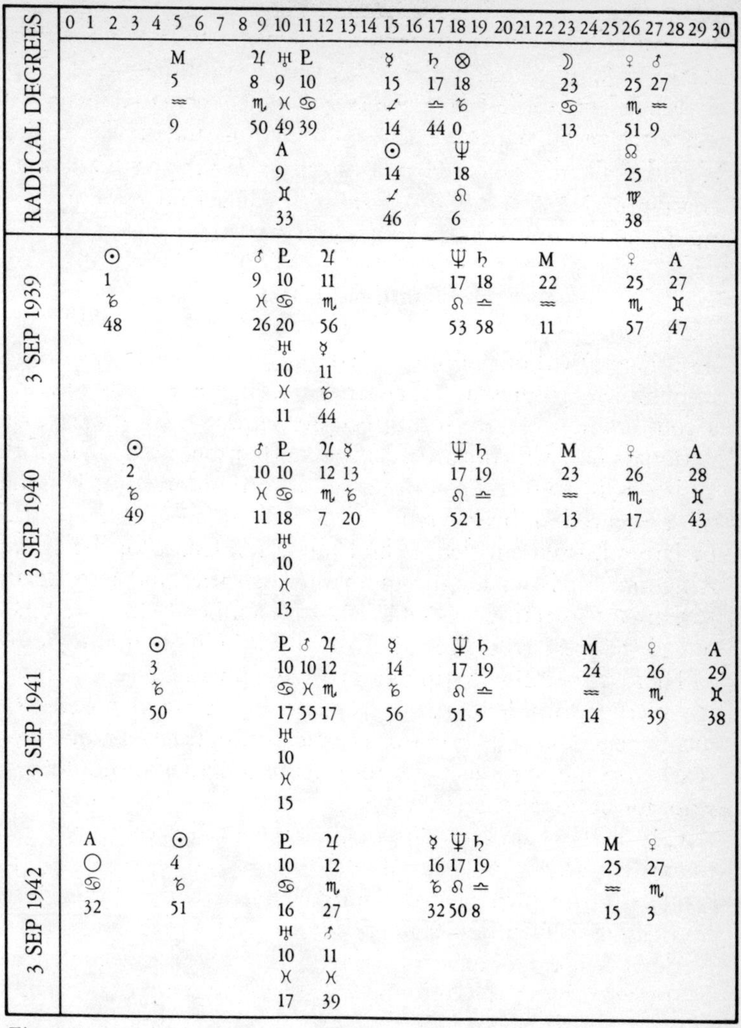

Fig. 5.5 — degree scale across the top: 0 1 2 3 4 5 6 7 8 9 10 11 12 13 14 15 16 17 18 19 20 21 22 23 24 25 26 27 28 29 30

Body	RADICAL DEGREES	3 SEP 1939	3 SEP 1940	3 SEP 1941	3 SEP 1942
☉	14°♐46′	1°♑48′	2°♑49′	3°♑50′	4°♑51′
M	5°♎9′	22°♒11′	23°♒13′	24°♒14′	25°♒15′
♃	8°♏50′	11°♏56′	12°♏7′	12°♏17′	12°♏27′
♅	9°♓49′	10°♓11′	10°♓13′	10°♓15′	10°♓17′
♇	10°♋39′	10°♋20′	10°♋18′	10°♋17′	10°♋16′
☿	15°♐14′	11°♏44′	13°♏20′	14°♏56′	16°♏32′
♄	17°♎44′	18°♎58′	19°♎1′	19°♎5′	19°♎8′
⊗	18°♑0′				
☽	23°♋13′				
♀	25°♏51′	25°♏57′	26°♏17′	26°♏39′	27°♏3′
♂	27°♒9′	9°♓26′	10°♓11′	10°♓55′	11°♓39′
A	9°♓33′	27°♓47′	28°♓43′	29°♓38′	0°♈32′
♆	18°♌6′	17°♌53′	17°♌52′	17°♌51′	17°♌50′
☊	25°♍38′				

Fig. 5.5

a trine aspect with progressed Jupiter, so that by victory in 1945 he is just beginning to separate — a truly amazing reflection of what actually happened!

Declaration of war = progressed Mars conjunct Uranus
Peace/Victory = progressed Mars trine Jupiter

Figure 5.6 illustrates the build-up of influences in the 1922 chart. Here we see the radical square between Sun–Mercury and Uranus.

	0	1	2	3	4	5	6	7	8	9	10	11	12	13	14	15	16	17	18	19	20	21	22	23	24	25	26	27	28	29	30
RADICAL DEGREES						M 5 ♒ 9			♃ 8 ♏ 50	♅ 9 ♓ 49; A 9 ♊ 33	♇ 10 ♋ 39				☉ 14 ♐ 46	☿ 15 ♐ 14		♄ 17 ♎ 44	⊕ 18 ♑ 0; Ψ 18 ♌ 6					☽ 23 ♋ 13		♀ 25 ♏ 51; ☊ 25 ♍ 38		♂ 27 ♒ 9			
3 SEP 1943	A 0 ♋ 55					☉ 5 ♊ 53					♇ 10 ♋ 15; ♅ 10 ♓ 20		♂ 12 ♓ 23; ♃ 12 ♏ 37					Ψ 17 ♌ 49	☿ 18 ♑ 7	♄ 19 ♎ 12						M 25 ♒ 40		♀ 27 ♏ 29			
3 SEP 1944		A 1 ♋ 48					☉ 6 ♑ 54				♇ 10 ♋ 13; ♅ 10 ♓ 20		♃ 12 ♏ 48	♂ 13 ♓ 7				Ψ 17 ♌ 47		♄ 19 ♎ 15; ☿ 19 ♑ 43							M 26 ♒ 42	♀ 27 ♏ 57			
8 MAY 1945 GERMAN SURRENDER			A 2 ♋ 24					☉ 7 ♑ 35			♇ 10 ♋ 12; ♅ 10 ♓ 22		♃ 12 ♏ 54	♂ 13 ♓ 37				Ψ 17 ♌ 47		♄ 19 ♎ 17	☿ 20 ♑ 47							M 27 ♒ 24	♀ 28 ♏ 16		
15 AUG 1945 JAPANESE SURRENDER			A 2 ♋ 38					☉ 7 ♑ 52			♇ 10 ♋ 12; ♅ 10 ♋ 22		♃ 12 ♏ 57	♂ 13 ♓ 49				Ψ 17 ♌ 46		♄ 19 ♎ 18		☿ 21 ♑ 13						M 27 ♒ 40	♀ 28 ♏ 24		

Fig. 5.5

On 2 December 1937 there was a solar eclipse at 10° Sagittarius, conjunct the Sun–Mercury position and exactly square Uranus; thus was the pattern sensitized. Inexorably, progressed Mars moved towards the highlighted degree. Meanwhile, on 28 May 1938, another solar eclipse fell opposite the first one, opposing Sun–Mercury and conjunct the Ascendant. The fatal pattern was given another charge of energy. By 1939, the progressed Mars had slipped into place and was joined in August by the progressed Moon. Everything was set for a dramatic event! Then, on 29 August 1939, a Full Moon (also a lunar eclipse), exploded above the whole conglomeration — five days later Britain was at war with Germany!

	5	6	7	8	9	10	11	12	13	14	15
1922 RADICAL SQUARE						♅ ♓					☿ ♐ ☉
SOLAR ECLIPSE 2 DEC. 1937						◑ ♐	SENSITIZATION				
SOLAR ECLIPSE 29 MAY 1938					◑ ♓						
PROG. ♂ 1939					♂ ♓		ACTIVATION				
PROG. ☽ AUG. 1939							☽ ♓				
FULL MOON 29 AUG. 1939		○ ♓					IGNITION				

Fig. 5.6

The original eclipse at 10° Sagittarius was ignited by a lunar eclipse 1.75 years after it had occurred. Now, as with the previous example, this falls a little short of the two-to-three year range suggested by Manik Chand Jain. Perhaps, in this case, we may justify a little latitude because of the extraordinary power of the pattern — *three* eclipses — and the exactness of the aspect between the first eclipse and the radical Uranus. Yet it is interesting that everything was delayed. Although Britain was officially at war, no battles were fought. It was not until six months later that the war began in earnest.

We must not forget the other radical pattern, the square between Mars and Venus; these bodies were in aspect throughout the war. Perhaps this contact is not as dramatic as the first one, but it is telling nevertheless, and gives added astrological emphasis to those critical years.

The first two years of the war were most perilous; Britain stood alone. She suffered massive aerial bombardment and fought off an attempted invasion. The intimate contact between Mars and Uranus

	21	22	23	24	25	26	27	28	29	30
1922 RADICAL SQUARE							♀ ♏	♂ ≈		
LUNAR ECLIPSE 18 NOV. 1937					● ☿					
LUNATION 15 AUG. 1939	☽ ♌									

Fig. 5.7

nicely describes the situation at that time. Once Mars had passed over Uranus, the danger of invasion began to recede. With the entry into the war of the United States and the German invasion of Russia, eventual victory was pretty well assured.

However, Britain remained at war for a number of years. All industrial output was geared to the war effort, most of the male workforce was under arms, and democratic government was virtually suspended; the Mars–Venus contact linking the sixth and tenth houses gives graphic testimony of this state of affairs.

Figure 5.7 shows how the radical square was agitated in a similar way to that in the first example. You will see how the aspect was sensitized by the lunar eclipse of November 1937; the lunation prior to the outbreak of war fell at 21° Leo, creating a Grand Cross in fixed signs, electrifying the whole pattern.

We have just described the correlations with the 1922 chart at the outbreak of war, What about the Battle of Britain? You may already have noticed common links between the charts of 973 and 1922. Figure 5.8 demonstrates how important parts of each chart are picked out by the same eclipses, how the transit of Uranus powerfully affected both charts, and how the Full Moon, which fell at the height of the Battle of Britain, squared everything from Aquarius.

This chapter has dipped briefly into the astrology of the Second World War from the British perspective; it is a rich and stimulating area of study. We can tell you that the Moon–Uranus conjunction in the chart of King George VI opposes the 973 chart Sun–Mars;

that throughout the war years Winston Churchill's progressed Moon was moving between 26° and 28° Scorpio, that the Jupiter of the London County Council chart was at 26° Taurus and opposed by Neptune, that the Uranus of the city of London chart falls at 29° Aquarius, and that the chart for the city of Coventry (decimated by enemy bombing) has the Moon at 25° Leo opposed to Venus. You will then realize that we haven't even glanced at the 1066, 1707 and 1801 charts. Perhaps you will be fired to dive into these charts for yourselves, as we have only scratched the surface and left much for you to do.

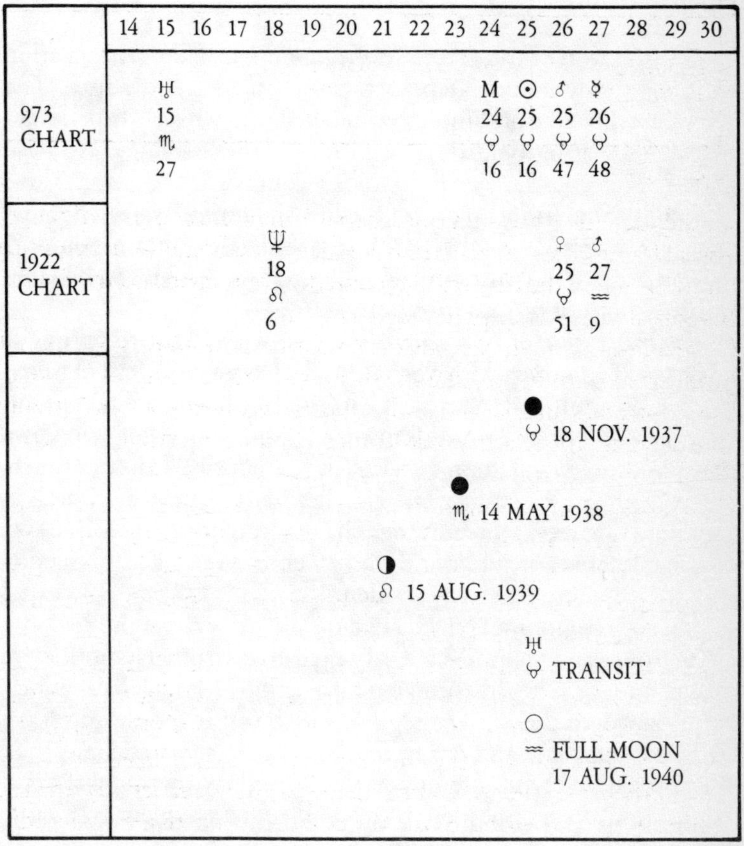

	14	15	16	17	18	19	20	21	22	23	24	25	26	27	28	29	30
973 CHART		♅									M	☉	♂	☿			
		15									24	25	25	26			
		♏									♈	♈	♈	♈			
		27									16	16	47	48			
1922 CHART					♆								♀	♂			
					18								25	27			
					♌								♈	♒			
					6								51	9			

● ♀ 18 NOV. 1937

● ♏ 14 MAY 1938

◐ ♌ 15 AUG. 1939

♅ ♀ TRANSIT

○ ♒ FULL MOON 17 AUG. 1940

Fig. 5.8

6.

NIGERIA

The dissolution of the great European empires led to the creation of many newly independent nations, particularly in Africa. The astrologer therefore has ample raw material with which to experiment in the fascinating field of political/mundane astrology. We have chosen Nigeria, the most populous country in Africa, for our demonstration. Formerly part of the British Empire, Nigeria became independent on 1 October 1960. It is a huge country of some 70 million souls of varying ethnic and religious groups, and even before independence it was a federation.

The Federation of Nigeria was invested with all the trappings of a Western democracy, with a Senate and a House of Representatives, elected by adult suffrage (except in the muslim north where the suffrage was confined to adult males). In addition, each region had a Governor, a Prime Minister, an Executive Council, a House of Chiefs and a House of Assembly. The Head of State, Queen Elizabeth II of Britain, was represented in Lagos by a Governor-General. In 1962, Nigeria became a republic and the Governor-General, Dr Nnamdi Azikiwe, became the first President.

From the beginning, Nigeria had problems, with various regions, racial groups and political leaders vying with each other for influence and advantage. The difficult general election of 1964 led to serious disturbances in the western region, which continued during 1965 and eventually law and order deteriorated to such an extent that the area became virtually ungovernable and civil war was feared.

Conditions were ripe for a *coup d'etat*, and it was planned for the first week of 1966, but this timing clashed with the Commonwealth Conference which had been arranged by the British Prime Minister, Harold Wilson. The conspirators politely waited for Mr Wilson to go home, and then, on 16 January 1966, they struck! Mutinous Ibo officers of the federal army staged the *coup* in which the Prime

Minister, the much respected Abubakar Tafawa Balewa, a number of high officials and senior army officers were murdered. General Ironsi ('Johnny Ironside') managed to contain the army and bring the situation under control but the Council of Ministers decided to hand over the responsibility of government to the army, and acting-President Azikiwe formally requested General Ironsi to assume power.

The General made valiant attempts to encourage the diverse interests within the country to act together for the benefit of Nigeria as a whole, and prevent the disintegration of the federation. In July 1966, Ironsi left Lagos on a tour of the country to sound out local opinion upon the future direction Nigeria should take. The 'January Revolution' had come to be regarded as an attempt to bring the country under Ibo control, so the general atmosphere was laden with suspicion. In July, a mutiny occurred in the western region and a number of Ibo officers were murdered by their northern troops.

The *coup* which led to the death of General Ironsi began at 11 p.m. on 28 July 1966 at Abeokuta barracks in the western region, when a Hausa officer led troups in the murder of three eastern officers. The mutiny spread. At the time of the *coup*, General Ironsi was the guest of Lieutenant-Colonel Fajuyi, Military Governor of the west, at Ibadan. At 9 a.m. on 29 July, Ironsi, Fajuyi and a Lieutenant Nwanko were arrested. According to Nwanko, who eventually managed to escape, Ironsi and Fajuyi were severely tortured and finally killed. After dawn on 29 July, a massacre of officers and men of eastern origin took place all over Nigeria with surprising speed and uniformity. The end result of the *coup* was that the controlling force in the north, the west and Lagos was the northern army under Lieutenant-General Yakubu Gowon. Although Gowon became head of state, his writ did not run in the predominantly Ibo eastern region where power was in the hands of the military governor, Lieutenant-Colonel Chukwuemeka Odumegwu Ojukwu.

During the Ironsi regime, proposals and official activity towards the unification of Nigeria met strong resistance in the traditional Muslim north but were well received by the Ibos of the east. General Ironsi himself had laid the blame for Nigeria's troubles on the previous rigid adherence to regionalism. On 24 May 1966, Ironsi announced over the radio the Constitution (Suspension and Modification) Decree which involved the abolition of the regions and their conversion into groups of provinces. The federation would cease to exist and Nigeria would become a unitary state.

Violent massacres of easterners resident in the northern region followed this decree, which was interpreted as an attempt by Ibos to take over and dominate Nigeria, and it was claimed tht 3,000 Easterners lost their lives.

As news of the killing of eastern soldiers within the federal army, on the heels of the July *coup*, spread back to the east, feelings ran high. At the instigation of Colonel Ojukwu, a meeting of representatives of the military governors was held on 9 August 1966 at which it was agreed that all troops should return to their regions of origin. The east returned the northern troops under its command; the northern troops stayed in the west. However, disarmed and unescorted eastern troops returning home were attacked and abused by a hostile population and 22 were executed at Ikeja after their return had been requested by Colonel Ojukwu. Opinion in the east now swung against Nigerian unification.

A constitutional conference was convened on 12 September 1966 at which the northern delegation asked that any new constitution should include a secession clause. The conference achieved nothing because it was interrupted by a new wave of violence against easterners throughout the northern region. It is alleged that Ibo men, women and children were subjected to an orgy of slaughter; some estimates give 30,000 Ibos slain, and 600,000 refugees fleeing to the safety of the east.

It is hardly surprisng that popular opinion in the eastern region was clamouring for secession. Nevertheless, continued attempts were made during the autumn of 1966 and the spring of 1967 to retrieve the situation, but it was not long before agreements made were broken and in the end Colonel Ojukwu was unable to accept proposals or trust assurances given by Colonel Gowon. Relations between the east and the rest of Nigeria worsened and in early May 1967 Gowon imposed a communications blockade on the east, virtually cutting it off from the outside world. On 26 May 1967, the Consultative Assembly of Chiefs and Elders gave Ojukwu a unanimous mandate to pull the eastern region out of the Federal Republic of Nigeria and declare it the sovereign state of Biafra. Colonel Ojuku read the declaration of Biafran independence to assembled journalists and diplomats in the small hours of 30 May 1967.

After the creation of Biafra, the federal government decided upon a 'police action' and invaded 'rebel' territory on 6 July. Federal forces captured Ogoja on 11 July, Nsukka on 15 July, and the oil terminal at Bonny, in a joint naval-military operation on 26 July. But when the secessionist army invaded the Mid-West on 9 August, and on

29 August attacked Lagos, it became clear that Nigeria had a full-scale civil war on its hands.

Federal forces finally ousted the secessionists from the Mid-West by 20 October, but there followed over two years of bitter and bloody civil war as battles were fought town by town and village by village into the Ibo heartland of Biafra. On 19 April 1968, Port Harcourt fell to the federal army, but despite the fact that they had lost their major port and airport, the Ibo heartland held out for another 21 months.

There was considerable support and sympathy for Biafra overseas. Moral and material support was obtained from Britain (although the Wilson Government appears to have supported Gowon), Europe and America, in response to claims that the northern Muslims were bent on the genocide of Biafran Christians. South Africa, Portugal and Rhodesia gave support, and Tanzania, Zambia, the Ivory Coast and Gabon recognized Biafra as a soverign state.

By mid-1969, the eventual defeat of Biafra was inevitable, but, in the face of great suffering, resistance continued until the very last moment. On 11 January 1970, when all was lost, Colonel Ojukwu fled to the Ivory Coast with his top advisors, and Lieutenant-Colonel Philip Effiong, head of the Biafran army, broadcast the end of secession.

On 1 October 1970, 10 years after independence, General Gowon announced a plan to return Nigeria to civilian rule in 1976. On 29 July 1975, while he was in Uganda attending the OAU conference, he was overthrown in a bloodless *coup*. The action was not unexpected; a number of senior Nigerians sensibly arranged to be out of the country while it took place. Gowon ended up in England as a student.

Let us pause now to consider the astrology of the following events:

16 January 1966, *coup d'état*, General Ironsi head of state.

28 July 1966, *coup d'état*, Ironsi murdered, Gowon head of state.

30 May 1967, Colonel Ojukwu declares Biafran independence.

6 July 1967, civil war begins.

12 January 1970, war ends, Biafran secession ends.

29 July 1975, Gowon overthrown in bloodless *coup d'état*

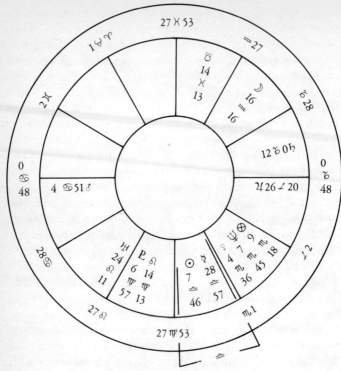

Fig. 6.1

NIGERIA INDEPENDENCE,
1 OCTOBER 1960,
00.00 GMT, LAGOS

The Nativity of Nigeria

You will see in the nativity of Nigeria (Fig. 6.1) how Mars rises. You will further note that Mars is in opposition to Saturn which is dignified in Capricorn, and that both Mars and Saturn are involved in a T-square with the Sun in Libra. The first house Mars emphasizes the importance of the military in the affairs of Nigeria. The opposition of Mars to Saturn indicates that the nation will suffer through the exercise of military power, particularly the common people, for Mars is in the sign of Cancer. The very opposition itself ideally illustrates the conflict of the military and the civil government. The head of state, shown by the Libran Sun, is square to both Mars and Saturn, suggesting that his function is to try and keep a balance between the two, and an unenviable position it is.

We may reflect for a moment upon the strength of Mars as opposed

to Saturn. Both are in angular houses, but Saturn is in his own sign
of Capricorn while Mars is in the sign of his fall. It may be deduced
from the relatively strong position of Saturn that although vigorous
conflict may be expected between the two power groupings, in the
end Saturn will prevail over the less strong Mars. Also, with Mars
sitting in the first house, conflict may be expected to damage Nigeria
herself. We know that Nigeria has suffered several military *coups
d'état*, and on three occasions the head of state was murdered. The
affliction from both points of the Mars–Saturn opposition to the Sun
(head of state) reflects these events. Further, the square of Mars to
the fourth house Sun is a powerful argument for civil war: Mars in
the fourth sign of Cancer, stabbing at itself in the first house, damages
the Sun in the fourth house, and the nation becomes stained with
its own blood. It is most appropriate that the sign of Cancer and
the fourth house of the chart are so emphasized here, for at the heart
of all Nigeria's troubles has been the rivalry between the diverse ethnic
groups and tribes that make up that complex nation.

Secondary Progressions

From the moment of Nigeria's independence, the Ascendant began
relentlessly to move, by secondary progression, towards a conjunction
with Mars. By the fifth anniversary of independence it was within
five minutes of arc of an exact conjunction. That fatal T-square was
about to be agitated, for it is a fact that when a progressed contact
is made to one arm of a T-square the energy of the whole pattern
is released. An astrologer would be justified in thinking that the
Nigerian people were about to experience a troublesome period.

This difficult period was bound to last for about 10 years, because
before the experience of that T-square could be worked out, the
progressed ascendant would have to move over the natal Mars, square
natal Sun and oppose natal Saturn. At the same time, the progressed
Midheaven would square natal Mars, oppose natal Sun and square
natal Saturn. For good measure, progressed Mars would be adding
his venom to the configuration too. And so a whole decade and more
was dominated by powerfully malefic aspects!

Figure 6.2 allows you to see at a glance the detailed progressed
aspects for Nigeria from 1965 to 1974, from the progressed planetary
positions calculated for the anniversary of Nigerian independence
for each of those years. The key movements, related to the events
we are considering, are those of the progressed Ascendant, progressed
Midheaven and progressed Mars. The progressed Ascendant was in

conjunction with radical Mars when law and order broke down and at the time of the first *coup d'état*; and progressed Mars was in square aspect with the radical Sun on the first and second occasion that the head of state was murdered. As civil war broke out, progressed Mars was still in contact with the radical Sun; the progressed Ascendant was closing to a conjunction with progressed Mars and

```
        0 1 2 .3 4 5 6 7  8 9 10 11 12 13 14 15 16 17 18 19 20 21 22 23 24 25 26 27 28 29 30
┌──────────────────────────────────────────────────────────────────────────────────────────┐
│ R │           A        ♂  P. Ψ  ⊗           ♄    ☊    ☽                   Ħ      ♃    M  ☿  │
│ A │           0        4  6  7  9           12   14   16                  24     26   27 28 │
│ D │           ♋        ♋  ♍  ♏  ♏           ♑    ♍    ♎                   ♌      ♐    ♓  ♎  │
│ I │           48       51 57 45 18          0    13   16                  11     20   53 57 │
│ C │                    ♀     ☉                                                              │
│ A │                    4     7                                                              │
│ L │                    ♏     ♎                                                              │
│   │                    36    46                                                             │
│ D │                                                                                         │
│ E │                                                                                         │
│ G │                                                                                         │
│ R │                                                                                         │
│ E │                                                                                         │
│ E │                                                                                         │
│ S │                                                                                         │
├──────────────────────────────────────────────────────────────────────────────────────────┤
│ 1 │        M   A  ☿ P. Ψ           ♀  ♄  ☉                              Ħ      ♃            │
│ O │        2   4  5 7  7           10 12 12                             24     26           │
│ C │        ♈   ♋  ♏ ♍  ♏           ♏  ♏  ♎                              ♌      ♐            │
│ T │        49  56 41 6  55         44 9  42                             25     57           │
│ . │                   ♂                                                                     │
│ 1 │                   7                                                                     │
│ 9 │                   ♋                                                                     │
│ 6 │                   7                                                                     │
│ 5 │                                                                                         │
├──────────────────────────────────────────────────────────────────────────────────────────┤
│ 1 │        M   A  P. Ψ             ♄    ☉                               Ħ      ♃            │
│ O │        3   5  7  7             12   13                              24     27           │
│ C │        ♈   ♋  ♍  ♏             ♏    ♎                               ♌      ♐            │
│ T │        48  46 8  57            11   41                              28     5            │
│ . │              ☿ ♂              ♀                                                         │
│ 1 │              6 7              11                                                         │
│ 9 │              ♏ ♋              ♏                                                          │
│ 6 │              58 33            57                                                         │
│ 6 │                                                                                         │
├──────────────────────────────────────────────────────────────────────────────────────────┤
│ 1 │          M   P. Ψ ☿           ♄  ♀  ☉                              Ħ      ♃            │
│ O │          4   7  7  8           12 13 14                             24     27           │
│ C │          ♈   ♍  ♏  ♏           ♏  ♏  ♎                              ♌      ♐            │
│ T │          47  10 59 14          13 11 40                             31     13           │
│ . │              A  ♂                                                                       │
│ 1 │              6  7                                                                        │
│ 9 │              ♋  ♋                                                                       │
│ 6 │              36 59                                                                       │
│ 7 │                                                                                         │
├──────────────────────────────────────────────────────────────────────────────────────────┤
│ 1 │          M P. Ψ ☿             ♄    ♀  ☉                            Ħ      ♃            │
│ O │          5 7  8  9             12   14 15                           24     27           │
│ C │          ♈ ♍  ♏  ♏             ♏    ♏  ♎                            ♌      ♐            │
│ T │          46 11 1  28           15   24 39                           33     21           │
│ . │            A  ♂                                                                         │
│ 1 │            7  8                                                                          │
│ 9 │            ♋  ♋                                                                         │
│ 6 │            26 25                                                                         │
│ 8 │                                                                                         │
├──────────────────────────────────────────────────────────────────────────────────────────┤
│ 1 │            P. Ψ ♂             ☿  ♄            ♀   ☉                 Ħ      ♃            │
│ O │            7  8  8             10 12          15  16                24     27           │
│ C │            ♍  ♏  ♋             ♏  ♏           ♏   ♎                 ♌      ♐            │
│ T │            13 4  50            41 17          38  39                36     29           │
│ . │            M A                                                                          │
│ 1 │            6 8                                                                           │
│ 9 │            ♈ ♋                                                                          │
│ 6 │            46 15                                                                         │
│ 9 │                                                                                         │
└──────────────────────────────────────────────────────────────────────────────────────────┘
```

Fig. 6.2

Fig. 6.2 contd.

Table note: each planet is listed under its whole-degree column (0–30, top header); the cell shows the planet glyph with its zodiac sign and arc-minutes. Where two bodies share a degree they are separated by " / ". Glyphs: A = Ascendant, M = Midheaven, ☉ Sun, ☽ Moon, ☿ Mercury, ♀ Venus, ♂ Mars, ♃ Jupiter, ♄ Saturn, ♅ Uranus, Ψ Neptune, ♇ Pluto, ☊ Node, ⊗ Part of Fortune.

	0	1	2	3	4	5	6	7	8	9	10	11	12	13	14	15	16	17	18	19	20	21	22	23	24	25	26	27	28	29	30
RADICAL DEGREES	A ♋48				♂ ♋51 / ♀ ♏36		♇ ♍57	Ψ ♏45 / ☉ ♎46		⊗ ♏18			♄ ♑0		☊ ♍13		☽ ♎16								♅ ♌11		♃ ♐20	M ♓53	☿ ♎57		
1 OCT. 1970								♇ ♍15 / M ♈45	Ψ ♏6	♂ ♋15 / A ♋5		☿ ♏52	♄ ♑20				♀ ♏51	☉ ♎38							♅ ♌39			♃ ♐38			
1 OCT. 1971								♇ ♍16	Ψ ♏8 / M ♈44	♂ ♋39 / A ♋55			♄ ♑22	☿ ♏1					♀ ♏5 / ☉ ♎37						♅ ♌41			♃ ♐46			
1 OCT. 1972								♇ ♍18	Ψ ♏10	M ♈44	♂ ♋3 / A ♋45		♄ ♑25		☿ ♏8					♀ ♏8 / ☉ ♎37					♅ ♌44			♃ ♐46			
1 OCT. 1973								♇ ♍19	Ψ ♏12		♂ ♋27 / M ♈43	A ♋35	♄ ♑27			☿ ♏13					♀ ♏32 / ☉ ♎36				♅ ♌46				♃ ♐4		
1 OCT. 1974								♇ ♍21	Ψ ♏14		♂ ♋50	M ♈43	♄ ♑30 / A ♋26				☿ ♏16					♀ ♏45 / ☉ ♎36			♅ ♌49				♃ ♐13		

they remained in close contact throughout the duration of the war. When Gowon was overthrown in 1975, the progressed Ascendant and Midheaven were in contact with Saturn and about to move away from the T-square, but progressed Mars would take a few years to detach himself from the third arm of that pattern. These remarkable configurations clearly demonstrate the troubles suffered by the

Nigerian people. The potential was there at the moment of
independence; a few years later that potential was invoked by the
progressed angles and Mars. The mines were laid. What produced
the spark?

Eclipses

We highlighted in the previous chapter how eclipse degrees will
remain dormant in the cosmos for several years, and how, when allied
with transits, they seem to produce the energy which encourages
manifestation of events within six months. With this example we
have a situation where the radical chart contains a strenuous T-square
which holds the promise of violence. We have seen how that T-square
was being invoked by secondary progressions during the years we
know were critical in the affairs of Nigeria. We must now discover
whether any eclipses falling between two and four years before the
events related to the radical and progressed patterns. In order to get
a complete picture, we have listed below all the eclipses, both solar
and lunar, that occurred between 1960 and 1975.

Solar eclipses		Lunar eclipses	
27.03.60	7° Aries	13.03.60	23° Virgo
20.09.60	9° Libra	5.09.60	13° Pisces
15.02.61	27° Aquarius	2.03.61	12° Virgo
5.02.62	16° Aquarius		
31.07.62	8° Leo		
25.01.63	5° Aquarius	6.07.63	14° Capricorn
28.07.63	28° Cancer	30.12.63	8° Cancer
14.01.64	24° Capricorn	25.06.64	4° Capricorn
10.06.64	20° Gemini	19.12.64	28° Gemini
9.07.64	17° Cancer		
4.12.64	12° Sagittarius		
30.05.65	9° Gemini	14.06.65	23° Sagittarius
23.11.65	1° Sagittarius		
20.05.66	29° Taurus		
12.09.66	20° Scorpio		
9.05.67	18° Taurus	4.04.67	4° Scorpio
2.11.67	9° Scorpio	18.10.67	24° Aries
28.03.68	8° Aries	13.04.68	23° Libra
22.09.68	0° Libra	6.10.68	13° Aries
18.03.69	28° Pisces		
11.09.69	19° Virgo		
7.03.70	17° Pisces	21.02.70	2° Virgo
31.08.70	8° Virgo	17.08.70	24° Aquarius

Solar eclipses		Lunar eclipses	
25.02.71	6° Pisces	10.02.71	21° Leo
22.07.71	29° Cancer		
20.08.71	27° Leo	6.08.71	14° Aquarius
16.01.72	25° Capricorn	30.01.72	10° Leo
10.07.72	19° Cancer	26.07.72	3° Aquarius
4.01.73	14° Capricorn	18.12.73	18° Gemini
30.06.73	8° Cancer		
24.12.73	3° Capricorn		
20.06.74	29° Gemini	4.06.74	14° Sagittarius
13.12.74	21° Sagittarius	29.11.74	7° Gemini
11.05.75	20° Taurus	25.05.75	4° Sagittarius
3.11.75	10° Scorpio	18.11.75	26° Taurus

A number of eclipses fell in relation to the chart of Nigeria between 1963 and 1967:

On 6 July 1963, a lunar eclipse at 14° Capricorn, conjunct radical Saturn.

On 30 December 1963, a lunar eclipse at 8° Cancer, conjunct radical Mars.

On 25 June 1964, a lunar eclipse at 4° Capricorn, in opposition to radical Mars.

On 9 July 1964, a solar eclipse at 17° Cancer in opposition to radical Saturn.

Thus was the radical Mars–Saturn/Sun T-square sensitized.

To recapitulate, 16 January 1966 saw the overthrow of the existing government structure, the murder of the Prime Minister and other high officials, and the imposition of what proved to be a military dictatorship under General Ironsi. On 28 July 1966, General Ironsi was murdered and Colonel Gowon emerged as the strong-man.

It is important to remember, as explained above, that when one arm of the radical T-square is activated by a major progression, the whole potential of the pattern is energized. At the time of these two events, the progressed Ascendant was conjunct radical Mars and the progressed Mars was square the radical Sun. Clearly the lunar eclipses of 14 July 1963 and 30 December 1963, falling at 14° Capricorn and 8° Cancer respectively, sensitized the degree area well in advance of events. We have found that the effects of lunar eclipses are delayed by approximately 2.5 years. Think of the eclipse as a mine laid about 2.5 years before an explosion is planned to occur, and think of major progressions as primers that set the mechanism in action. What then provokes the actual explosion?

Lunations and Pleniluna

In mundane/political astrology, a planetary pattern within a radical chart, which holds promises of a certain character, may be sensitized several years in advance of events by an eclipse. The year in which the events may be expected to manifest may be determined from the year in which major progressions activate the potency of the radical pattern. When a lunation (or Full Moon) then falls in sharp angular relationship to the whole sensitized and activated pattern, events sympathetic to the symbolism of the radical scheme may be expected to manifest with a month at most, but usually within two weeks.

On 23 December 1965, a lunation fell at 1° Capricorn.

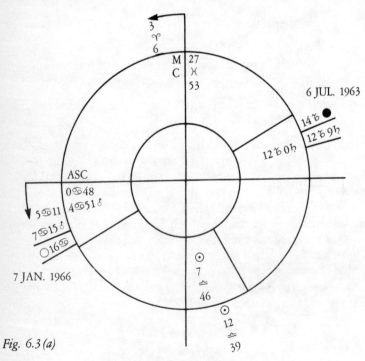

Fig. 6.3 (a)

COUP D'ETAT, 16 JANUARY 1966,
GENERAL IRONSI HEAD OF STATE

On 7 January 1966, a Full Moon fell at 16° Cancer.

On 2 July 1966, a Full Moon fell at 10° Capricorn.

On 18 July 1966, a lunation fell at 25° Cancer.

See what happens when we set out the radical pattern with relevant secondary progressions, and superimpose upon them the lunar eclipses and Full Moons in logical order.

Coup d'état 16 January 1966
See Fig. 6.3 (a).

1 The 6 July 1963 lunar eclipse, at 14° Capricorn, fell 2.5 years before the *coup*, sensitizing the radical T-square through a conjunction with Saturn.
2 The T-square is activated by secondary progressions: progressed

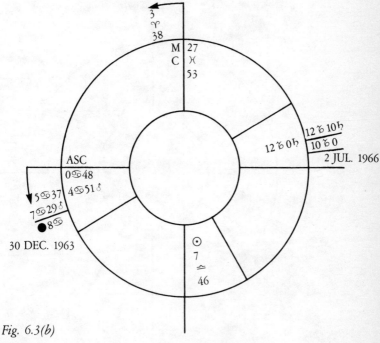

Fig. 6.3(b)

COUP D'ETAT, 28 JULY 1966,
GOWON HEAD OF STATE

Ascendant conjunct Mars and progressed Mars square the Sun.
3 On 7 January 1966, just nine days before the event, a Full Moon
fell at 16° Cancer in opposition to the eclipse degree, igniting the
whole pattern.

Coup d'état 28 July 1966
See Fig. 6.3 (b)

1 A lunar eclipse fell at 8° Cancer, 2.6 years before this *coup*,
sensitizing the radical T-square through a conjunction with Mars
and a square to the Sun.
2 The activation of the T-square through secondary progressions is
still potent as in the previous example.
3 Ignition is provided by a Full Moon falling at 10° Capricorn, on
2 July 1966, 26 days before the event.

The war between Nigeria and newly created Biafra began on 6
July 1967, and ended in defeat for Biafra on 12 January 1970.

The effective range of a solar eclipse is rather longer than a lunar

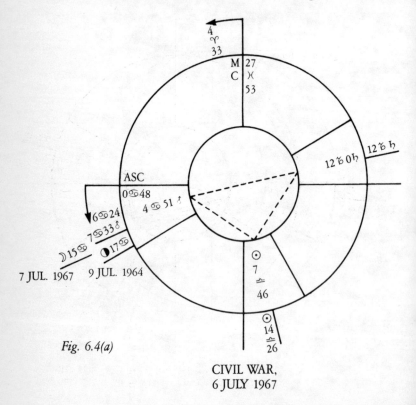

Fig. 6.4(a)

CIVIL WAR,
6 JULY 1967

eclipse — from 2.5 to 5 years, depending, it is said, upon the length
of the eclipse itself. The solar eclipse of 9 April 1964 at 17° Cancer
fell a few days short of the three years before the outbreak of civil
war. On 7 July 1967, the day after the war began, there was a New
Moon at 15° Cancer. Figure 6.4(a) illustrates the sequence.

1 *Sensitization* — solar eclipse at 17° Cancer in opposition to the
radical Saturn and square the progressed Sun.
2 *Activation* — progressed Ascendant square the radical Sun; the
progressed Midheaven square radical Mars.
3 *Ignition* — lunation at 15° Cancer on the day after the event.

Defeat of Biafra
See Fig. 6.4(b)

On 24 April 1967, a lunar eclipse fell at 4° Scorpio, right on the
national Venus, and, on 2 November 1967, a solar eclipse fell at 9°
Scorpio, conjunct the national Neptune (actually between Neptune

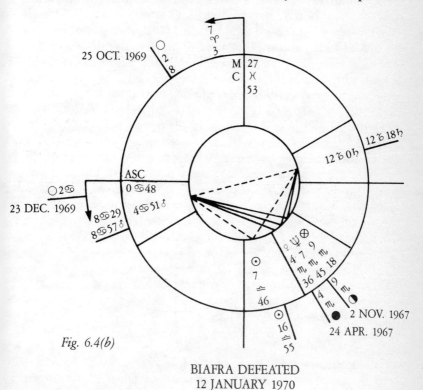

Fig. 6.4(b)

BIAFRA DEFEATED
12 JANUARY 1970

and Fortuna). You will see that Venus and Neptune are in radical conjunction in the fifth house of the chart, and both of them are well aspected to the Mars–Saturn opposition. Surely this is an indication of peace, national rejoicing, even euphoria? Venus is the planet of victory, and her good radical aspect to Mars does suggest victory for Nigeria. In any matter of contest, Nigeria has a great advantage through its rising Mars in trine aspect to a fifth house Venus (this is one of the positive interpretations that may be given to a very difficult national Mars).

Our researches lead us to believe that a delayed-action lunar eclipse tends to be 'confirmed' by a Full Moon (plenilunum) falling close to an actual event, while a delayed-action solar eclipse tends to be 'confirmed' by a New Moon (lunation) falling close to an event. There were no confirming lunations in the month preceding the official peace, but the Full Moon before the event did fall at 2° Cancer, in trine aspect to the lunar eclipse degree. A Full Moon also occurred on 25 October 1969 (seeming to confirm the lunar eclipse at 4° Scorpio). It would seem from stellar indications that effective peace came within the month succeeding the October Full Moon, although official peace was delayed until January 1970. Quoting what Michael Crowder said in his book *The Story of Nigeria*: 'By mid-1969 it had become clear that it was only a matter of time before Biafra would fall to the Federal Forces. But Ojukwu refused to concede defeat despite the very considerable suffering continued resistance was inflicting on his people. Only as the Federal Troops closed in on his last strongholds in late December did Ojukwu begin to consider abandoning the fight.'

By this time the progressed Ascendant had passed beyond the point of opposition with radical Saturn, but it was still just in contact with progressed Saturn (separating). The progressed Midheaven however, was still square both radical and progressed Saturn but separating, and the progressed Mars, although now about to be overtaken by the progressed Ascendant, had not yet perfected its opposition to Saturn. Nigeria's troubles were not over.

1973 was a big year for eclipses; three of these were solar: 4 January, 14° Capricorn; 30 June, 8° Cancer; 24 December, 3° Capricorn.

The Overthrow of General Gowon
See Fig. 6.5.

General Gowon was ousted on 29 July 1975; 2.5 years before he was overthrown, the first solar eclipse of 1973 fell at 14° Capricorn

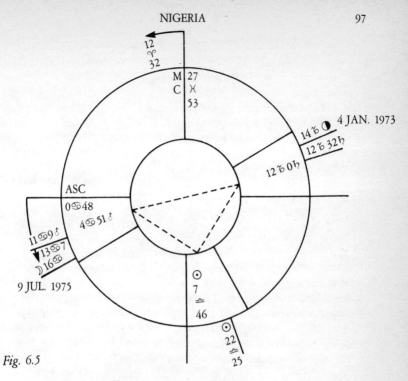

Fig. 6.5

COUP D'ETAT, 29 JULY 1975,
GOWON OVERTHROWN

(that most sensitive degree for Nigeria, conjunct national Saturn). The lunation prior to the event took place on 9 July 1975 at 16° Cancer, thus opposing the eclipse degree and the radical Saturn. This *coup* was achieved without apparent loss of life, and it would seem that Gowon was well advised to be out of the country when it happened (you will note that Mars was hardly involved here).

The solar eclipse of 30 June 1973 was extremely powerful. It was of unusually long duration — some five hours. There will not be another eclipse of such length for 177 years. It fell at 8° Cancer, between the radical and progressed positions of the national Mars, igniting once again that fatal Mars–Saturn–Sun T-square.

The lunation of 1 January 1976 fell at 10° Capricorn, opposing the eclipse degree and providing another explosion. There was a further attempted *coup* which was reported to have been unsuccessful. However, the head of state was murdered in the process, so the object of the perpetrators might well have been achieved.

Just after the overthrow of Gowon in 1976, one of your authors was lecturing on the astrology of Nigeria since independence. He ended his lecture with the following observations.

That brings us up-to-date as far as Nigeria is concerned, but there
is more to come yet! The third solar eclipse of 1973 fell at 3° Capricorn
on 24 December, that is, conjunct the national Mars and Ascendant.
It looks as if there is another explosion to come. When can it be
expected? The New Moon of 27 June this year falls at 6° Cancer.
Within a month of that lunation it seems likely that the military will
have another go, and judging by previous experience, the head of
state might get the 'chop'. Unless he has an astrologer who can warn
him to be out of the country, his position seems perilous. I await events
with interest.

Broadly speaking, once this eclipse has worked itself out, there are
no more that will fall across the fatal angles for a number of years,
and the progressed angles and the progressed Mars will have passed
beyond effective orb of the sensitive degrees we have been considering.
It would seem, therefore, that whoever gains control in Nigeria this
summer is likely to keep it for some time. Having said that, there
might just be danger points for some two years or so, at times when
a lunation strikes the degree of the June 1973 solar eclipse, because
it was so unusually powerful, but on balance I believe that the heat
is coming out of the Nigerian situation. Progressed Sun is closing
to a sextile of that Sagittarian Jupiter, and in due course the progressed
Midheaven will trine Jupiter — that must be a prosperous indication.

At this time, your author was in contact with a Nigerian, resident
in London, who had close contacts with high officials of the Nigerian
government. On 28 June 1976, the astrologer received the following
information: during the previous week six officers had approached
the Nigerian Chief of Staff and proposed that President Obasanjo
be removed and replaced by himself; the Chief of Staff reported
the matter to the President, a probable *coup* was forestalled, and
the six officers were shot.

Nigeria continued to be ruled by the military until 1979, when
civilian government was restored. Following a general election in 1983,
in the early hours of 31 December, the military took over again.
Leading officials of the civilian government were arrested and
eventually brought before military tribunals and charged with
corruption. In the 20 years since independence, Nigeria has had a
civilian government for 10 years and a military one for 10 years.

Summary
In this chapter we have attempted to illustrate how:

1 The horoscope of a nation responds to secondary progressions in a similar way to a human nativity.

2 Both solar and lunar eclipses may sensitize areas of a radical chart several years in advance of events.

3 When secondary progressions activate eclipse-sensitized radical patterns, New and Full Moons can ignite those sensitized/activated patterns, provoking the radical potential to manifest into experience within a few weeks.

4 There is a tendency for New Moons to confirm solar eclipses and Full Moons to confirm lunar eclipses.

7.

KITTY HAWK PROGRESSED

On 14 December 1903, at Kill Devil Hill, North Carolina, USA, Wilbur Wright won the honour of being the first to attempt powered flight from his brother Orville, on the toss of a coin. Fate ignored the decision of chance, for Wilbur's attempt did not succeed. Three

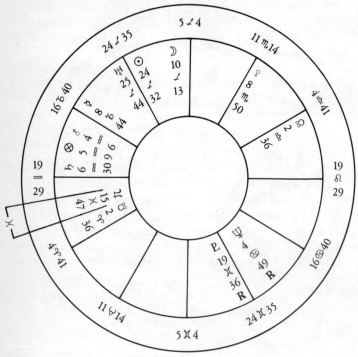

KITTY HAWK,
17 DECEMBER 1903, 15.35 GMT,
36°2' N, 75°42' W

Fig. 7.1

days later Orville took his turn, boarded *Flyer 1* (later to be named *Kitty Hawk*), took off without assistance and stayed aloft for 12 seconds. Man's bid for conquest of the air had begun, and just 66 years later Neil Armstrong set foot on the Moon.

An astrological map for this moment (Fig. 7.1) marks the beginning of man's quest for mastery of the air, and it is entirely appropriate for a Sun–Uranus conjunction in the aspiring sign of Sagittarius, with the Moon close to the Midheaven in the same sign. The Mars–Saturn conjunction in Aquarius seems to symbolize 'powered flight', and the importance of the moment for communication is shown by Venus, ruler of the third house, on the cusp of the ninth house, applying by trine to a dignified Jupiter in the first house. The chart is not without its difficulties however. The Sun–Uranus conjunction opposes Pluto and squares Jupiter, creating a T-square in mutable signs.

It did not take mankind very long to harness powered flight for the purposes of warfare and destruction, creating a new dimension of terror in human experience, but air travel has shrunk the world and brought her peoples closer together, making possible a breadth of international understanding unthinkable a century ago. Thus enshrined within the moment of '*Kitty Hawk*' is the potential for a revolution in relationships between the ordinary people of the world, which surely must serve the fraternal ideal of Aquarius.

Accidents

Air travel is probably safer than most other forms of transportation, but when accidents do occur there is often considerable loss of life. Certain years have been particularly marked by major tragedies. In 1970 at Tenerife, in the worst aviation accident yet recorded, two aircraft collided on the runway, causing the death of 583 people; 346 died near Paris in 1974; the Chicago air disaster two years later claimed 271 lives, and 269 were killed when a Korean airliner was shot down when it strayed into Soviet air space. But the worst year for civil aviation yet was 1985/86; one appalling accident after another sent shock-waves across the world. These are some of the major accidents that occurred:

Accident	Date	Latitude	Longitude	Killed
Bilbao, Spain	19 February 1985	43°16′N	02°56′W	148
Air India (off Irish coast)	23 June 1985	51°02′N	12°48′W	329

Accident	Date	Latitude	Longitude	Killed
Tokyo	12 August 1985	37°25'N	135°49'E	524
Manchester	22 August 1985	53°30'N	02°15'W	54
Gander	12 December 1985	48°56'N	54°34'W	256
Guatemala	18 January 1986	30°58'S	59°47'W	93
Challenger explosion	28 January 1986	28°30'N	80°36'W	7
Mexico	31 March 1986	19°00'N	102°00'W	167
East Berlin	12 December 1986	52°32'N	13°24'E	71

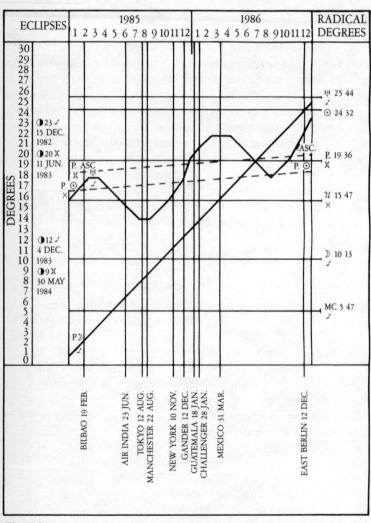

Fig. 7.2

Why was the year 1985/86 so tragic for air travel? If there is any verity in astrology, we can expect such a period to be reflected in the potential of that dramatic moment when man first flew in an aeroplane. Indeed, the whole experience of aviation should be intimately connected with *Kitty Hawk*.

Uranus rules aviation and also has a reputation for sudden accidents, particularly in the sign of Sagittarius. As we have seen, Uranus is prominent in the *Kitty Hawk* chart, being conjunct the Sun and in opposition to Pluto. Sagittarius is associated with long-distance travel. The Moon at the Midheaven is linked by strenuous T-square with Pluto and Jupiter, the ruler of the tenth house.

By 1985, Uranus by transit, was in the final stages of the 84-year cycle which would bring him back to his natal place. Indeed, he had already passed over the radical Midheaven, entered the tenth house, and made a conjunction with the radical Moon. Meanwhile, as 1985 opened, the *Kitty Hawk* progressed Moon moved into Sagittarius. Figure 7.2 plots the courses of Uranus and progressed Moon in relation to important radical degrees and the dates of the above mentioned accidents. It also shows the course of the progressed Ascendant and progressed Sun over the two-year period. During the year 1985/86 Uranus was never far away from involvement with the Moon/ Jupiter/Pluto T-square, and progressed Moon made contact with all the sensitive degrees over the same period.

Secondary Progressions

When Orville Wright first rose into the air, Pluto was at 19°36' Gemini. When that chart is progressed to the date of the Tokyo crash, Pluto has reached 18°41' Gemini. By the 81st anniversary of the *Kitty Hawk* flight (17 December 1984), the progressed Ascendant was approaching a conjunction with progressed Pluto. Figure 7.2 also shows how this progressed Ascendant conjunct Pluto aspect was in operation throughout 1985/86, and meanwhile the progressed Sun in Pisces was moving up to square Pluto — thus the energy of the radical T-square was doubly invoked. With this strenuous pattern made potent, it is hardly surprising that the period was marred by a series of horrific accidents. By 12 August, the date of the worst accident near Tokyo, the progressed Ascendant was within a few minutes of conjunction with progressed Pluto. The following table shows the exact position of the progressed Ascendant and Sun, in relation to Pluto, for each of the accidents we have mentioned, as well as the transit of Uranus and the position of the progressed Moon:

Accident	Date	P. Asc.	P. Sun	P. Pluto	T. Uran	P. Moon
Bilbao, Spain	19 Feb. 1985	18°30′Gem.	16°50′Pis.	18°41′Gem.	17°34′Sag.	02°30′Sag.
Air India	23 Jun. 1985	18°50′Gem.	17°11′Pis.	18°41′Gem.	15°18′Sag.	06°54′Sag.
Tokyo	12 Aug. 1985	18°58′Gem.	17°19′Pis.	18°41′Gem.	14°00′Sag.	08°40′Sag.
Manchester	22 Aug. 1985	18°59′Gem.	17°21′Pis.	18°41′Gem.	13°58′Sag.	09°01′Sag.
Gander	12 Dec. 1985	19°17′Gem.	17°39′Pis.	18°41′Gem.	18°21′Sag.	12°56′Sag.
Guatemala	18 Jan. 1986	19°23′Gem.	17°45′Pis.	18°41′Gem	20°29′Sag.	14°14′Sag.
Challenger	28 Jan. 1986	19°24′Gem.	17°47′Pis.	18°41′Gem.	20°58′Sag.	14°34′Sag.
Mexico	31 Mar. 1986	19°38′Gem.	17°57′Pis.	18°41′Gem.	22°22′Sag.	16°43′Sag.
East Berlin	12 Dec. 1986	20°13′Gem.	18°39′Pis.	18°41′Gem	22°26′Sag.	25°30′Sag.
Radical Pluto				19°36′Gem		

During the period 1982/84, the following solar eclipses, which appear relevant to the above positions, occurred: 15.12.82, 23° Sagittarius; 11.06.83, 20° Gemini; 04.12.83, 12° Sagittarius; 30.05.84, 09° Gemini.

Figure 7.3 shows the radical *Kitty Hawk* chart, with the progressions and transits from 19 February 1985 to 12 December, 1986, which have a bearing on our study, together with the four solar eclipses.

Imagine that the two sets of eclipses carved two furrows of sensitivity across the chart several years in advance, the 23° Sagittarius and 20° Gemini eclipses broadly aligning with the Sun–Uranus opposition to Pluto, and the 12° Sagittarius and 9° Gemini eclipses with the Moon–Jupiter–Pluto T-square.

Then, as 1985 opens, the progressed Ascendant moves to activate Pluto by conjunction, realizing the potential of the two strenuous radical patterns which were already sensitized by the eclipses. Close on the heels of the Ascendant, the progressed Sun, which has an effective orb of 1½°, is moving to square Pluto.

Throughout the same period, transiting Uranus is hovering around in the tenth house, never far away from an opposition to Pluto. Meanwhile, the movement of the progressed Moon through the tenth house coincides remarkably with one of the worst series of accidents in the history of civil aviation.

Astrologically, it is entirely reasonable that the radical *Kitty Hawk* chart should give promise of disaster, and that *Kitty Hawk* progressed should indicate when the radical promise is likely to manifest. Yet *Kitty Hawk* is set for Kill Devils Hills, North Carolina, and the accidents occurred in all parts of the world. What kind of pattern would emerge if we relocated *Kitty Hawk* for the place of an accident, and progressed the relocated chart for the date of the accident?

Kitty Hawk Relocated

From our list of disasters, we shall extract the Tokyo accident, as it

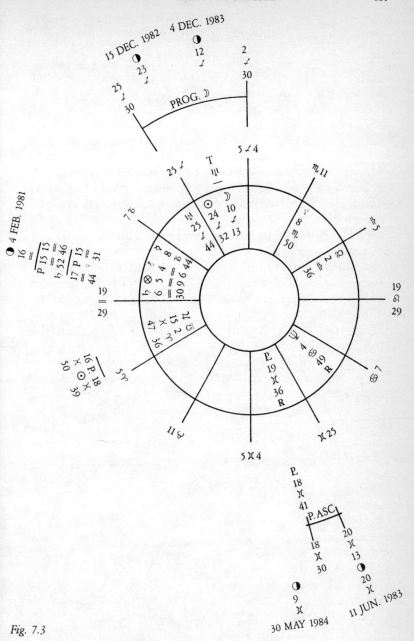

Fig. 7.3

KITTY HAWK PROGRESSED,
19 FEBRUARY 1985 — 12 DECEMBER 1986

was the worst recorded disaster involving a single aircraft, to give a full and detailed illustration.

Tokyo crash

A Japan Airlines Boeing 747 with 524 people on board crashed into a storm-swept mountain north-west of Tokyo on 12 August 1985.

Flight 123, packed with passengers returning home for a religious festival, left Tokyo's Haneda Airport at 9.12 a.m. GMT bound for Osaka. At 9.31 a.m. the pilot radioed that the starboard rear door was damaged and he had announced a state of emergency on the aeroplane. Eight minutes later, air control was told that the rear door had been destroyed and an emergency descent would take place. When a controller asked if the plane was heading back to Haneda, a voice in the cockpit shouted, 'Yes please.' Minutes later a gasping voice said, 'Please tell us where we are. We are unable to control.'

Apparently the pilot attempted an emergency landing at the US

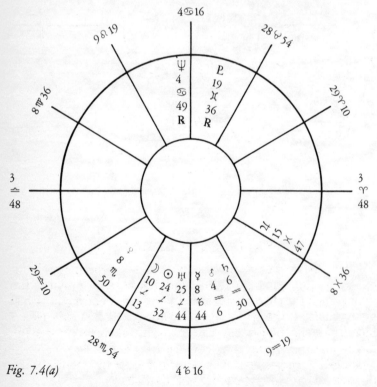

Fig. 7.4(a)

KITTY HAWK RELOCATED TO 37°25′ N 135°49′ E

base at Yokota. There was heavy cloud and storms in the rugged
Nagano area as the aircraft limped in at low altitude. It vanished
from the radar screens at 9.59 a.m. GMT and a minute later a Japanese
Air Force jet saw a high burst of flame in the mountains. Of the
524 passengers, only four survived. The site of the crash was 6,000
feet up Mt Osukada and Mt Ogura.

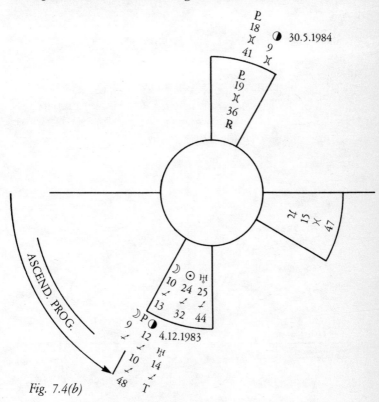

Fig. 7.4(b)

PROGRESSED TO 12 AUGUST 1985

Figure 7.4(a), the relocated chart, puts the Sagittarian stellium
opposing Pluto across the third–ninth houses with Jupiter in the
sixth. When the chart is progressed for the accident (Fig. 7.4(b)),
the Ascendant is within half a degree of a conjunction with the radical
Moon, invoking the T-square. The eclipse had already sensitized the
Moon–Pluto opposition, but it is fascinating to find the progressed
Moon exactly opposing the Gemini eclipse for the month of the
disaster. Here then is the order of activation:

Radical promise — Moon–Jupiter–Pluto T-square.

Sensitization — the eclipses.

The year — progressed ascendant conjunct radical Moon.

The Month — progressed Moon opposite Gemini eclipse.

The time — MC of accident chart conjunct progressed Moon and opposite eclipse.

An incredible alignment? Take another example.

Challenger

On 28 January 1986, a spellbound world watched the televised final countdown of the USA space shuttle *Challenger* as it prepared for lift-off. This latest space venture was to be rather special, because among the crew of seven was Christine McAuliffe, a schoolteacher,

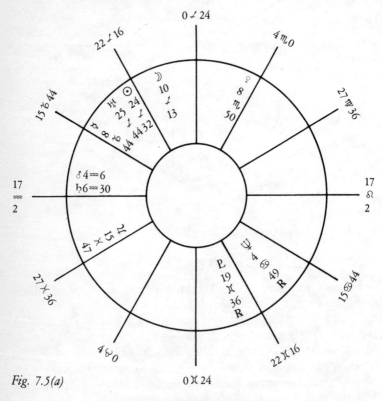

Fig. 7.5(a)

KITTY HAWK RELOCATED
TO CAPE CANAVERAL

who had been selected from numerous applicants to be the first civilian in space. *Challenger* lifted cleanly off the launch pad at 11.38 a.m., with the normal blazing exhaust behind it. One minute after the launch, when the spacecraft had reached a height of nine miles, it turned into a ferocious fire-ball. All on board perished.

In terms of human life this was a comparatively small disaster, but it was certainly the most dramatic, and it was witnessed by millions of viewers world-wide.

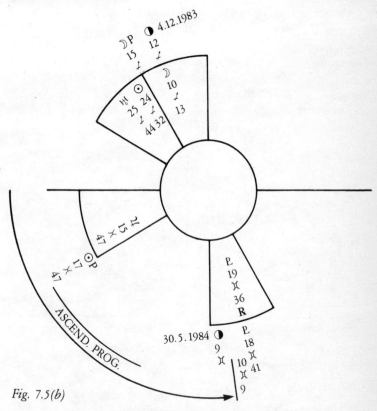

Fig. 7.5(b)

PROGRESS TO 28 JANUARY 1986

There is not a great deal of difference between the chart for *Kitty Hawk* set for its original location and that for its relocation to Cape Canaveral, just 4° on the Midheaven and 2° on the Ascendant (see Fig. 7.5(a)). Yet when the relocated chart is progressed (see Fig. 7.5(b)), the Ascendant has only reached 10° Gemini. Once again, it is the radical Moon–Jupiter–Pluto T-square that is activated, this time by the Ascendant's opposition to the Moon, and it is the same

pair of eclipses that sensitized the radical pattern about two years
previously. On this occasion, the progressed Moon is not in exact
aspect with an eclipse point, but she is not far off the midpoint of
radical Moon/Pluto. The order of activation is as follows:

Radical promise — Moon–Jupiter–Pluto T-square.

Sensitization — the eclipses.

The year — the progressed ascendant opposite the radical Moon.

The month — no exact indication.

The time — MC of accident chart conjunct the progressed moon
and opposite eclipse.

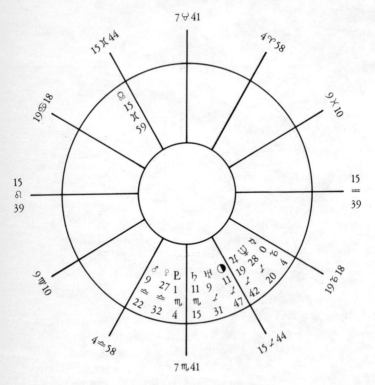

SET FOR 37°25′ N, 35°49′ E

Fig. 7.6(a)   SOLAR ECLIPSE 4 DECEMBER 1983

The eclipse at 12° Sagittarius occurred on 4 December 1983 (1.7 years before the Tokyo accident, 2.2 years before the *Challenger* accident). The eclipse at 9° Gemini occurred on 30 May 1984 (1.3 years before the Tokyo accident, 1.9 years before the *Challenger* accident). We have seen how these eclipse points were intimately involved in the two accidents through radical *Kitty Hawk* and *Kitty Hawk* progressed, but the following questions need to be considered:

1 Do either of the eclipse charts, when set for the location of the accidents, and judged of themselves, give any indication of the tragedies?
2 If so, do they conform to the rules of timing suggested by Ptolemy?

Figure 7.6(a) shows the chart for the eclipse of 4 December 1983 set for the location of the Tokyo accident, and Fig. 7.6(b) gives the

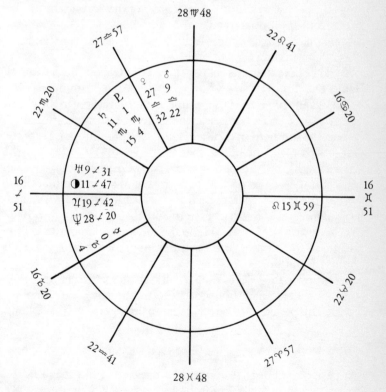

Fig. 7.6(b)

chart for the same eclipse but set for Cape Canaveral.

The Tokyo chart has the eclipse degree in the fourth house, framed on the one side by Uranus and the other by Jupiter. Uranus, being closely conjunct the eclipse, could be designated as Lord, but Jupiter is also very close and in dignity. There are obvious correlations between this chart and aviation accidents. First, there is the prominence of the sign of Sagittarius which, by its nature, has dominion over voyages and long-distance travel; secondly, there is the status of Uranus which has an association with both aviation and accidents. It is also worth noting that the Sun is Lord of the Chart, and the Moon ruler of the unfortunate Twelfth House, while powerful Jupiter rules the eighth. There is potential tragedy in these aspects, and the originator of the misfortune is Uranus. The astrologer would perhaps prefer the crucial connection, the eclipse--Uranus conjunction, to be more authoritatively placed — distinctly angular rather than tucked away in the fourth house. The Cape Canaveral chart, on the other hand, brings the eclipse to within a few degrees of the Ascendant. In this case the Sun appropriately rules the ninth house and the Moon the eighth. It may be significant that the nodes fall across the Ascendant–Descendant angles.

We do believe that this eclipse threatens aviation, both through Uranus and Jupiter. Now what about traditional timing?

This was an *Annular* eclipse, visible as a partial eclipse in the north-eastern part of South America, the extreme south-eastern part of Canada, the southern tip of Greenland, Iceland, Europe (except the northern part but including the British Isles), Africa (except the extreme south), and the south-western part of Asia. The eclipse began at 09.41 hrs GMT and ended at 03.21 hrs GMT. The annular phase began in the nothern part of the Atlantic Ocean, crossed Africa near the equator, ended in north-eastern Somalia and lasted from 10.48 hrs GMT until 14.14 hrs GMT. So the total duration of this eclipse was 5 hours 39 minutes, and the duration of the annular phase was 3 hours 26 minutes.

According to the rules of Ptolemy, the greater range of this eclipse, based upon a year for an hour of eclipse duration, is 5 years 7 months 25 days. This period must be divided into three equal parts as follows:

Eclipse date: **4 December 1983**

First period: 1 year 10 months 18 days = 22 October 1985
Second period: 1 year 10 months 18 days = 10 September 1987
Third period: 1 year 10 months 18 days = 28 July 1989

At Tokyo, the eclipse fell in the fourth house and is therefore nearest the Descendant, and so the greatest effects may be expected to manifest in the third period. Since the accident occurred in 12 August 1985, the ancient formula does not work in this case. The eclipse at Cape Canaveral fell nearest the Ascendant and should therefore manifest to the greatest extent during the first period, but the accident occurred on 28 January 1986, so it does not work out in this example either.

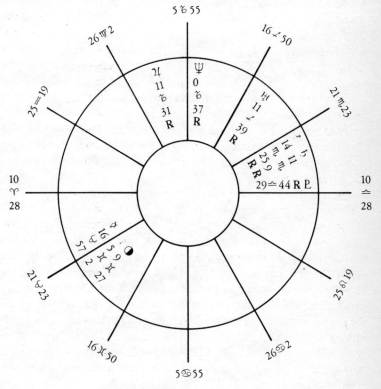

SET FOR 37°25′ N, 135°49′ E

Fig. 7.7(a)   SOLAR ECLIPSE, 30 MAY 1984

Now look at Fig.7.7(a), which takes the second eclipse of the pair and sets it for the two locations as before. Once again the chart for the Tokyo accident does not make the eclipse angular, but Uranus is again in the ninth sign and in very close aspect to the eclipse degree, this time by opposition. Further, Uranus is in the mortal eighth house, and it may be thought something of a confirmation that Mars, ruler of the Ascendant and eighth house, is moving retrograde to a conjunction of Saturn in the eighth sign. The Cape Canaveral chart (Fig. 7.7(b)) puts the eclipse at the Midheaven, and the Mars–Saturn conjunction (Mars is ruler of the eighth and ninth houses) in the third house (communication). We suggest that the close relationship of the eclipse with Uranus in Sagittarius again threatens air travel.

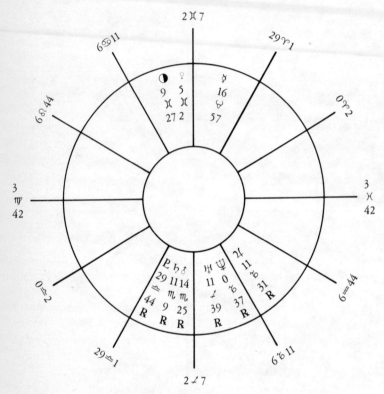

SET FOR 28°30′ N, 80°36′ W

Fig. 7.7(b)   SOLAR ECLIPSE, 30 MAY 1984

This annular eclipse occurred on 30 May 1984, and was visible as a partial eclipse from Hawaii, the eastern part of the Pacific Ocean, North America (except the north-west), Central America, the West Indies, the extreme north-west of South America, the Arctic regions, the Atlantic Ocean, Greenland, Iceland, Europe (including the British Isles), and north-west Africa. The eclipse began at 13.54 hrs GMT and ended at 19.35 hrs GMT. The annular phase began in the Pacific Ocean, crossed Mexico, the Gulf of Mexico, the south-eastern part of the United States, the Atlantic Ocean and Morocco and ended in Algeria. The annular phase lasted from 14.58 hrs to 18.32 hrs GMT.

The total duration of this eclipse was 5 hours 41 minutes, equating to 5 years 8 months 7 days, which when divided in the traditional way appears as follows:

Eclipse date: **30 May 1984**

First period: 1 year 10 months 22 days = 22 April 1986
Second period: 1 year 10 months 22 days = 14 March 1988
Third period: 1 year 10 months 22 days = 6 February 1990

The eclipse chart set for Tokyo shows the eclipse nearest the Ascendant and therefore it is the first period above that is relevant); The accident took place on 12 August 1985, so this example conforms to the ancient rule. At Cape Canaveral, the eclipse fell at the Midheaven, so the potential of the chart may be expected during the second period, but the accident actually happened within the first period on 28 January 1986.

In these two examples, where eclipses fell several years prior to the accidents and clearly relate to the radical *Kitty Hawk* chart and to *Kitty Hawk* relocated and progressed, the traditional formula for *timing* is relevant in only one out of four possibilities. While the timing may be awry, we can say that eclipse degrees remain potent in the cosmos for a number of years after their occurrence, and may act as sensitizers upon a radical chart, so that the potential of the radix will manifest when secondary progressions and/or major transits align themselves with the eclipse degrees. It is possible that eclipse degrees may have a potency equated with as many years as hours of eclipse duration, but the timing of manifestation appears to rest, in the first instance, with the secondary progressions emanating from the radix.

We would now like to work through one more example which picks up an alternative strenuous radical pattern in the *Kitty Hawk* chart.

Manchester

On 22 August 1985, 54 passengers on a holiday flight bound for

Corfu died when the cabin of their Boeing 737 jet turned into an
inferno of burning fuel while the aircraft was taking off from
Manchester Airport. Flight KT328 was taking off at about 100 mph,
travelling along Manchester's main runway at 7.13 a.m., when the
disaster struck. 83 passengers and crew members escaped.

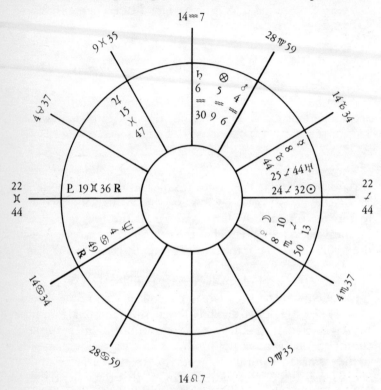

Fig. 7.8(a)

KITTY HAWK RELOCATED TO
MANCHESTER

Figure 7.8(a) shows *Kitty Hawk* relocated to Manchester, and Fig.
7.8(b) isolates the relevant secondary progression at the date of the
accident.

In this case it is not the Sagittarian stellium of *Kitty Hawk* that
is invoked but the radical square between Saturn–Mars and Venus,
and it must be highly significant that Saturn–Mars occurs in the
ninth house at Manchester.

You will see that the radical square was sensitized by a pair of
eclipses at 8° Leo and 5° Aquarius some four years before the accident.

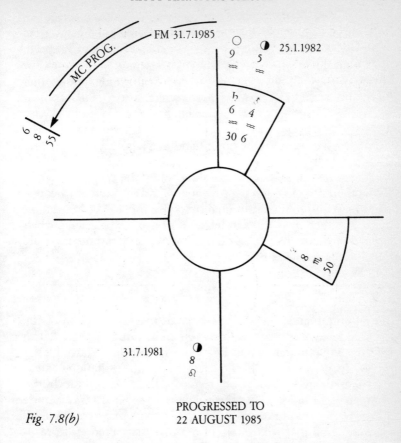

Fig. 7.8(b)

PROGRESSED TO
22 AUGUST 1985

On the day of the tragedy, the progressed Midheaven was at 6°55′ Taurus, in square to the radical Saturn and applying to an opposition of Venus. The Full Moon before the accident was closely linked with the pattern at 9° Aquarius.

Eclipse of 31 July 1981 — This was a total eclipse of the Sun which began at 01.11 hrs GMT and ended at 06.20 hrs GMT; the total phase began at 02.18 hrs GMT and ended at 06.14 hrs GMT. The path of totality began at the eastern edge of the Black Sea, crossed Central Asia and ended in the central part of the Pacific Ocean. The partial phase was visible from Eastern Europe, Saudi Arabia (except the western part), Asia (except the southern part), the Arctic regions, northern Greenland, and the north-west of North America. The full duration of this eclipse was 5 hours 9 minutes.

Eclipse of 25 January 1982 — This was a partial eclipse which began at 02.50 hrs and ended at 06.34 hrs GMT, a duration of 3 hours 44 minutes. It was visible from Antarctica and most of New Zealand.

It is doubtful whether the latter eclipse should enter into our calculations at all, being a partial eclipse visible only on the other side of the world. It is very much less powerful than a total or annular eclipse, but assuming that its period of potency did extend to 3 years 9 months, it would cover the period of the Manchester accident. The former total eclipse, on the other hand, has a potency span of over six and a half years.

When the eclipses are set for Manchester, the eclipse degree in each case occurs closest to the Ascendant, and therefore neither one would respond to the traditional timing formula. Also, we cannot say that either chart gives indications of aviation accidents when judged of themselves. This example serves only to underline the conclusions extracted from the first two.

Summary

It is a central tenet of the astrological art that the moment of any beginning has enshrined within itself all its future potential. The quality of that potential may be judged from a chart drawn for the initiatory moment. The likely timing of the manifestation of areas of potential can be measured by certain well tried techniques by the competent astrologer. Thus the moment of the *Kitty Hawk* launch — the beginning of powered air-flight — contains within itself the promise of all that will develop from that first faltering lift-off.

We have seen how the radical *Kitty Hawk* chart contains varying indications, some positive and some negative. For the purposes of demonstration we have concentrated upon several stenuous patterns which suggest tragedy and destruction.

By the well tested technique of secondary progressions we have advanced the radical moment to a year which saw unprecedented loss of human life through aviation accidents, and we have found that the unkind planetary configurations present at the initiatory moment were powerfully invoked to potency.

We have further sought to discover whether solar eclipses falling up to five years before this unhappy period had any relationship with the radical chart. It transpired that *Kitty Hawk*, both radical and progressed, was subjected to a barrage of solar eclipses during that time.

We also discovered that when *Kitty Hawk* was relocated to the place of each accident and then progressed, relevant aspects were in operation in every case, and that the eclipses aligned themselves with these patterns too. The following table below summarizes the details in each case.

Column 1 identifies the particular accident, Column 2 gives the date of the accident, Column 3 shows the Ascendant, and Column 4 the Midheaven of the *Kitty Hawk* chart when relocated to the place of the accident. Column 5 shows the progressed Ascendant and Column 6 the progressed Midheaven of the relocated chart progressed to the date of the accident. Column 7 gives the progressed Moon for the date of the accident. The most prominent aspect of the progressed relocated chart is also noted. At the end of the Table are listed all the solar eclipses falling between 1980 and 1984; each eclipse is identified by a small letter of the alphabet, and these letters are set against positions given in column 5, 6, and 7, to show which eclipse aspected by conjunction, square, or opposition any progressed angle position or the progressed Moon. The capital letters T, A and P indicate a total, annular, or partial eclipse respectively.

1	2	3	4	5	6	7
Place	Date	R. ASC.	R. MC	P. ASC.	P. MC	P. Moon
Bilbao	19.2.85	9°49'Gem.	13°26'Aqu.	16°31'Leo b	5°44'Tau.d	2°30'Sag.k
(Key aspect: Midheaven progressed square radical Mars—Saturn)						
Air India	23.6.85	6°59'Gem	6°59'Gem.	13°45'Leo a	26°21'Ari.	6°54'Sag.j
(Key aspect: progressed Moon opposite relocated Ascendant)						
Tokyo	12.8.85	3°48'Lib.	4°16'Can.	10°48'Sag.j	27°2'Vir.	8°40'Sag.j
(Key aspect: Ascendant progressed conjunct radical Moon)						
Manchester	22.8.85	22°44'Gem.	14°7'Aqu.	22°7'Leo a	6°55'Tau.d	9°01'Sag.ji
(Key aspect: Midheaven progressed square radical Saturn)						
Gander	12.12.85	17°38'Pic.	24°44'Sag.	15°52'Can.	17°51'Pic.h	12°56'Sag.ji
(Key aspect: Midheaven progressed opposite Pluto progressed)						
Guatemala	18.1.86	20°32'Pic.	19°56'Sag.	3°18'Gem.k	13°8'Pic.i	14°14'Sag.i
(Key aspect: Sun progressed square Pluto progressed)						
Challenger	28.1.86	16°58'Aqu.	00°24'Sag.	10°41'Gem.j	23°38'Aqu.	14°34'Sag.i
(Key aspect: Ascendant progressed opposite radical Moon)						
Mexico	31.3.86	27°17'Cap.	9°14'Sco.	12°55'Tau.b	2°38'Aqu.d	16°43'Sag.h
(Key aspect: Sun progressed square Pluto progressed)						
E. Berlin	12.12.86	5°56'Can.	00°09'Pic.	3°33'Vir.k	24°15'Tau.	25°30'Sag.g
(Key aspect: Moon progressed conjunction radical Sun—Uranus)						

The Eclipses

a	10.08.80	18°17'Leo T	b	04.02.81	16°02'Aqu.A	c	31.07.81	07°51'Leo T
d	25.01.82	04°54'Aqu.P	e	21.06.82	29°47'Gem.P	f	20.07.82	27°43'Can.P
g	15.12.82	23°05'Sag.P	h	11.06.83	19°42'Gem.T	i	04.12.83	11°47'Sag.A
j	30.05.84	09°26'Gem.AT	k	27.11.84	00°50'Sag.T			

We have found no convincing evidence to support the detailed timing theory of Ptolemy, but it does seem clear that solar eclipse degrees remain potent in the heavens for a number of years after

their occurrence, and become activated when they are agitated by
the progressions of a chart, particularly when aspected by conjunction,
square, or opposition.

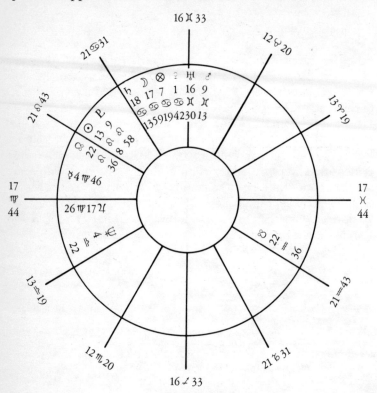

Fig. 7.9

HIROSHIMA,
5 AUGUST 1945, 23.15 GMT,
34°30′ N, 132°30′ E

It may reasonably be asked what value this exercise has in the
business of prediction. Can the astrologer look ahead and warn of
potential aviation accidents? We belive we have demonstrated that
an overall scenario may be gleaned from the basic *Kitty Hawk* chart
when progressed and aligned with relevant eclipses. This will allow
the interested astrologer to forecast difficult years for aviation in
general. It does not seem possible to indicate likely accident locations,
but it is a fact that most accidents occur on take-off or landing, and
a special study of major airports, or of airports which are of particular
interest to the individual, using a relocated *Kitty Hawk* chart, would
be valuable.

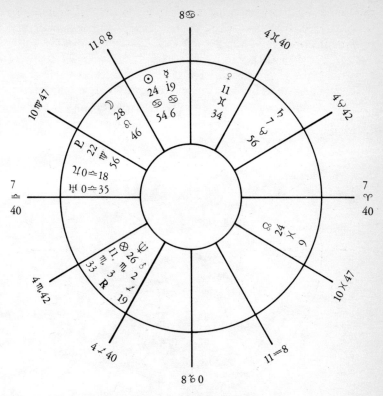

APOLLO MOONSHOT,
17 JULY 1969, 16.16 GMT,
28°30′ N, 80°36′ W

Fig. 7.10

Postscript

If there had not been a *Kitty Hawk* or its equivalent, man would
not have taken to the air. If man had not taken to the air he would
not have launched himself into space. If man had not had an
aeroplane there would not have been war in the air and he would
not have dropped bombs. The most horrific consequence of *Kitty
Hawk* must surely have been the explosion of the atom bomb at
Hiroshima on 6 August 1945 at 8.15 a.m. (5 August 1945 at 23.15
GMT). (See Fig. 7.9.) Possibly the greatest positive manifestation
of the potential of the *Kitty Hawk* chart to date was the launch
of Apollo XI, on 17 July 1969 at 16.16 hrs GMT from 28°30′ N,
80°36′ N, which carried Neil Armstrong on his historic mission to

set foot upon the Moon on 20 July 1969 at 20.18 hrs GMT (See Fig. 7.10).

We think we have given you enough charts to consider in this chapter, but if you choose to relocate *Kitty Hawk* to the places concerned, progress the relocated chart and discover if any solar eclipses, falling up to five years before the events, aligned themselves with progressed aspects, we can promise you a most intriguing study.

8.
TWO DISASTERS

The Titanic

John Jacob Astor IV (Fig. 8.1) boarded the ill-fated White Star liner *Titanic* at Southampton on 10 April 1912. The fabulously wealthy

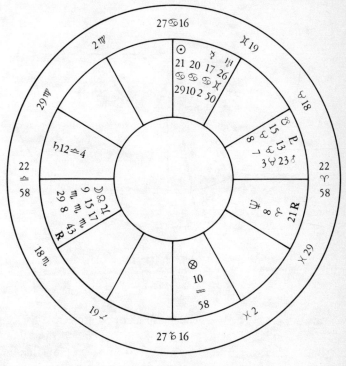

J.J. ASTOR IV
13 JULY 1864, 17.26 GMT
41°50′ N, 74°0′ N

Fig. 8.1

48-year-old Astor was accompanied by his 19-year-old wife of seven months, Madeleine. Four days later he assisted his pregnant wife into No. 4 lifeboat, stepped back, lit a cigarette and waved as it was lowered into the sea. John Jacob Astor IV was one of the 1,523 people to perish in the world's greatest sea disaster; 711 were saved.

The Launch

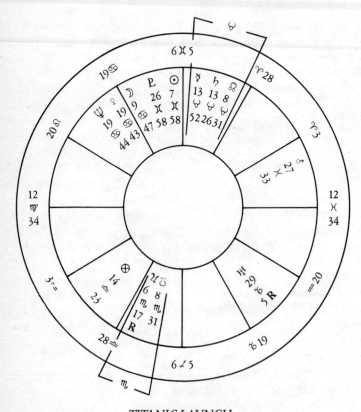

TITANIC LAUNCH,
30 MAY 1911,
Fig. 8.2   12.13 GMT, 54°35′ N, 5°56′ W

No famous person cracked a bottle of champagne across the bows of the *Titanic* at her launching on 31 May 1911 at Harland and Wolff's yard, Belfast. It was a tradition of the White Star Company that none of its liners was 'christened'. The imminence of launch was signalled by a red rocket a few minutes before noon. At 12.13 p.m., a second rocket ascended, the order to launch was given and the great ship entered the water 'shortly after 12.15', according to the Belfast *Telegraph*. The chart for the launching (Fig. 8.2), is drawn for 12.13 p.m.

It was not very clever to launch this great 'unsinkable' ship when Mercury, ruler of the Ascendant, was conjunct Saturn in the ninth house of voyages. This unhappy conjunction opposes Jupiter and the south node in the third house. There is a sextile from Mercury to Venus which does not perfect within Taurus–Gemini.

The strong Cancer Moon applies at once to a trine of Mars, and then to an opposition of Uranus (the Moon's final aspect before changing sign). This famous sea disaster has been much studied by astrologers over the years, and some have professed themselves surprised that the ship ended so tragically when a powerful Moon linked with Mars by *trine* aspect. By tradition Mars is naturally malefic. In this chart he rules the eighth and ninth houses and squares a tenth house Pluto. He occupies his own triplicity, which gives him strength, and thus intensifies his maleficence. None of these conditions are helpful, but they pale into insignificance before the fact that he occupies the degree of the evil fixed star Scheat. According to the old astrologers, Scheat causes 'extreme misfortune, murder, suicide, and drowning'. Another evil fixed star in the area was Markab, a white star situated on the wing of Pegasus; its name means a 'saddle', 'ship', or 'vehicle'. The approximate 1912 position of Markab was 22°15' Pisces, and of Scheat 28°08' Pisces.

It does not really matter at what angle the Moon points her finger at Mars when he is so ill-placed; the beneficial effects normally associated with a trine will not mitigate the maleficence of Scheat. The trine could be saying, 'I don't want to worry you but there's a nasty fixed star over there,' while a square would scream, 'Help! Scheat's coming to get me.'

This is a most inauspicious chart — no astrologer can deny it. Mars, ruler of the eighth house in watery Pisces, highlighted by a lunar aspect, square Pluto, and brutalized by Scheat, is ominous enough, but this pattern is given sinister support by Mercury–Venus opposing Jupiter and the south node, and Moon–Venus opposing Uranus.

Departure

The maiden voyage of the *Titanic* began at 12.15 p.m. on 10 April 1912 when she departed from the White Star dock at Southampton with 955 passengers and a crew of 909. It was not a clean start. Her vast bulk caused such a displacement of water that the *New York*, secured at berth 36, suffered an enormous strain as she passed, and broke her moorings. *New York*'s stern drifted out towards the great liner and came within four feet of colliding with her stern. Captain Smith of the *Titanic* ordered his vessel 'full astern', and she eventually moved backwards towards the White Star dock. This incident caused a delay of an hour before the ship finally sailed off to Cherbourg. She arrived at the French port at 6.35 p.m., disembarked 22 cross-channel passengers, took on a further 274, and left for Ireland at 8.10 p.m. She arrived at Queenstown the following day at 11.30 a.m.

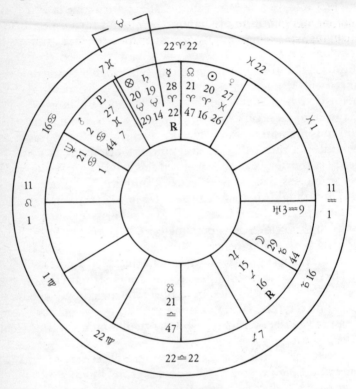

TITANIC SAILING,
10 APRIL 1912,
Fig. 8.3   12.15 GMT, 50°54′ N, 1°25′ W

Seven very lucky local passengers got off, one sensible crewman deserted, and 120 souls embarked. The *Titanic* departed Queenstown at 1.30 p.m. with 1,320 passengers and 908 crew, and headed west across the Atlantic towards her appointment with destiny.

The departure chart (Fig. 8.3) is hardly more auspicious than that of the launch. To set sail on a long voyage with Mercury retrograde at the Midheaven, with the Moon applying to the conjunction of Uranus (lord of the eighth house), which is itself quincunx Mars was, to say the least, unfortunate. Venus exalted in the ninth house is beautiful, although she does square Pluto, and in spite of all her silver-tongued charm she can be a treacherous bitch. She chose this moment to ally herself with Scheat—see how she nestles to him — just 42'' from his 1912 position.

By noon 12 April, the ship had logged 386 miles; by noon 13 April, she had covered a further 519 miles, and by the following noon another 546 miles. And so she sped on, her crew busy with their tasks and her passengers relaxing in their appropriate class of luxury.

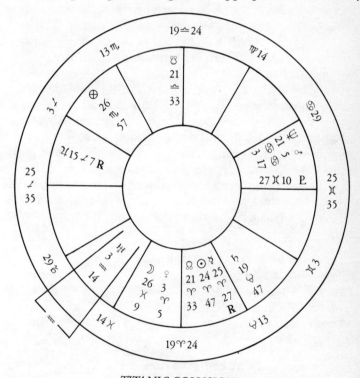

TITANIC COLLISION,
15 APRIL 1912, 3.00.56 GMT,
Fig. 8.4   41°46′ N, 50°14′ N

Other ships travelling along the busy Atlantic route radioed warnings of ice at various times during the 14 April: the *Caronia* at 9 a.m., the *Baltic* at 1.42 p.m., the *Amerika* at 1.45 p.m., the *Californian* at 7.30 p.m. and the *Mesaba* at 9.40 p.m. At 10.30 p.m. the passing

Rappahanock signalled by morse lamp that she had just run through heavy ice. At 11 p.m. the *Californian* tried to transmit another warning but was cut off by the *Titanic's* wireless operator.

Shortly after Seven Bells (11.30 p.m.) the lookout sounded his alarm bell and telephoned the bridge, 'Iceberg right ahead.' The First Officer took immediate avoiding action and gave orders to the engine room: 'Stop. Full speed astern.' The collision, when it came, was not that obvious to many. One passenger likened it to going over 'about a thousand marbles', and another to 'an extra heave of the engines', but down in the bowels of the ship a stoker heard a noise like thunder, and saw a line of water pouring through a thin gash in her side. The gash, which had penetrated the steel plates, exposed an area of about 12 square feet to the sea. The damage penetrated the forepeak tank, holds 1, 2, and 3, and the forward boiler room. The *Titanic* could float with her first four compartments flooded, but not with five.

It could be said that the collision chart (Fig. 8.4) has little relevance unless set against other charts. Could angular Pluto represent the iceberg? But look at the Moon, a little just over midway between Markab and Scheat! The time of the collision was recorded as 11.40 p.m. ship's time, and eight minutes later the Midheaven was exactly conjunct the south node, the Ascendant just having cleared an opposition with Pluto. It took nearly three hours for the ship to sink, by which time the Moon had reached 27°34' Pisces (see Fig. 8.5).

See what a fascinating thread Scheat spins through this whole affair:

1912 position of Markab (violent death)	22°15' Pisces
1912 position of Scheat	28°08' Pisces
'Launch' Mars (ruler of the eighth house)	28°17' Pisces
'Departure Venus in the Ninth house	27°26' Pisces
'Collision' Moon	26°09' Pisces
'Sinking' Moon	27°34' Pisces

A Pertinent Lunation

The *Titanic* was not even a year old when she floundered. From launch to sinking there had elapsed about 10½ months. It is remarkable indeed that the 'sinking' Moon was 43' of the 'launch' Mars, but of course the Moon would make that contact once a month during her transit of the zodiac. What marked out April 1912 as fatal?

If the launch chart is progressed on the basis of a year for a day, the only significant movement in such a short time will be that of

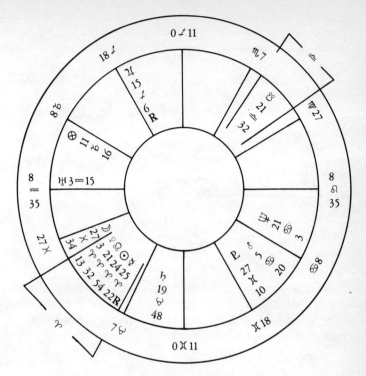

Fig. 8.5

TITANIC SINKING,
15 APRIL 1912, 5.40.56 GMT,
41°46′ N, 50°14′ W

the progressed Moon, she had only reached 23° Cancer by the time of the accident, so there is nothing remarkable to be gleaned from secondary progressions.

When the sailing chart is set against the launch chart, it is startling to find the Moon transiting the 'launch' Uranus, as well as the previously mentioned transit of Venus of the 'launch' Mars.

Between the launch and the maiden voyage, two eclipses occurred, one solar and one lunar. The solar eclipse on 22 October 1911, just less than six months before the sailing, fell at 28° Libra. This eclipse squares the 'launch' Uranus, which is picked up again by the 'sailing' Moon, and the eclipse degree is opposed by the 'sailing' retrograde Mercury. A lunar eclipse fell just nine days before the 'sailing' on 1 April 1912 at 12° Libra, but this degree does not really make strong contact with either chart. In order to find the contact we are looking for, we must turn to New Moons and Full Moons. The following list gives all of these between the launch and the sinking:

New Moons	Degree	Full Moons	Degree
25.06.11	04° Cancer	11.06.11	20° Sagittarius
25.07.11	02° Leo	11.07.11	18° Capricorn
24.08.11	00° Virgo	10.08.11	17° Aquarius
22.09.11	29° Virgo	08.09.11	15° Pisces
22.10.11*	28° Libra	08.10.11	14° Aries
20.11.11	27° Scorpio	06.11.11	13° Taurus
20.12.11	28° Sagittarius	06.12.11	13° Gemini
19.01.12	28° Capricorn	04.01.12	13° Cancer
18.02.12	28° Aquarius	02.02.12	13° Leo
18.03.12	28° Pisces	03.03.12	12° Virgo
17.04.12	27° Aries	01.04.12*	12° Libra

* Eclipses

There it is! The New Moon *before* the event fell at 28° Pisces —
Scheat again! This lunation puts the final touch to an extraordinary
pattern of contacts with a fixed star traditionally associated with
extreme misfortune and drowning.

1912 Scheat		28°08' Pisces
'Launch' Mars (ruler of eighth house)	30 May 1911	28°17' Pisces
Previous lunation	18 March 1912	27°58' Pisces
'Departure' Venus (in the ninth house)	10 April 1912	27°26' Pisces
'Collision' Moon	15 April 1912	26°09' Pisces
'Sinking' Moon	15 April 1912	27°34' Pisces

While the persistent appearance of Scheat at every important
moment for the *Titanic* screams warnings from the heavens to the
astrologically aware, it is the lunation which lays the mine, 'departure'
Venus which lights the fuse, and the transiting Moon which produces
the final explosion.

J.J. Astor IV

Many famous people perished in the *Titanic* disaster, but we have
the birth data (unconfirmed) of J.J. Astor IV as at 12.30 LMT 13

July 1964, Rhinebeck, New York, USA. It makes sense that such a wealthy man should have Jupiter on the second cusp and in Scorpio, the sign of inherited wealth. Scorpio, being the eighth sign, is also associated with death. So is Pluto, the natural ruler of Scorpio, which is opposed to Jupiter in the nativity, and that opposition tightly encloses the nodes.

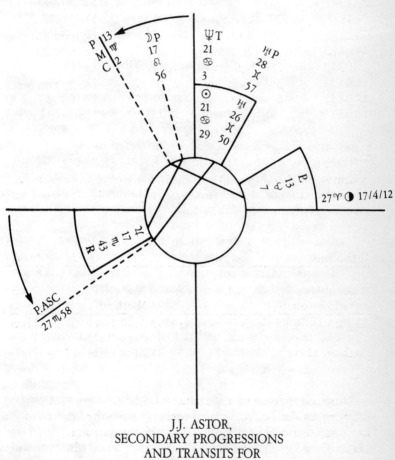

J.J. ASTOR,
SECONDARY PROGRESSIONS
AND TRANSITS FOR
Fig. 8.6   15 APRIL 1912, .3.0.56 GMT

As the *Titanic* struck the iceberg, J.J. Astor's progressed Midheaven was within two minutes of an exact trine with his radical Pluto, and the progressed Moon was square to Jupiter; thus both ends of the Jupiter–Pluto opposition were activated (see Fig. 8.6). This appears to be the key aspect, but two quincunx contacts were also in operation. The progressed Sun was quincunx the progressed Neptune in the sixth house, and the progressed Ascendant was just entering orbs of quincunx with ninth house progressed Uranus. A most appropriate transit of Neptune was within 26′ of conjunction with the radical Sun. The solar eclipse which occurred two days after the disaster on 17 April fell at 27° Aries, square to the Sun and Neptune transit, but Scheat seems to have had little to do with J.J. Astor's chart.

Chernobyl

When the hand of God sends a great storm to flatten the Earth and chasten the arrogance of man, we can feel philosophical about it and the inevitable human tragedy which accompanies such demonstrations of natural power. Yet, no such comfortable feelings arise when disaster strikes as the direct result of man's exploitive manipulation of nature. So when in Pripyat, in cherry-blossom time, the Ukrainian spring was horribly contaminated by radioactive poisons pouring from the devastated Chernobyl nuclear power station, shocked populations could only wait impotently as the noxious cloud, borne upon the wind, spread across Western Europe.

The suffering of those poor souls directly involved at the scene of the disaster and its aftermath is obvious enough, but God alone knows how many others will, in due course, suffer serious sickness and die owing to this man-made catastrophe.

The Chernobyl nuclear reactor exploded at 1.23.40 EET on 26 April 1986, sending a great fireball to illuminate the night sky, and mark the point of the tragedy.

Six eclipses fell during the 12 months before the explosion, three solar and three lunar. It will be remembered that according to tradition the *immediate* effects of a solar eclipse may be expected to manifest within the first four-month period (following the eclipse) when it occurs nearest the Eastern Angle, during the second four-month period when nearest to the MC, and during the third four-month period when nearest to the Western Angle. The immediate effects of a lunar eclipse should be felt within the month following its occurrence, during the first, second, or third period of 10 days, according to the angle nearest to which it fell.

When we set the eclipse charts for Pripyat, the solar eclipse which occurred on 19 May 1985 casts its shadow over the period covering the disaster, but so does the one which fell on 9 April 1986. The material lunar eclipse fell just two days before the disaster; in this case the eclipse was nearer to the North Angle than any other, but since tradition does not mention this angle, we take it as being nearest to the East — thus its effects should be immediate.

We should not dismiss any chart out of hand which might cast some light upon an event and the old astrologers held that solar eclipses tend to affect rulers and great men, while lunar eclipses have a particular connection with Nature and the common people. So if we consider the effects and implications of the Chernobyl disaster, it is obvious that the lunar eclipse of 24 April 1986 should first command our attention. This chart (Fig. 8.7) contains ample symbolism of the nature of the nuclear disaster.

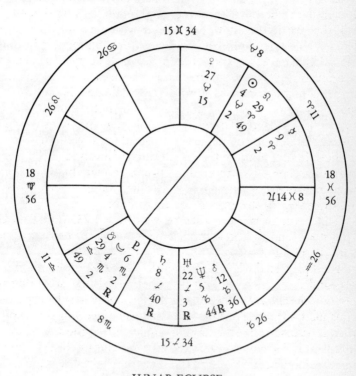

LUNAR ECLIPSE,
24 APRIL 1986,
12.47 GMT, 51°20′ N, 30°21′ E

Fig. 8.7

The most potent planet in the chart is Pluto because it is conjoined with the eclipse degree. Thus the people (Moon) are exposed to the unscrupulous rays of Pluto in the noxious sign of Scorpio, and the conjunction occurs upon the third cusp, which appears to describe a poisonous cloud very neatly.

This chart, set for Pripyat, has the fourth cusp almost exactly at the midpoint between Saturn and Uranus in Sagittarius. Sagittarius is as notorious for accidents as is Uranus for sudden explosions. The fourth house of a chart set for a town describes the fabric of that town. Mars–Neptune, as noxious a combination as you can get, are still within orbs of conjunction in Capricorn, and within the confines of the fourth house.

The eclipse degree, 4° Scorpio, does make a close applying aspect to Neptune (sextile), but what this chart appears to lack is any linking factor to bring together the evil nature of Uranus–Neptune–Mars. It could be argued that there is enough potential in Moon–Pluto alone to explain the event, but how we wish we would find some recognizable agent to link together explosive Uranus with noxious Neptune–Mars.

Parallels

We are perhaps as guilty as most modern astrologers in failing to give adequate recognition to *parallels of declination*. It sometimes happens that the heavens will find an opportunity of bashing the student across the head, so that his attention is drawn to something important. This is just such an occasion. For when one takes note of parallels, this is the fascinating and telling pattern that emerges:

Date	Time	Moon	Mars	Uranus	Neptune	
24.04.86	12.47	13°15′S	23°43′S	23°17′S	22°13′S	Lunar eclipse
25.04.86	12.00	18°59′S	23°43′S	23°17′S	22°13′S	
25.04.86	23.24	21°26′S	23°43′S	23°17′S	22°13′S	Accident
26.04.86	03.29	22°13′S	23°43′S	23°17′S	22°13′S	
	09.17	23°17′S	23°43′S	23°17′S	22°13′S	
	11.50	23°43′S	23°43′S	23°17′S	22°13′S	
26.04.86	12.00	23°45′S	23°43′S	23°17′S	22°13′S	
27.04.86	12.00	26°54′S	23°43′S	23°17′S	22°13′S	
28.04.84	12.00	28°07′S	23°43′S	23°16′S	22°13′S	
29.04.86	12.00	27°24′S	23°43′S	23°16′S	22°13′S	
30.04.86	12.00	24°56′S	23°43′S	23°16′S	22°13′S	
01.05.86	12.00	21°05′S	23°43′S	23°16′S	22°13′S	
02.05.86	12.00	16°17′S	23°43′S	23°16′S	22°13′S	

See how Mars and Uranus were in half a degree of parallel over
the 11 days we have isolated, and Neptune within one and a half
degrees of those two. Now see what happens when we enter the path
of the Moon. She starts off on the eclipse at 13° S, by noon on 25
April she is at 19°, then, within half a day of the disaster, she perfects
parallel with Neptune, Uranus and Mars in turn. The cloud
(Neptune) of radioactive poisons (Uranus) forms in the atmosphere
and begins to move (Mars) across the Continent!

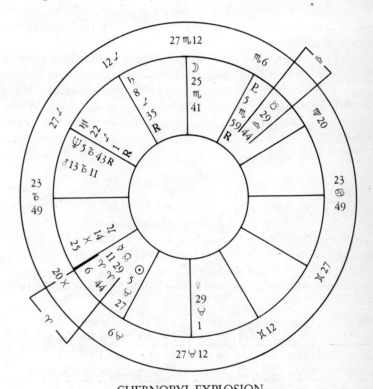

CHERNOBYL EXPLOSION,
25 APRIL 1986,
Fig. 8.8   23.23.40 GMT, 51°20′ N, 30°20′ E

The chart for the explosion itself (Fig. 8.8) contains an extraordinary
opposition between the Moon and Venus across the MC–IC —
extraordinary, not merely because of the angularity of the opposition,
but because Venus is ruler of the fourth house and on the degree
of the Pleiades (the Weeping Sisters), a fixed star cluster of evil
influence said to cause sorrow and violent death. If we had the exact

co-ordinates of the reactor, we would not be surprised if Venus sat exactly upon the IC.

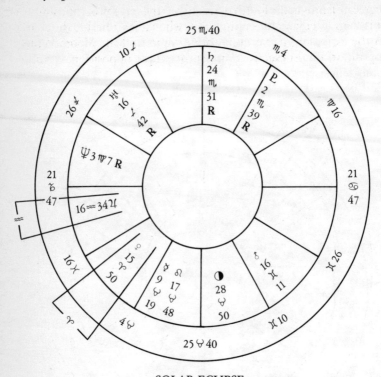

Fig. 8.9

SOLAR ECLIPSE,
19 MAY 1985,
21.42 GMT, 51°20′ N, 30°20′ E

Solar Eclipses

According to ancient rule, we have a solar eclipse chart which should or might have some bearing upon this horrendous event. The eclipse occurred way back on 19 May 1985, but because the eclipse degree is nearest the Western Angle, this chart (Fig. 8.9) has a range of a year, and its effects may be expected to manifest within the third four-month period from the date of the eclipse, and thus it was potent at the time of the disaster. Some of us, of the horary persuasion, were concerned by this eclipse because the degree falls upon the Pleiades and opposes Saturn, and that vicious opposition has no mitigation. When set for Pripyat, the opposition is angular across the MC–IC, with Saturn (ruler of the chart) at the Midheaven. With the Moon as ruler of the seventh house of foreign relations, this chart speaks of serious loss of prestige for the Soviet Union, and the eclipse degree in Taurus in the fourth house afflicts the very soil of the country. This chart is remarkable enough but, when it is set beside the chart for the explosion, it is quite astounding to find the Moon–Venus opposition almost exactly conjunct the eclipse opposition — some coincidence!

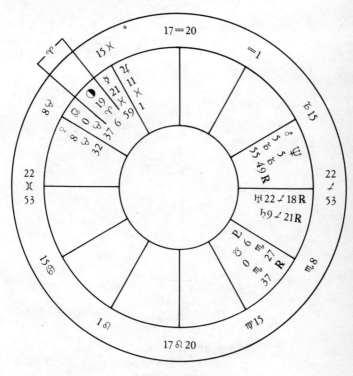

Fig. 8.10

SOLAR ECLIPSE,
9 APRIL 1986,
06.9 GMT, 51°20′ N, 30°20′ E

There is a case for taking the solar eclipse of 9 April 1986 (see Fig. 8.10) as having potency at the time of the disaster as well, because the eclipse degree is pretty well equidistant between the Ascendant and Midheaven, but the composition of the chart is hardly relevent to the event. We have strong indications from the solar eclipse of 19 May 1985 which is intimately connected with the moment of explosion, and from the lunar eclipse of 24 April 1986.

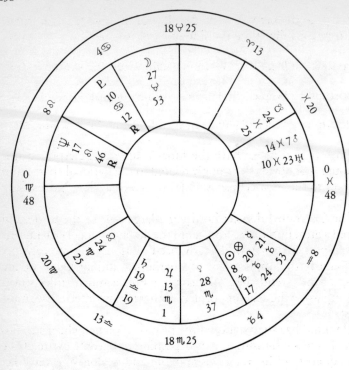

Fig. 8.11

USSR,
30 DECEMBER 1922,
18.00 GMT, 55°45′ N, 37°34′ E

The Soviet Chart

The whole question of a foundation chart for the Soviet Union is
still open, and will remain so until someone takes the trouble to
investigate the matter thoroughly. In *Mundane Astrology*, Michael
Baigent gives two possibilities. He does not favour the one we produce
here (Fig. 8.11), but we show it because of the remarkable link it
has with this eclipse chart. Once again, that degree area in late Taurus-
Scorpio is highlighted, and once again across the MC–IC. We like
this chart for its debilitated Venus in the fourth house. The Soviet
Union has continually suffered from bad harvests, and if we extend
the theme a little it can easily be permitted to encompass the
poisoning (Scorpio) of the earth (fourth house). The nature of Venus
may also explain collective farms, the devastation experienced during
the last war and the 'scorched earth' policy adopted by the Russians
against their invaders. It would take meticulous research to justify

this chart as the nativity of the USSR, but in this particular case it
fits in beautifully. Note the line of contacts:

National chart Moon   27°53′Taurus 10th/Venus   28°37′Scorpio 4th

Solar eclipse   Eclipse 28°51′Taurus   4th/Saturn 24°34′Scorpio MC

Explosion   Venus   29°01′Taurus   4th/Moon   25°41′Scorpio MC

On top of this, we have the lunar eclipse of 24 April, which
although not obviously strongly related to the national chart given
here, or to the solar eclipse, stands on its own as descriptive of the
event.

The Chernobyl disaster horrified a large part of the world and
caused a great public reaction against the development of civil nuclear
power, particularly from the 'advanced' nations. It is too early yet
to quantify the implications of Chernobyl, and although we are
tempted to extend these observations into a much fuller study,
encompassing the astrology of all the other nations affected, we must
resist.

Mankind has always abused the beautiful planet which sustains
him. There are signs that he is beginning to become aware of the
consequences of his voracious appetite and exploitive genius. Let
us hope he comes to full consciousness before it's too late.

9.

EUROPE ABLAZE

The Third Reich

After the defeat of Germany in the First World War, the British Prime
Minister, David Lloyd George, favoured putting the Kaiser and the
German army leaders on trial 'as an example to the future'. Field-
Marshal von Hindenberg accused Lloyd George of having the
thoughts of 'a reincarnated Roman Imperator', wishing to drag
German political leaders behind the British chariot to increase his
own popularity. 'He thinks by this means to terrorize 60 millions
of Germans even unto the third generation. Mr Lloyd George is
mistaken. Instead he will implant the most implacable hatred, a
hatred that can give no assurances to promise a permanent peace
for the world.' The Kaiser was exiled to Doorn in Holland, and Lloyd
George did not get his Roman triumph. All the same, in defeat
German hatred smouldered, until the blast of an ex-corporal's oratory
stirred the ashes into a white-hot inferno.

When Adolf Hitler became Chancellor of Germany on 30
January 1933, the Nazi state came into being, and a reign of terror
descended upon the German people. The terror was to grow and
spread beyond the bounds of that unfortunate country, and career
unchecked throughout Europe. Twelve years and millions of lives
later, with the Continent in smouldering ruins, it was finally
contained.

Charles Carter gives the data for Nazi Germany as 30 January 1933
at 11 a.m. CET (*An Introduction to Political Astrology*), which he
took from Goering's book *Germany Reborn*. The chart for this
moment is also given in *Mundane Astrology* (Baigent, Campion,
and Harvey). William L. Shirer, in *The Rise and Fall of the Third
Reich*, quotes Franz von Papen as follows:

At about half past ten the members of the proposed Cabinet met in my house and walked across the garden to the Presidential palace, where we waited in Meissner's office. Hitler immediately renewed his complaints about not being appointed Commissioner for Prussia. He felt that this severely restricted his power. I told him . . . the Prussian appointment could be left until later. To this Hitler replied that if his powers were to be thus limited, he must insist on new Reichstag elections.

This produced a completely new situation and the debate became heated. Hugenberg, in particular, objected to the idea, and Hitler tried to pacify him by stating that he would make no changes in the Cabinet, whatever the result might be . . . By this time it was long past eleven o'clock, the time that had been appointed for our interview with the President, and Meissner asked me to end our discussion, as Hindenburg was not prepared to wait any longer. At last we were shown in to the President . . . Hindenburg made a short speech about the necessity of full co-operation in the interests of the nation, and we were then sworn in. The Hitler Cabinet had been formed.

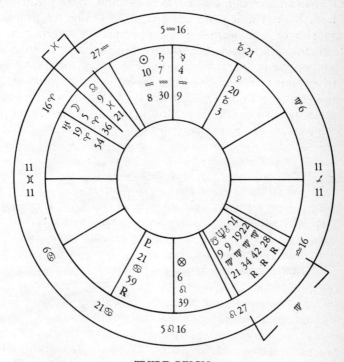

THIRD REICH,
30 JANUARY 1933,
11.00 GMT, BERLIN

Fig. 9.1

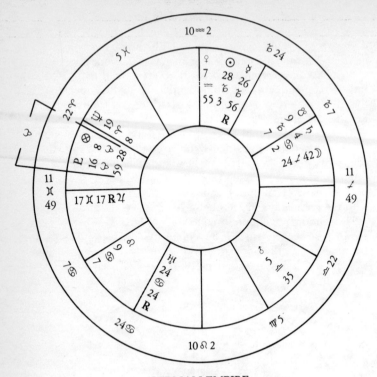

GERMAN EMPIRE,
18 JANUARY 1871
12.51.28 GMT, BERLIN

Fig. 9.2

From this account, it would seem that the beginning of the Third Reich was nearer noon than eleven o'clock, thus the chart given here (Fig. 9.1) is set for noon. We also show in Fig. 9.2 the map for the German Empire, which some astrologers say holds good for Germany until this present day. Doubtless, each chart in its own way will reflect the fortunes of the German people.

The chart for the beginning of the Third Reich is of immense importance to any astrologer, for this was the moment when, acting quite constitutionally, the president of Germany let Adolph Hitler loose upon the world. A devil incarnate was given legal authority, and without delay embarked upon a career of murder. He murdered enemies, friends and neighbours; he murdered nations, he murdered races, and in the end he murdered himself.

With Sun–Saturn at the Midheaven and the Sun in mutual reception with Uranus, it is not surprising that this regime was

	0 1 2 3 4 5 6 7 8 9 10 11 12 13 14 15 16 17 18 19 20 21 22 23 24 25 26 27 28 29 30

GERMANY NAZI STATE
RADICAL POSITIONS

☿ M ☽ ♄ ☊ ♆ A   ♅ ♇
4 5 5 7 9 9 11   19 22
♒ ♒ ♈ ♒ ♓ ♍ ♓   ♈ ♋
9 16 36 30 21 34 11   54 59
             ☉   ♐ ♃
             10   19 22
             ♒   ♍ ♍
             8   42 28
                      ♀
                      20
                      ♉
                      8

CONSCRIPTION
16 MAR. 1935

☽   M ♄   ♆   ☉   A   ♐ ♅ ♇ ♀
1   7 7   9   12   13   19 19 21 22
♈   ♒ ♒   ♍   ♓   ♍ ♈ ♋ ♉
38   25 45   30   17   48   24 58 56 42
           ☿   ♃
           7   22
           ♒   ♍
           43   19

RHINELAND
7 MAR. 1936

           ♄ ♆   ☽   A   ♂ ♅ ♇   ♀
           7 9   13   14   19 19 21   23
           ♒ ♍   ♈   ♓   ♍ ♈ ♋   ♉
           52 29   20   58   15 59 55   55
           M ☿   ☉   ♃
           8 9   13   22
           ♒ ♒   ♒   ♍
           24 22   17   14

ANSCHLUSS
11 MAR. 1938

         ☽ ♄ ♆ M   ☿   ☉   A ♐ ♅ ♇   ♀
         7 8 9 10   12   15   17 18 20 21   26
         ♓ ♒ ♍ ♒   ♓ ♍ ♈ ♋   ♉
         12 7 26 27   49   19   17 54 3 53   26
                                         ♃
                                         22
                                         ♍
                                         4

CZECHOSLOVAKIA
15 MAR. 1939

         ♄ ♆ M   ☿ ☉   A ♐ ♅ ♇   ⚷
         8 9 11   14 16   18 18 20 21   27
         ♒ ♍   ♒ ♓   ♓ ♍ ♈ ♋   ♉
         14 25 28   33 21   25 42 5 51   41
                           ☽   ♃
                                    19   21
                                    ♓   ♍
                                    15   59

Fig. 9.3(a)

Degree scale (columns): 0 1 2 3 4 5 6 7 8 9 10 11 12 13 14 15 16 17 18 19 20 21 22 23 24 25 26 27 28 29 30

GERMANY NAZI STATE — RADICAL POSITIONS

Point	°	Sign	′
☿	4	♒	9
M	5	♒	16
☽	5	♈	36
♄	7	♒	30
☊	9	♓	21
♆	9	♍	34
A	11	♓	11
☉	10	♒	8
♅	19	♈	54
♇	21	♋	59
♃	19	♍	42
δ	22	♍	28
♀	20	♉	3

POLAND — 1 SEPT. 1939

Point	°	Sign	′
♄	8	♒	17
♆	9	♍	24
M	11	♒	56
☿	15	♒	22
☉	16	♍	49
♂	18	♈	36
A	18	♓	56
♅	20	♈	6
♇	21	♋	51
♃	21	♍	57
☽	24	♓	51
♀	28	♉	16

SPRING OFFENSIVE — 9 APR. 1940

Point	°	Sign	′
☽	2	♋	12
♄	8	♒	21
♆	9	♍	23
M	12	♒	33
☿	16	♒	26
☉	17	♒	26
♂	18	♈	29
A	19	♓	35
♅	20	♈	7
♇	21	♋	50
♃	21	♍	54
♀	29	♉	1

RUSSIA — 22 JUN. 1941

Point	°	Sign	′
♀	0	♒	32
♄	8	♒	30
♆	9	♍	21
M	13	♒	46
☽	16	♋	59
♂	18	♏	12
☿	18	♒	32
☉	18	♒	39
♅	20	♈	9
A	20	♓	53
♇	21	♋	49
♃	21	♍	47

USA AT WAR — 11 DEC. 1941

Point	°	Sign	′
♀	1	♒	7
♆	9	♍	20
♄	8	♒	33
M	14	♒	15
♂	18	♏	6
☿	19	♒	22
☉	19	♒	7
♅	20	♈	10
A	21	♓	22
♇	21	♋	48
♃	21	♍	44
☽	22	♋	52

Fig. 9.3(b)

| | 0 1 2 3 4 5 6 7 8 9 10 11 12 13 14 15 16 17 18 19 20 21 22 23 24 25 26 27 28 29 30 |

**GERMANY
NAZI STATE**

**RADICAL
POSITIONS**

```
              ☿  M ☽ ♄      ☊ ♆  A                    ♅    ♇
              4  5 5 7      9 9  11                   19   21
              ≈  ≈ ♈ ≈      ♓ ♍  ♓                    ♈    ♋
              9  16 36 30   21 34 11                  54   59
                            ☉                         ♂    ♃
                            10                        19   22
                            ≈                         ♍    ♍
                            8                         42   28
                                                      ♀
                                                      20
                                                      ♍
                                                      3
```

**STALINGRAD
2 FEB. 1943**

```
        ♀           ☽    ♆               M      ♂    ♅ ☿ ♇  A
        2           7    9               15     17   20 21 21 22
        ≈                ♍               ≈      ♍    ♈ ≈ ♋  ♓
        33          23   19              24     49   13 24 47 33
                         ♄                            ☉    ♃
                         8                            20   21
                         ≈                            ≈    ♍
                         41                           17   38
```

**ASSASINATION
ATTEMPT
20 JUL. 1944**

```
        ♀           ♆                    ♂      ♅ ♃ ♇    ☿    ☽
        4           9                    17     20 21 21 24   26
        ≈           ♍                    ♍      ♈ ♍ ♋    ≈    ♌
        22          16                   26     16 29 45 2    26
                    ♄                    M             ☉    A
                    8                    16            21   24
                    ≈                    ≈             ≈    ♓
                    52                   53            46   2
```

**HITLER'S
SUICIDE
30 APR. 1945**

```
        ♀      ☽    ♆                    ♂   M  ♅ ♃ ♇       ☿
        5      6    9                    17  17 20 21 21     25
        ≈      ♍    ♍                    ♍   ≈  ♈ ♍ ♋       ≈
        20     46   15                   14  40 17 25 45     26
                    ♄                               ☉       A
                    8                               22       24
                    ≈                               ♓
                    57                              33       48
```

Fig. 9.3(c)

described as 'the new order', and, bearing in mind the dictatorial nature of the negative Saturnian Aquarian, it is interesting that the Germans set about reordering Europe with revolutionary speed, ruthless efficiency and clinical detachment. The Mars–Jupiter conjunction in Virgo linked to Pluto in Cancer seems descriptive of the Nazis' obsession with racial purity, and the quincunx aspect of that conjunction with Arian Uranus is indicative of the manner in which they gave practical effect to that obsession.

Let us take a look at how the progressions worked out during the 12 years of the regime's existence in Figs. 9.3(a), (b) and (c).

They really fall into four broad phases: firstly, conscription in 1935, the march into the Rhineland in 1936, and the *Anschluss* (incorporation of Austria into the Reich) in 1938; secondly, the invasion and subjugation of Czechoslovakia and Poland and the outbreak of war with Great Britain and France; thirdly, the western offensive which within six weeks brought Denmark, Norway, Belgium, Holland, Luxembourg and France under German domination; and finally the invasion of Russia, the entry of the United States into the war, and the defeat of Germany.

Phase 1 — Having spent two years reorganizing Germany and drawing total power to himself, Hitler announced conscription: the *progressed Midheaven is conjunct the radical and progressed Saturn*. With the Midheaven still in contact with Saturn, Hitler takes his first big gamble, gives expression to his power and marches into the Rhineland. German generals have admitted that if France had intervened at this point the German army would have been forced to retreat, and Hitler would probably have fallen. But, the Germans were welcomed by the Rhinelanders and Hitler's gamble paid off.

Next, Hitler arranges for the annexation of Austria, his homeland, and forms one united German Reich. Again the Germans were well received by the majority of the Austrian population: *the progressed Midheaven is conjunct the radical Sun (ruler of the fourth house)*. You can see that the radical chart shows the Ascendant in wide square with Mars. The Ascendant has been progressing to perfect that square with the Lord of War, and Mars has been retrograding towards the advancing Ascendant. Hitler has taken over two territories, populated by people of German blood, and he has not had to resort to armed conflict to do it. So far so good.

Phase 2 — Now Hitler tries an audacious and dangerous gamble. Under the pretext of protecting the German minority in Czechoslovakia from ill-treatment, he decides to take over the country.

This time he invades a neighbouring sovereign state, subdues it, and declares a protectorate: *the progressed Ascendant has linked with retrograding Mars.* Germany has gone to war and risked the retaliation of Britain and France. Hitler declares that Czechoslovakia is his last territorial demand in Europe, and to their undying shame the great powers agree to sacrifice that sad country for the sake of peace. 'Czechoslovakia has ceased to exist,' boasted the Führer.

Having won against all the odds, Hitler goes for a double and six months later invades Poland: *the progressed Ascendant has perfected the square with retrograding Mars and is approaching a sextile with Arian Uranus and a square with radical Mars; the radical quincunx is now fully invoked.* After this naked and unprovoked aggression, which was supported by Russia in a secret agreement, Britain and France finally declare war on Germany.

Phase 3 — After a period of comparative inactivity, Hitler launched his western offensive in the spring of 1940. *The power of radical Mars-Jupiter quincunx Uranus (Uranus in mutual reception with the Sun) is now in full spate as the progressed Ascendant perfects its sextile with Uranus.* Norway and Denmark are invaded on 9 April 1940 and Belgium, Holland and Luxembourg on 10 May 1940. French and British forces engage the enemy. The British Expeditionary Force is driven into the sea, but manages to escape in the remarkable Dunkirk evacuation. France capitulates on 22 June 1940. Throughout the summer, Germany attempts to break Britain by aerial bombardment before invading. After the Battle of Britain, the invasion plans abandoned, Hitler, now master of Europe, turns his gaze East.

The stupendous success of German arms during this period appears linked with the influence of Uranus in Aries which is mutually received by the tenth house Sun.

Phase 4 — When Hitler followed in the footsteps of Napoleon and invaded Russia, on 22 June 1941: *the progressed ascendant is leaving the sextile of Uranus and is approaching a square of progressed Jupiter, but the progressed Sun is moving to sextile Uranus (radical reception).* Now begins a mammoth struggle, as German forces make great early progress in Russia, and Hitler felt able to announce to a deliriously happy German populace on 3 October 1941 that the Soviet Union was finished.

Following the Japanese attack on Pearl Harbour, the United States of America finally entered the conflict on 11 December 1941, but Hitler was quick to declare war on them first: *the progressed Sun is now closing with radical Uranus and standing conjunct progressed Mercury (Ascendant ruler).*

German forces suffered serious reverses during the winter of 1941/42 but recovered brilliantly, so that by the end of the summer of 1942: 'On the map the sum of Hitler's conquests looked staggering . . . German troops stood guard from the Norwegian North cape on the Arctic to Egypt, from the Atlantic at Brest to the southern reaches of the Volga river on the border of central Asia.' (*The Rise and Fall of The Third Reich* by William Shirer). Hitler's refusal to allow retreat, his interference with the strategy of his generals, the indomitable fighting spirit of the Red Army aided by the vicious Russian weather, and Allied action in other spheres, stopped him in his tracks. When in early 1943 the Russians eliminated the German Sixth Army at Stalingrad, and the Axis forces in North Africa surrendered: *the progressed Sun is separating from its sextile with Uranus and approaching a quincunx with progressed Jupiter, while progressed the Ascendant is square Jupiter.*

The attempt on Hitler's life on 20 July 1944 seems well symbolized by the *progressed Sun exactly quincunx Pluto*, and when he commits suicide on 30 April 1945, *the progressed Sun, from the tenth house, is almost exactly quincunx Jupiter in the fifth house (eighth from the tenth), and forms a finger-of-fate with Jupiter—Pluto; also the progressed Midheaven is separating quincunx of progressed Mars.*

National Secondary Progressions

We have just seen an example of the secondary progressions for the Third Reich which seem to work very well and confirm the validity of the map we have suggested. Now let us look at several specific examples for some of the nations which were on the receiving end of German aggression. Maps for most of the nations concerned exist, but often they are not very reliable or the source is obscure. However, we have selected the maps of Czechoslovakia and Poland for the Phase 2; Norway and Belgium, for Phase 3; and the United States and Russia for phase 4. We do not have maps for Denmark or Luxembourg, and the chart for France — the Third Republic — does not respond to secondary progressions.

Czechoslovakia

See Fig. 9.4. Czechoslovakia is a Central European republic incorporating the lands of the old kingdom of Bohemia (Bohemia, Moravia and part of Silesia), the Slovak territory of former Hungary, and the autonomous territory of Carpathian Ruthenia. Czecho-

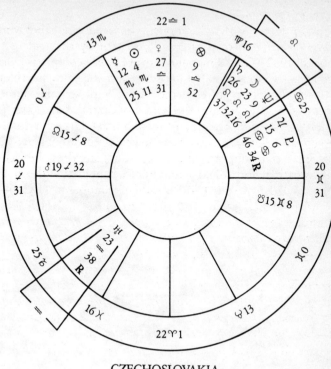

Fig. 9.4

CZECHOSLOVAKIA,
28 OCTOBER 1918,
10.00 GMT, PRAGUE

slovakia emerged from the aftermath of the First World War as an independent republic, being formerly part of the Austro-Hungarian Empire. At the 1923 census the principal nationalities were represented as follows: Czechoslovak 66.6%; German 23.4%; Magyar 5.6%; Jew 1.6%; Pole 0.6%. The substantial German minority was strongest in the industrial zones.

In the closing stages of the First World War, the great powers officially recognized the right of Czechoslovakia to complete independence. On 14 October 1918, Dr Benes announced the establishment of an interim Czechoslovak government in Paris. This interim government was recognized by France on 15 October and by Italy on 24 October. Meanwhile the interim government itself proclaimed the independence of the Czechoslovak nation by a declaration in Washington. Following the capitulation of Austria–Hungary during the night of 27/28 October, the National Committee at Prague proclaimed the independence of the Czechoslovak state

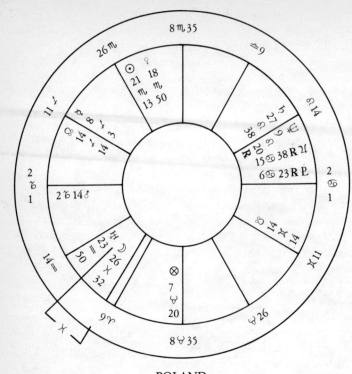

POLAND
14 NOVEMBER 1918,
Fig. 9.5   09.30 GMT, WARSAW

by its first law on 28 October. The time is quoted by Carter as
'about 11 a.m. LMT'. The map for this moment shows a strong Venus
at the Midheaven and Mars at the Ascendant, which is quite
promising, but an eighth house Moon–Saturn conjunction in Leo
opposes second house Uranus in Aquarius. Mercury, ruler of the
seventh, while in good aspect to a strong Jupiter, is squared by eighth
house Neptune.

Poland

See Fig. 9.5 this chart, given by Carter for the proclamation of the
Polish Republic, is generally accepted as a reliable map for Poland.
The Treaty of Versailles (28 June 1919), the assentors to the Covenant
of the League of Nations, and the signatories of the Treaty of Peace
guaranteed the independence of Poland which was reconstituted
within the limits of the eighteenth century 'Polish Commonwealth'.

The Polish-Soviet War of 1920 ended with the establishment of
Poland's borders with Russia, to the benefit of Poland. In 1926, a

coup d'état by Marshal Pilsudski resulted in a more authoritarian regime. In 1935, a new constitution gave the president dictatorial powers. The internal affairs of Poland were not assisted by the multiplicity of nationalities and political parties. In 1921 the population was made up as follows: Poles 69.2%; Ruthenians and Ukrainians 14.0%; Jews 7.8%; White Russians 3.9%; Germans 3.8%; Lithuanians 0.3%; Others 1.0%

In October 1938, after the Munich Agreement, Poland happily took her share of dismembered Czechoslovakia (Teschen and Czech Silesia), but when Hitler made demands for frontier rectifications in 1939 and was resisted, Poland was doomed. Germany invaded on 1 September and the country was partitioned between Germany and the USSR under the terms of the Nazi–Soviet pact. Part of Poland was incorporated into the Reich, while the central and southern parts were administered as a colony. The territories occupied by the USSR were incorporated into the Byelorussian and Ukrainian Soviet Socialist Republics.

The Polish chart has two major stressful patterns.

1 Jupiter and Pluto are conjunct in Cancer in the seventh house of war. It is a wide conjunction (9°), but retrograde Jupiter is moving back towards retrograde Pluto, so it is an applying conjunction. From the Ascendant exalted Mars is within orbs of opposition to Pluto, and although Mars is not within orbs of Jupiter, it is applying to opposition.

2 Sun–Saturn–Uranus combine to form a T-square in fixed signs, and this is a violent pattern. Apart from the obvious economic difficulties suggested by Uranus afflicted in the second house, it indicates restrictive and dictatorial regimes (Uranus in Aquarius and Saturn in Leo), symbolizing the constant struggle between the two rulers of government — democratic and revolutionary Uranus against imperial Saturn in Leo, made the more intense Scorpionic Sun.

The strength of Mars rising suggests the fierce sense of national identity associated with the Poles; Jupiter exalted in Cancer shows the power of the Church which the later Communist regime has been unable to eradicate, and the link between Mars–Pluto across the horizon holds the promise of war.

When Hitler invaded Czechoslovakia on 15 March 1939 (see Fig. 9.6), the Midheaven had progressed to a conjunction of Mercury (ruler of the seventh house), and the Sun had progressed to square the Moon and Uranus, thus forming a T-square and activating the radical opposition. The only transit of note was Uranus hovering around the opposition point to Mercury. On the invasion of Poland

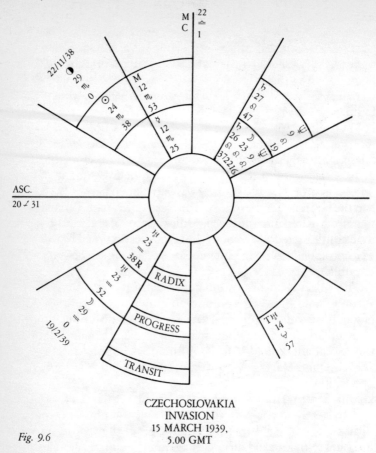

CZECHOSLOVAKIA
INVASION
15 MARCH 1939,
5.00 GMT

Fig. 9.6

on 1 September 1939 (see Fig. 9.7), the progressed Midheaven was
in contact with the radical T-square through a square aspect to Saturn,
and the progressed Moon was poised to pass over the Ascendant and
the radical Mars. Meanwhile, transiting Uranus had moved neatly
into position in Taurus to turn the radical T-square into a fixed Grand
Cross, and Mars was appropriately transiting the progressed
Ascendant.

Note, for the moment, how the solar eclipse of 22 November 1938
(29° Scorpio) involved itself with the radical/progressed patterns of
both charts, and how the New Moons before each event fell in sharp
relationship with it.

The United Kingdom
After the attack on Poland, Britain and France finally declared war

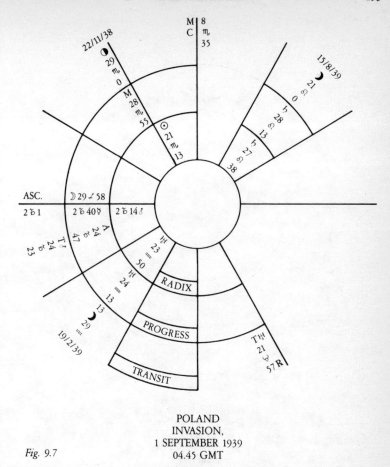

POLAND
INVASION,
1 SEPTEMBER 1939
04.45 GMT

Fig. 9.7

on Germany; the British ultimatum expired at 11 a.m. GMT on 3
September 1939.

It seems astrologically apt that, at the declaration of war, the United
Kingdom Mars was activated. The progressed Ascendant was in trine
to Mars, thus invoking the radical Mars–Venus square, and the
progressed Mars was not only square the radical Ascendant but
conjunct Uranus, with the progressed Moon closely involved with
progressed Mars and Uranus in the eleventh house. The United
Kingdom chart appears in Chapter 5, and Fig. 9.8 picks out the
relevant pattern. Note once again how the same eclipse and New
Moons activate this chart as well as the Czechoslovak and Polish maps.

We think that these secondary progressions for Phase 2 give
credence to the radical charts, and although some rectification may

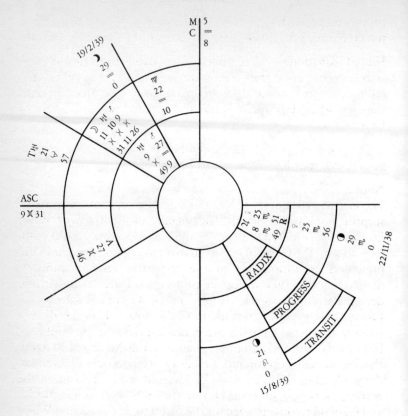

UNITED KINGDOM
AT WAR,
3 SEPTEMBER 1939,
10.00 GMT

Fig. 9.8

prove reasonable upon further study, the timings cannot be far off the mark.

The solar eclipse of 22 November 1938 fell at 29°02′ Scorpio, and it is fascinating how intimately this degree linked in with all three national charts given above.

Czechoslovakia — Progressed Sun invoking by square the Moon–Saturn opposition with Uranus; solar eclipse falling at 29° Scorpio, sensitizing the pattern and within less than 2° of an exact square with progressed Saturn; the New Moon before the invasion on 19 February 1939 provided the ignition.

Poland — Radical Sun–Saturn–Uranus T-square activated by progressed Midheaven; solar eclipse sensitizing the pattern by conjunction with the progressed Midheaven; the New Moon before the event on 15 August 1939 at 21° Leo ignites. Transit of Uranus.

United Kingdom — Progressed Ascendant trine radical Mars activating the radical Mars–Venus square; solar eclipse at 29° Scorpio falling close to Venus and square to Mars; the New Moon prior to the event at 21° Leo square Venus and opposed to Mars. Transit of Uranus.

The solar eclipse of 22 November is beginning to assume importance, but let's move on to Phase 3.

Norway

The German conquest of Denmark and Norway took everyone by surprise, not least the British. The operation *Weseruebung* ('Weser Exercise') was ordered to begin at 3.15 a.m. GMT on 9 April 1940. At 3.20 a.m. the German representatives in Copenhagen and Oslo presented an ultimatum to the respective foreign ministers demanding that they accept the protection of the Reich, without delay and without resistance. King Christian of Denmark surrendered promptly, but Norway resisted from the outset. King Haakon of Norway, brother to King Christian, made it clear that he would not be bullied or intimidated by Germany. On the evening of 10 April, the Norwegian government broadcast its rejection of German demands from the little town of Elverum, and called upon the Norwegian people to resist. During the battle for Norway, British and German troops engaged for the first time in the Second World War, at Lillehammer. But the ship carrying British artillery was sunk, the infantry suffered badly from German air attacks, and Allied forces were forced to evacuate. The King and members of his government were moved to Tromsö in the far north on 29 April where they set up a provisional government. Meanwhile, Allied forces managed to drive the Germans from Narvik, but eventually adandoned it to the Germans in favour of concentrating on the Western Front. Finally, King Haakon and his government were boarded onto the British cruiser *Devonshire* on 7 June 1940, and taken to exile in London. The King returned to Oslo on 7 June 1945.

Norway is an ancient kingdom and we know of no date for its foundation. Carter gives the chart for Norway's separation from Sweden as 7 June 1905, at 10.30 a.m. CET, and noted 'may be about half an hour later'. We have seen a time of 10 a.m., although the source cannot be recalled, and such limited investigations as we have been able to carry out tend to support this timing, so we produce it here (Fig. 9.9).

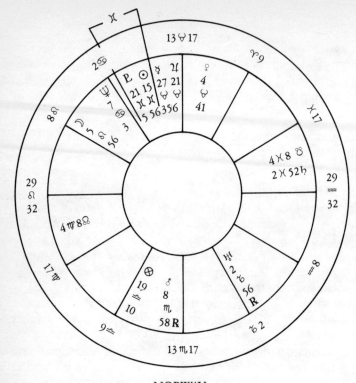

NORWAY,
7 JUNE 1905,
09.00 GMT, OSLO

Fig. 9.9

The map, when progressed to the invasion (Fig. 9.10), fairly bristles
with symbolism of the event:

1 The difficult conjunction between Sun–Pluto in the tenth house
is neatly activated by both progressed angles, Midheaven conjunct
the Sun and Ascendant square Pluto. It was exactly five years from
King Haakon's departure to his return, and there are 5° between
the Sun and Pluto. This conjunction itself can be interpreted as
showing the exile of the King from his native land, and also the nature
of the Nazi government of the country which increased in brutality
as time went on, with the progressed Midheaven moving closer to
Pluto. The progressed Ascendant square Pluto at the time of invasion
describes the nature of the experience the Norwegian people suffered.

2 The progressed Moon from the fourth house opposes Jupiter in
the tenth and also stands quincunx to Pluto. The Norwegian people
(Moon) in their own land (fourth house) are separated (opposition)

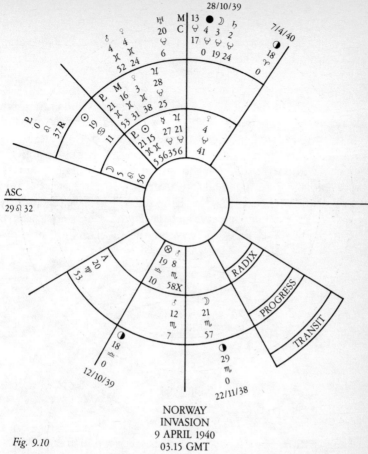

Fig. 9.10

NORWAY
INVASION
9 APRIL 1940
03.15 GMT

from their government and monarch (tenth house Jupiter) and
afflicted (quincunx) by the experience of war (Pluto).

3 The progressed Sun squares Fortuna, and this pattern was struck
by a solar eclipse from 18° Aries only two days before the invasion.

4 Progressed Mars, which was moving very slowly at the time, was
to pass across the IC during the occupation, clearing it by half a degree
by 1945.

5 The radical T-square between the Moon, Venus and Mars was
activated by a lunar eclipse less than six months before the event,
and on the very day the Moon would transit the eclipse degree.

6 The ruler of the tenth house, which may be taken to signify the
King, is Venus. Venus had progressed to 4° Gemini and attracted
a conjunction from the transiting Mars–Venus conjunction on the
fateful day. The King left the country on 7 June 1940 (transiting

Venus at 13° Cancer, conjunct radical Neptune, went retrograde on
6 June).

You will notice once again how the solar eclipse of 22 November
1938 affected this chart.

Belgium

King Leopold of the Belgians tried desparately to remain neutral.
He repudiated his country's alliance with Britain and France, but
when German forces invaded his land on the pretext of preserving
that neutrality, he appealed to the alliance for assistance and got
it. Then, without consultation and against the advice of his ministers,
he surrendered unconditionally on 29 May, undermining the position
of the Anglo-French forces. The King refused to leave the country
and lead a government-in-exile; he believed the Allies were finished.

Carter gives V. E. Robson's map for the proclamation of inde-

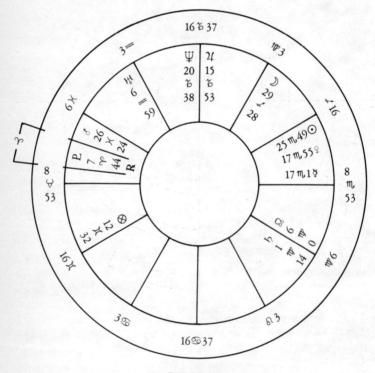

BELGIUM,
18 NOVEMBER 1830,
Fig. 9.11   15.06 GMT, BRUSSELS

pendence (15.06 hrs GMT, 18 November 1830, at Brussels, Fig. 9.11).
It has a full seventh house, with Mars (ruler of the seventh) in
the twelfth house square on eighth house Moon. At the invasion
(see Fig. 9.12), progressed Mars had moved to oppose the Sun in
the seventh house, and the progressed Ascendant at 21°16' Leo was
just 4° away from perfecting a T-square with that opposition. It is
possible that the timing is a little later, for it would make astrological
sense if the pattern was exact. This chart is also powerfully affected
by the previously mentioned solar eclipse of 22 November 1938.

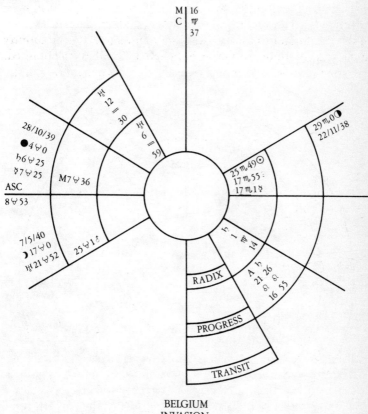

Fig. 9.12

BELGIUM
INVASION,
10 MAY 1940, 19.00 GMT

Barbarossa

Hitler launched 'Operation Barbarossa', the invasion of Russia, on
22 June 1941 at 3.30 a.m. MET, and thereby sealed his fate. The
chart for Soviet Russia favoured by us appears in Chapter 8 in

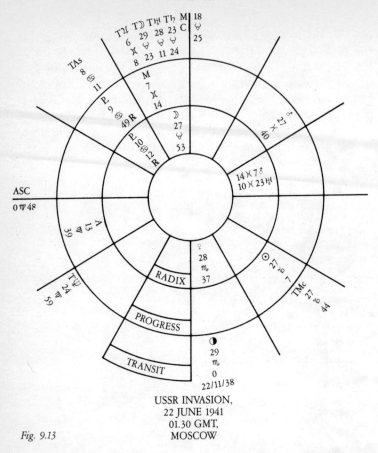

Fig. 9.13

USSR INVASION,
22 JUNE 1941
01.30 GMT,
MOSCOW

connection with the Chernobyl disaster. Figure 9.13 shows the progressions for the invasion.

A conjunction of Mars–Uranus appears in the seventh house in the radical chart. That conjunction is well aspected by Jupiter, Pluto and the Sun, but it is a vicious combination to have in the house of war and holds the promise of great conflict. Eventual victory is doubtless shown by Jupiter's aspect and his mutual reception with Mars, though over 20 million Russians perished in the war. The scale of the suffering may be associated with Pisces, the square between Jupiter–Neptune (joint rulers of the eighth house) and the twelfth house position of Neptune. Also notable is the opposition of Moon–Venus across the tenth–fourth houses squaring Ascendant–Descendant.

As the German guns opened fire, the progressed Ascendant had moved to oppose Mars, while progressed Mars in the eighth house was sexile the progressed Sun in the fifth, and they were to remain within close aspect throughout the war. The transits for the event are remarkable. Uranus was conjunct the Moon and in opposition to Venus with Saturn closing up to meet him. Neptune was poised to transit the opposition point of progressed Mars, and Jupiter was within a degree of the progressed Midheaven. The transiting Moon was at 29°23′ Taurus, the Ascendant of the invasion chart was coming to a conjunction of radical and progressed Pluto, and the Midheaven was conjunct the progressed Sun and sextile progressed Mars. We hardly need mention the importance of the solar eclipse of 1938 at 29° Scorpio.

United States of America

With some diffidence we decided to look at the chart of the United States, because there is much disagreement as to which one is correct. That it should be drawn for 4 July 1776 at Philadelphia is certain; it is the timing that is questionable. Carter gave the chart which appeared in the *1940 Year-Book* of the American Federation of Astrologers, which has an Ascendant of 20°11′ Gemini and Mars rising. Others have favoured an Ascendant of 8°47′ Gemini with Uranus rising, and there are some who prefer 13°32′ Libra. Michael Baigent, writing in *Mundane Astrology*, argues for 12°12′ Sagittarius, which is attributed to the English Astrologer Ebenezer Sibly, who apparently got his information from masonic connections in America.

A similar problem confronts the astrologer with almost any national chart, for to be certain of its validity it must be justified in art! Yet, without an exhaustive study of the history of each nation in relation to its proposed chart, such justification is impossible. Meanwhile, we must work with what we have, and seek such evidence as seems reasonable to us. We do like Uranus rising in Gemini for a nation which has always been so intimately involved with new developments in communications, the car, radio, aeroplanes, telephone, films, television, space-travel, etc. To us reserved Europeans, Americans seem natural and uninhibited communicators. We also like Aquarius on the Midheaven with the Aquarian Moon in the tenth house. The American presidency is very like a monarchy, but it is an ultra-democratic Aquarian monarchy which allows its citizens to elect the 'king' every four years, where even judges and dog-catchers must face the electorate, and any humble man or woman may aspire to the highest office in the land. For these reasons we produce Fig. 9.14 without making dogmatic claims for it.

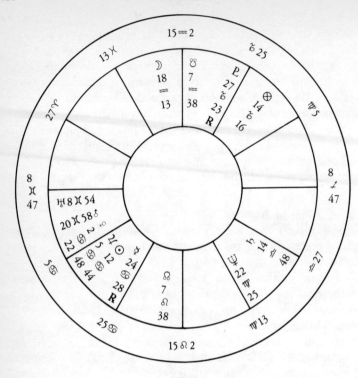

USA
4 JULY 1776,
Fig. 9.14   7.19.15 GMT, PHILADELPHIA

After the treacherous attack by Japan on Pearl Harbour, America
entered the war. For the second time in 25 years, she mobilized the
flower of her youth and sent them to fight and die on the battle-
fields of the lands of their ancestors. Many American soldiers would
have found themselves fighting against the peoples from whom they
sprang — German Americans against Germans, Italian Americans
against Italians. It takes little imagination for the astrologer to equate
this state of affairs with the radical opposition between retrograde
Mercury (ruler of the first house) in Cancer and Pluto in the ninth
house of the United States chart. It just so happened that the
secondary progressions for Pearl Harbour (see Fig. 9.15) show this
opposition activated by the progressed Midheaven, with a transit
of the Moon at the time of the attack, and the Moon herself conjunct
that progressed point. The radical opposition between Mercury–Pluto
was also squared by the progressed Ascendant, as was progressed
Jupiter (ruler of the seventh house), and progressed Mars in Aries

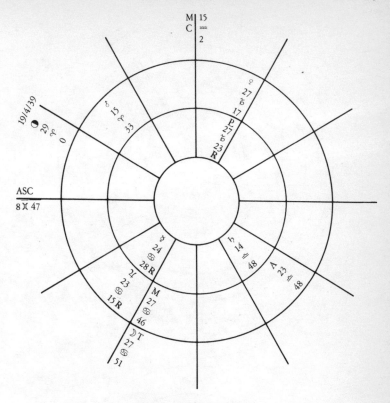

Fig. 9.15

USA — PEARL HARBOUR,
11 DECEMBER 1941,
7.19.15 GMT, PHILADELPHIA

was opposite the radical Saturn in the seventh sign of Libra.

This is the first chart produced in connection with the war which does not have contacts with the solar eclipse of 22 November 1938 at 29° Scorpio. In this case the solar eclipse, which fell six months later at 29° Aries, seems to draw all the radical and progressed indications together.

War Eclipses?

If Ptolemy was right, there should have been a powerful solar eclipse visible in Europe and falling at some time within the five years prior to the outbreak of war, giving an indication of the coming disaster. Not so! Between 1927 and 1954 no total solar eclipse was visible in Europe. There was one on 19 June 1936 which swept from Greece to Central Asia and Japan with a period of totality of 2.5 minutes.

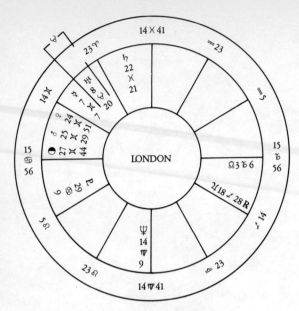

TOTAL SOLAR ECLIPSE,
19 JUNE 1936,
5.15 GMT

Fig. 9.16(a)

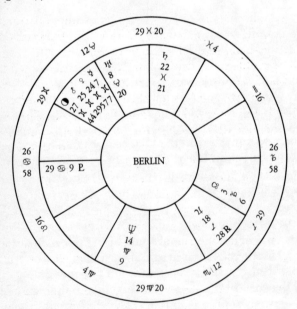

Fig. 9.16(b)

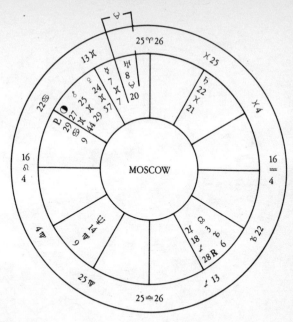

Fig. 16(c)

There was another of exceptionally long duration (totality 7.1 minutes), which was visible in the Pacific Ocean and Peru, on 8 June 1937. If we abandon the Ptolemy's requirement that the eclipse should be visible to be effective in a certain area, we can take the 19 June 1936 eclipse and recognize it as a chart descriptive of war. Figures 9.16(a), (b) and (c) show the eclipse set for London, Berlin, and Moscow respectively. Throughout Europe, this eclipse occurred nearest the eastern horizon, so its effects both immediate and extended should have expired long before the outbreak of war, if traditional rules are followed. The extended effects of the 1937 eclipse (see Fig. 9.17) would have encroached on the beginning of the war, because it fell nearest the Western Angle. A case could be made for it as a war eclipse, but its path was confined between latitudes 12° S and 10° N. In the absence of any total solar eclipse fulfilling the requirements of duration and visibility for such a momentous event as the Second World War, we are obliged to fall back on astrological common sense.

We have never been happy about the claim that the effects of a solar eclipse, as symbolized in the chart for that eclipse, may extend beyond a year according to the angle nearest to which it fell and

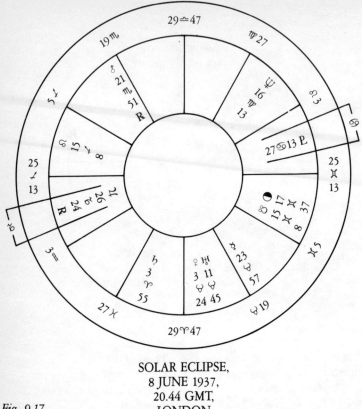

SOLAR ECLIPSE,
8 JUNE 1937,
20.44 GMT,
Fig. 9.17   LONDON

the duration of the eclipse from first to last contact. However, we
do believe that the power of the eclipse degree persists in the cosmos
for two to three years, perhaps longer in the case of an eclipse of
long duration, and that it has an effect when radical and progressed
patterns in national charts relate intimately to that eclipse degree.
You have seen how, in the case of Czechoslovakia, the eclipse degree
falling in strong angular relationship with the radical-progressed
pattern was ignited by the New Moon at 29° Aquarius just 24 days
before the invasion; a similar situation pertained with the charts of
Poland, Norway, Belgium, the United Kingdom and Russia. Thus,
the solar eclipse degree of 22 November 1938 appears to have cast
its influence over 2 years 7 months. It was the next solar eclipse, on
19 April 1939, falling at 29° Aries, which appears to have activated
the United States chart about 2 years 8 months after it occurred.
    We also believe that an eclipse chart may symbolize events that

will happen within the year following, and there is some evidence
to suggest that the angle nearest the eclipse degree does give a guide
as to timing. Although it was the German invasion of Poland which
brought Britain and France into the war, very little happened until

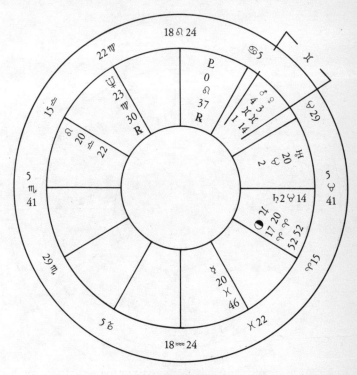

SOLAR ECLIPSE,
7 APRIL 1940, 20.20 GMT
Fig. 9.18   LONDON

Hitler launched his western offensive on 9 April 1940 — just two
days after the annular solar eclipse at 18° Aries. Between this eclipse
and the next on 1 October 1940 at 8° Libra, Germany occupied
Western Europe and most of Scandinavia, and the United Kingdom
fought the Battle of Britain and suffered the London blitz. The chart
for this eclipse (Fig. 9.18), set for London, shows the eclipse degree
in the sixth house of the armed forces in the military sign of Aries
conjunct Jupiter; the whole of Europe was mobilized and at battle.
The military sign of Scorpio rises with its ruler, Mars, conjunct Venus
(ruler of the seventh house of war), in the eighth house of death.
Mercury, ruler of the eighth, opposes Neptune. Saturn is at the

Descendant, and Uranus, whose transit closely affected most of the national charts we have discussed, sits menacingly in the seventh. Whether this is the war eclipse or not, it is the eclipse which heralded the war proper. We can see the sense of it, if only with the value of hindsight.

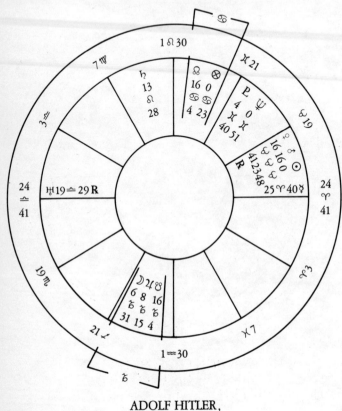

ADOLF HITLER,
20 APRIL 1889
Fig. 9.19   17.26.48 GMT, 48°15′ N, 13°3′ E

The War Leaders

On 20 April 1889, at 5.27 p.m. GMT at Braunau am Inn in Austria, Adolf Hitler (see chart shown in Fig. 9.19), the future war-lord and Führer of Germany, was born in humble circumstances of peasant stock. On 30 January 1933, Hitler became Chancellor of Germany and the Third Reich was born. Seven years later, with Europe under his domination, his victorious forces held sway from the Pyrenees to the Arctic Circle. Five years after that, he was to perish by his own hand as his 'Thousand Year Reich' crumbled and burned about him.

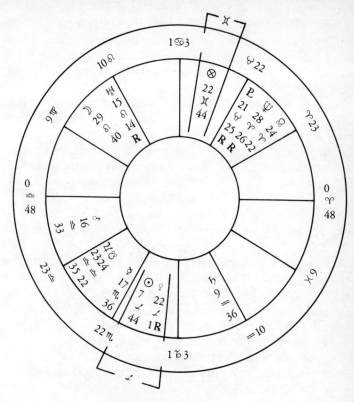

WINSTON CHURCHILL,
30 NOVEMBER 1874
Fig. 9.20 01.35 GMT, 51°50′ N, 1°22′ W

On 30 November 1874, at 1.35 a.m. at Woodstock in England, Winston Churchill (see chart shown in Fig. 9.20) was born, a member of the privileged ruling class, in Blenheim Palace. We have spent some time on Churchill's chart, and we are not altogether satisfied with the birth time 1.30 a.m., given by Elizabeth Longford in an authorized biography. This time would put the last degree of Gemini at the Midheaven and the last degree of Virgo at the Ascendant. Previous astrologers seem to have made it later by five minutes so that cardinal signs fall at the angles, and there is logic in that. The strongest case rests with the Moon, for it makes total sense that the Midheaven should be ruled by the Moon in Leo upon the fixed star

Regulus. Depending upon which method of secondary progression one employs, there is a case for making the birth time later and a case for making it earlier. For the moment we'll stay with 1.35 a.m.

Churchill's youth was adventurous. His early political career was meteoric, but it came to grief in the First World War. Between the Wars he suffered a period in the political wilderness. He did not endear himself to the establishment when he supported King Edward VIII during the abdication crisis, and he constantly rattled the government by warning against Hitler's antics in Europe. When Hitler invaded the Rhineland in 1936, Churchill saw that war was inevitable. After the great powers sold out Czechoslovakia at Munich and Neville Chamberlain held up the pathetic piece of paper declaring 'peace in our time', Churchill said: 'The Government had to choose between War and Shame. They chose Shame and they will get War too.'

After war was declared, Prime Minister Chamberlain lasted only a few months, and on 10 May 1940, Churchill became Prime Minister at the age of 65, and entered his 'finest hour'.

From the capitulation of France on 22 June 1940 until December 1941, when the United States came into the war in the wake of Pearl Harbour — 18 months in which Britain stood alone — Hitler and Churchill glared at each other across the channel. They personified the contest, the all-conquering German war-Lord on the one hand, the symbol of European resitance on the other.

Both men, in their own way, were gifted orators. Hitler's oratory had a great deal to do with his political success, as one would expect from Moon–Jupiter in the third house, in trine aspect with the Sun, Lord of the Midheaven. Churchill was a Sagittarian; with the Sun in the third house so all the great enthusiasm and aspiration of the sign was geared to communication. He was a magician with the English language, a spell-binder, whose speeches on the wireless to a nation on the verge of defeat, on the edge of invasion, struck a chord of defiance and optimism in every heart, and inspired everyone to stick it out until the war was won for never once did he even hint that eventual victory would not be ours. During the Battle of Britain, Churchill made a broadcast to the nation which contained these immortal words:

> Hitler knows that he will have to break us in this island or lose the
> war. If we can stand up to him, all Europe may be free and the life
> of the world move forward into broad sunlit uplands. But if we fail,
> then the whole world, including the United States, including all that
> we have known and cared for, will sink into the abyss of a new Dark

Age made more sinister, and perhaps more protracted, by the lights of perverted science. Let us therefore brace ourselves to our duties, and so bear ourselves that, if the British Empire and its Commonwealth last for a thousand years, men will say 'this was their finest hour'.

Churchill has Mars–Jupiter in the first house, with Jupiter on the fixed Star Arcturus (the nature of Mars–Jupiter), and the Sun in the third house on the Fixed Star Antares (the nature of Mars–Jupiter), and this is a military star. His life was devoted to writing and politics, but it was war that marked his fortune and misfortune. He took part in the battle of Omdurman, the last cavalry charge of the British Army, and he won his first parliamentary seat because he won fame in the Boer War. He rose to his zenith as First Lord of the Admiralty in the First World War, but he was brought down by responsibility for the Gallipoli fiasco. His immortality came from the Second World War, but he was cast out of office as soon as victory was won. Despite the varying fortunes, Churchill was made by war.

Hitler, on the other hand, sought immortality through war — a strange thing to do, one might think, with Mars in Taurus. However, Mars is conjunct Venus, the chart ruler, and, in mutual reception with a Capricorn Moon, though square the tenth house Saturn.

The astrological explanation for Hitler's rise to lead the German nation must have something to do with his tenth house Saturn in Leo (Führer), and not a little to do with the Sun, Lord of the MC trine Moon–Jupiter. The extraordinary thing is that if Hitler had stopped at Czechoslovakia he might still be Führer of a Greater German Reich at the age of 98. But he couldn't stop; he had to take on the British Empire and the Russian Empire at the same time; he had to get one over on Napoleon — and he came so close to succeeding that one can still shudder at the thought of it.

Roosevelt

When Franklin D. Roosevelt (see chart shown in Fig. 9.21) took the oath as president for the first time on 4 March 1932, the American financial system was on the point of collapse and one third of the work force was unemployed. This great Aquarian president promptly set about reforming the banking system to ensure that another stock market crash could not occur. He introduced many, often controversial, measures for the relief of the hard-pressed American people. The unemployed were given work to do, farmers and home-owners were given security, organized labour was given rights of collective bargaining. His policies 'effected a revolution in American

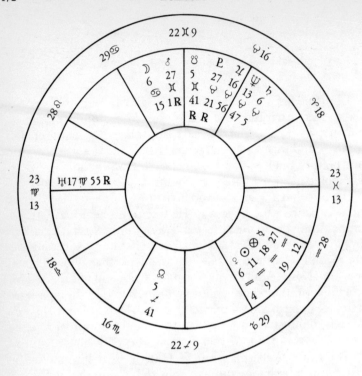

FRANKLIN D. ROOSEVELT,
31 JAN. 1882
Fig. 9.21   1,41 GMT, 40°45′ N, 73°58′ W

politics'. Roosevelt used radio to give 'fireside chats" to the people, seeming to take them into his confidence while discussing the political issues of the day. Not surprisingly he was re-elected in 1936 and 1940, and finally again in 1944 when the nation was at war.

In the early part of the war, Roosevelt proved a staunch ally to beleaguered Britain and developed a special relationship with Winston Churchill. Later, after America with her vast resources of manpower and material had entered the conflict and the end was in sight, Churchill foresaw the post-war ambitions of Stalinist Russia and wished to adjust the Allied strategy accordingly. Roosevelt was seduced by 'Uncle Joe' Stalin, however, and Churchill could not prevail. Roosevelt did not live to see the consequences, or to hear Churchill coin a new phrase at Fulton Missouri in 1946: 'From Stettin in the Baltic to Trieste in the Adriatic, an *iron curtain* has descended across the continent.'

Some Key Progressions

We regret that we do not have a reliable chart for Joseph Stalin, but we can examine some of the key progressions for Hitler, Churchill and Roosevelt.

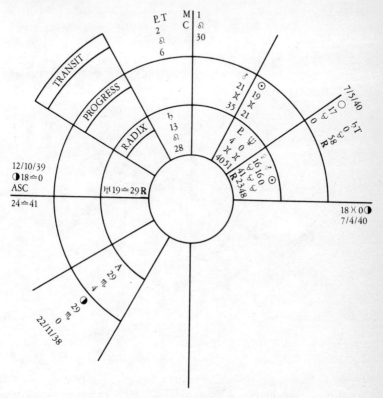

Fig. 9.22

ADOLF HITLER
OUTBREAK OF SECOND WORLD WAR,
1 SEPTEMBER 1939

Figure 9.22 shows Hitler's secondary progressions, transits, etc., for the beginning of the Second World War. Saturn and Uranus are in radical sextile, and when Hitler became Chancellor of Germany the progressed Sun was appropriately in exact sextile with Saturn from the sign of Gemini. During the six years between 1933 and 1936, when he was busily drawing all power unto himself within his own country, and swallowing-up the Rhineland, Austria, and Czechoslovakia, the progressed Sun was moving between that sextile aspect of Saturn and a trine aspect of Uranus. As he moved into Poland, and thus precipitated the war, the aspect with Uranus was exact, and the progressed Sun was moving to within orbs of conjunction of progressed Mars in the ninth house. The progressed Ascendant at 29° Scorpio was poised to move across the opposition point of the radical eighth house Neptune–Pluto conjunction; Pluto was transiting at the Midheaven, and Saturn was transiting the radical Sun. A pair of solar eclipses should be noted: one, at 18° Libra, occurred five weeks after the outbreak of war; the other at 18° Aries, occurred two days before the western offensive, when the war began in earnest. We cannot ignore the remarkable fact that the progressed ascendant was conjunct the degree of the solar eclipse of 22 November

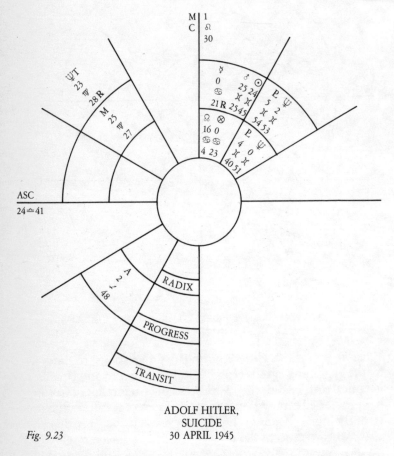

ADOLF HITLER,
SUICIDE
Fig. 9.23   30 APRIL 1945

1938, the eclipse which has proved so potent in the national charts we have considered in this chapter. As a sort of bonus, the Full Moon of 7 May 1940, at a time when German arms were everywhere successful, fell upon Hitler's radical Mars–Venus conjunction in the seventh house.

Figure 9.23 shows the major contacts operating when Hitler committed suicide on 30 April 1945. The progressed Sun is less than a degree from a conjunction with progressed Mars, and the progressed Midheaven is all but exactly square Mars. The progressed Ascendant has now moved to oppose progressed Neptune in the eighth house within five minutes of arc, and Neptune is transiting the progressed Midheaven. No eclipses accentuate these patterns.

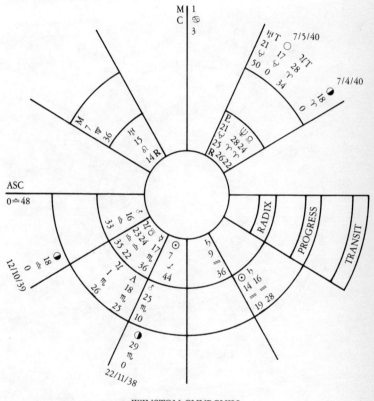

Fig. 9.24

WINSTON CHURCHILL,
PRIME MINISTER,
10 MAY 1940

When Winston Churchill became Prime Minister on 10 May 1940, (see Fig. 9.24), his progressed Sun was opposing his eleventh house Uranus, which stands radically sextile first house Mars, and is moving towards a conjunction with progressed Saturn. Remember that Churchill's natal Sun was conjunct the military fixed star Antares, and it was as he assumed the political leadership of the British Empire that the progressed Midheaven slid into square aspect with it, invoking the radical Sun–Saturn sextile. At an age when most sensible men retire to their firesides and rose gardens, Churchill's hour had finally come! Uranus, of course, forms part of the T-square involving Mercury and Pluto in fixed signs. In fact, through the progression of Saturn, the T-square had become a Grand Cross, and it is activated through the progressed Sun–Uranus opposition and the progressed Ascendant conjunct Mercury. Uranus was transiting

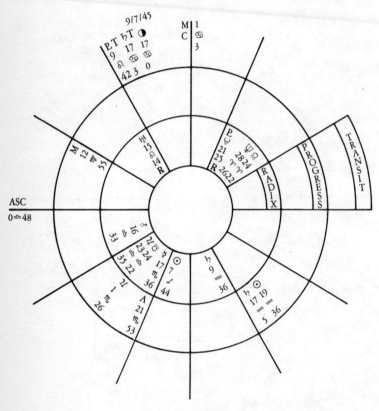

WINSTON CHURCHILL,
RESIGNATION,
Fig. 9.25   27 JULY 1945

radical Pluto, and Jupiter radical Neptune. The 18° Aries–Libra pair of eclipses invoked Churchill's Mars–Jupiter conjunction, and the 1938 eclipse of 29° Scorpio fell at a point equidistant between an opposition to Pluto and a conjunction with the Sun.

Fig. 9.25 shows the situation at Churchill's resignation. You will
see how the progressed Ascendant is just separating from the
opposition with Pluto and thus disengaging itself from the Grand
Cross. The progressed Sun is neatly separating from orbs of aspect
to Saturn (the progressed Sun has an effective orb of 1½°), and Pluto
is transiting in opposition to Saturn. With Saturn transiting the tenth
house, at a point square radical Mars and trine radical Mercury, the
solar eclipse of 9 July 1945 (two days after the General Election which
rejected the Conservative Party), fell conjunct the transiting Saturn.

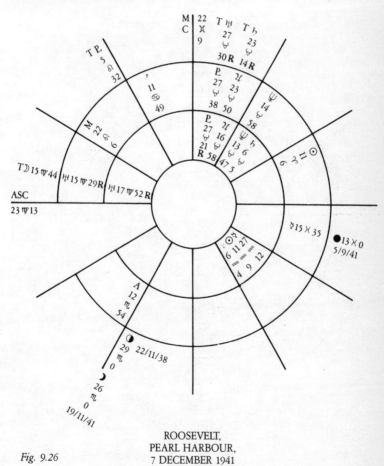

Fig. 9.26

ROOSEVELT,
PEARL HARBOUR,
7 DECEMBER 1941

When the treacherous attack on Pearl Harbour brought the
Americans into the global conflict, Roosevelt's progressed Sun
was square to his progressed tenth house Mars (Fig. 9.26). The

progressed Ascendant was in opposition to radical Neptune and the progressed Midheaven was coming towards a square with progressed Jupiter in the ninth house. Transiting Uranus was in conjunction with radical/progressed Pluto, and transiting Saturn conjunct progressed Jupiter. See also how Pluto was opposed by the 1938 eclipse (29° Scorpio), and how the New Moon before the attack fell conjunct that eclipse degree. Progressed Mercury (chart ruler) was opposing progressed Uranus, and the Moon at the moment of the Pearl Harbour attack was conjunct Uranus.

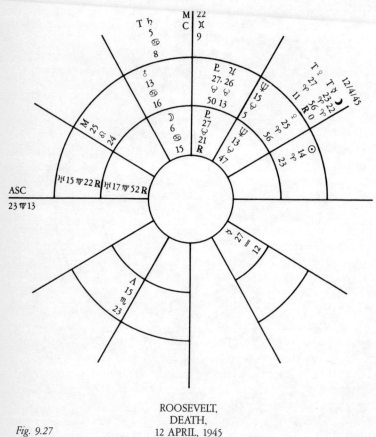

Fig. 9.27

ROOSEVELT,
DEATH,
12 APRIL, 1945

At Roosevelt's death (see Fig. 9.27), progressed Venus had moved into the eighth house, the progressed Midheaven was square progressed Venus, and Venus and Mercury were transiting on either side of progressed Venus. Also, on the very day of death, a New Moon fell conjunct progressed Venus. The progressed Ascendant was just separating from an opposition of progressed Neptune, and Saturn was transiting tenth house Moon.

A touch of synastry

From Fig. 9.28 you will see that when Winston Churchill became Prime Minister on 10 May 1940, Hitler's progressed Sun was in trine aspect with radical Uranus and chasing a conjunction with progressed Mars. See also how Churchill's progressed Midheaven was in square aspect with the radical Sun on the Fixed Star Antares (in the constellation of Scorpio), and how the progressed Sun was stuck between the radical and progressed positions of Uranus, and moving towards a conjunction with progressed Saturn.

As one would expect, there are a number of contacts between the charts of Hitler and Churchill, but it is most interesting to see how Churchill's nodes fall across Hitler's horizon, with Jupiter at the Ascendant, and how Churchill's Uranus is within 2° of Hitler's Saturn, and closely linked therefore with Hitler's Saturn–Venus–Mars T-square. Notice how the position intensifies when Churchill becomes Prime Minister, and therefore the personification of opposition to Hitler's ambitions. His Uranus has moved by progression to within 18′ of Hitler's Saturn; their progressed Saturns are opposed to each other within 18′; and Churchill's progressed Sun is set to oppose Hitler's progressed Sun and conjunct his own, squaring as it does so Hitler's Mars–Venus conjunction. Churchill's exact progressed Sun–Saturn conjunction would occur some 18 months after this date and coincide with the lowest point in British war fortunes — Rommel's successes in North Africa and the fall of Singapore to the Japanese. At that point Churchill's progressed Sun stood exactly square to Hitler's Mars–Venus conjunction. Taking account of the New Moon on 7 May 1940, falling at 17° Taurus, it could be said that this lunation set the chain of events in motion.

When Hitler committed suicide, his progressed Sun had finally caught up with Mars to form the conjunction, and this conjunction was in trine to the radical Ascendant. But Mars is the eighth house ruler, and the progressed Ascendant has neatly moved in to square the conjunction. Remarkably, the progressed Ascendant for the Third Reich chart at Hitler's suicide was 24°48′ Gemini, throwing in its lot with Hitler's Sun–Mars conjunction. At this point Churchill's Sun, which was opposed to Hitler's Saturn at the beginning of the war, had moved into trine aspect with Hitler's Uranus.

You may find it interesting that Churchill's progressed Ascendant (having started the war on the Fixed Star Serpentis) has reached an

	0 1 2 3 4 5 6 7 8 9 10 11 12 13 14 15 16 17 18 19 20 21 22 23 24 25 26 27 28 29 30

HITLER NATAL

	♃	♄	♂ ♀	♅	A
	8	13	16 16	19	24
	♉	♌	♆ ♆	♎	♎
	15	28	23 41	29	41

HITLER 10 MAY 1940

	☽	♄	♅	☉	♂
	10	16	17	20	22
	♏	♌	♎	♓	♓
	34	10	58	0	3

HITLER 30 APR. 1945

	A ♆	♄ ♅	☉ ♂
	2 2	16 17	24 25
	♐ ♓	♌ ♎	♓ ♓
	48 53	38 54	45 25

CHURCHILL NATAL

	☉ ♄	♅ ♂	♇ ♃ ♉
	7 9	15 16	21 23 24
	♐ ♒	♌ ♎	♀ ♎ ♎
	44 36	14 33	25 35 21

CHURCHILL 10 MAY 1940

	M ☽	♅	☉ ♄ ☽ 7/5/40
	7 9	13	14 16 17
	♏ ♉	♌	♒ ♒ ♆
	38 49	10	54 28 0

CHURCHILL 30 APR. 1945

	♅	♄	☉	A
	12	17	19	21
	♌	♒	♒	♏
	57	3	21	43

HITLER NATAL

	♇ ☽ ♃	♄	♂ ♀ ♅	♉
	4 6 8	13	16 16 19	25
	♓ ♉ ♉	♌	♆ ♆ ♎	♈
	40 31 15	28	23 41 29	40

HITLER 11 DEC. 1941

	☽ ♇	♄ ♅	☉ ♂
	4 5	16 17	21 23
	♐ ♓	♌ ♎	♓ ♓
	15 50	19 56	31 7

ROOSEVELT NATAL

	♉ ☽	☉	♆	♃
	5 6	11	13	16
	♓ ♋	♒	♋	♋
	41 15	9	47	56

ROOSEVELT 11 DEC. 1941

	♄ A ♆
	11 12 14
	♋ ♏ ♋
	15 54 58

Fig. 9.28

opposition with Pluto at victory. He had fulfilled his purpose; his use at an end, and three months later he was rejected at the polls in the General Election. 'I was out in the street,' as he later remarked.

It is also worth looking at some of the more obvious contacts between Hitler and Roosevelt. Their radical Moons are opposed. Roosevelt's south node falls upon Hitler's Pluto, his Sun is opposed to Hitler's Saturn, and his Jupiter links with Hitler's Mars–Venus conjunction. At Pearl Harbour, when America entered the war, Roosevelt's progressed Ascendant was moving to oppose Hitler's Saturn.

These are just a few of the most obvious contacts between the charts of three great war leaders. A full synastric study, involving the charts of Stalin, all the leaders and monarchs of occupied countries, as well as the outstanding generals on both sides and the Mikado of Japan, would justify a book in its own right.

The Dominant Eclipse

We may not have been able to find a chart which could be designated 'The War Eclipse', but what has emerged is the all-pervading influence of the solar eclipse of 22 November 1938 at 29° Scorpio! It has figured powerfully in every national chart except that of the United States, and has even carried its weight through to the charts of three of the war leaders we have considered. For the record, we present the chart here, set for London (Fig. 9.29).

Preamble to Final Chapters

The last three chapters of this book are concerned with ordinary people. Our researches have shown that syzygies, taken on their own, are usually of little account when related to natal charts. Their value is seen when allied with *secondary progressions* and/or *transits*, when they appear to act as *timers*. In this section we use the nativities of three people to demonstrate how syzygies linked with the progressions at important times in their lives. Our subjects are not famous, just humble citizens contending with the uncertainties of life, attempting to survive and find happiness.

Students of astrology will be aware that the generally accepted method of progressing planets is 'a-day-for-a-year'; the planets are advanced one unit of daily motion for each year of life. This is simple enough until one has to contend with the angles (the Midheaven and the Ascendant), because there are several ways of determining

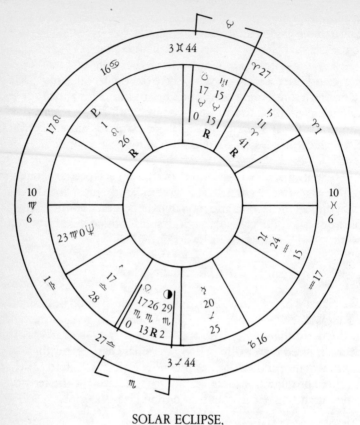

SOLAR ECLIPSE,
22 NOVEMBER 1938
00.06 GMT,
Fig. 9.29   LONDON

the length of a day, and thus several different ways of advancing the
angles.

All our demonstrations of secondary progressions so far have
employed the solar arc in longitude technique to move the Midheaven
by the arc, measured in ecliptic longitude, between the radical to
the progressed Sun. We have found this method consistently reliable,
and it has the great advantage of simplicity. However, now and then
one comes across a chart which does not appear to respond to this
method. In such cases our experiments have shown that the method
employed by Kepler, moving the MC by the same arc as the progressed
Sun measured in right ascension, yields good results. Very often there
is very little difference in the result whatever method is employed.

It all depends upon the time of year the subject was born, for the daily motion of the Sun will vary between 57'11" and 61'11", according to season.

As an example of the variation possible, consider the case of France. We mentioned in the previous chapter that the chart for the third republic (4 September 1879, 16.36 hrs GMT, 48°50' N, 2°20' E) did not respond to secondary progressions which seemed to relate to the war experience. Note here the radical and the progressed planetary positions, with the MC advanced by the solar arc in longitude for the capitulation of France on 22 June 1940:

	Radix	**Progressed**
Sun	11°54' Virgo	20°56' Scorpio
Moon	8°55' Capricorn	17°28' Cancer
Mercury	8°28' Libra	15°31' Scorpio
Venus	18°02' Leo	14°51' Scorpio
Mars	27°26' Cancer	8°25' Virgo
Jupiter	22°55' Gemini	25°03' Gemini
Saturn	22°00' Sagittarius	26°29' Sagittarius
Uranus	25°09' Cancer	26°32' Cancer
Pluto	18°53' Taurus	17°53' Taurus
Midheaven	27°13' Scorpio	6°15' Aquarius
Ascendant	27°13' Capricorn	7°15' Gemini

No really convincing aspects appear which would explain the Battle of France and the following capitulation, but when the angles are progressed by Kepler's method, the Midheaven progresses to 28°01' Capricorn and the Ascendant to 26°00' Taurus. It will then be seen how the progressed Midheaven is opposed to the radical seventh house Mars–Uranus conjunction, which is far more appropriate to the event.

One of your authors, who for years had regularly employed solar arc in longitude, was always puzzled by the lack of a convincing progressed aspect to explain his marriage. His birth time had to be correct within a minute or so because it was recorded in his father's diary. When he eventually applied Kepler's method, a convincing aspect appeared and the puzzle was solved.

We do not wish to make a case for any particular one of the five methods of progressing angles variously employed; the individual astrologer must be guided by his own experience. We would point out, however, that the Kepler method has been applied in Chapter 11.

10.

LAVINIA'S MARRIAGE

Background

There was a New Moon on 9 January 1940 at 13.54 GMT. Less than

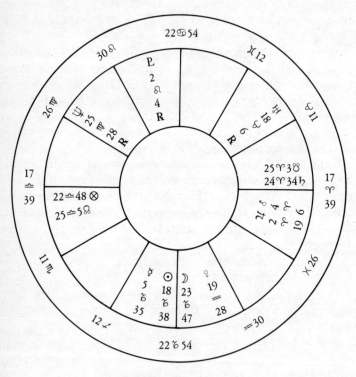

NATIVITY OF LAVINIA,
10 JANUARY 1940,
0.39.35, 50°26′ N, 3°34′ W

Fig. 10.1

12 hours later Lavinia was born (Fig. 10.1). She grew up happily in a modest but loving and secure family environment in a beautiful part of the country. It was a time of war, however, and although she was well removed from the terrors of fire and devastation experienced in other parts of the country, she did not know her father for some years. He was enlisted in the Army on 30 September 1940, and did not return to take his place in the family until 1 May 1945.

Lavinia had all the energy and athletic prowess one might expect from the angular and cardinal New Moon, and the powerful sixth house Mars conjunct Jupiter. She grew into a slim, attractive, vivacious young woman, with a happy disposition and many friends.

The Moon in Capricorn ensured that Lavinia was quite strictly brought up, but her home life was harmonious. Her parents loved each other deeply and remained in love for the 51 years of their married life. She did not experience domestic conflict; to her it was natural that husband and wife treated each other with consideration and respect. Such was the model of marriage she was set by her parents.

It is said that the relationship between Sun and Moon in a nativity shows the relationship of the parents as seen by the native in childhood, and the position and condition of Saturn in a woman's chart will describe her experience of and relationship with her Father. The conjunction of Sun and Moon in Lavinia's chart symbolizes the close harmony which existed between her parents, and the profound effect it had upon her home life (fourth house).

Yet the astrologer must look askance at angular Saturn, squaring the New Moon from Aries, and wonder whether everything was as wonderful as our report suggests, for at the very least there would seem to be a promise of stress between the native and her father. For the sake of the art, it is worth going a little deeper.

Moon square Saturn — The Moon's influence, which is traditionally associated with the mother, is at her most powerful during the first seven years of life. For the first years of her life Lavinia did not know her father. She was aware of him, of course, and dreamed of the day he would come home, but he was not to become a potent force in her life until he was demobilized. During his absence Lavinia's mother endeavoured to play the father's role as well as her own, and she was under constant stress due to her isolation and continual worry over the fate of her husband.

Sun square Saturn — When her father did return, estranged by enforced absensce and hardened by the violent experience of war, the reality of his presence did not accord with the dream. Patience was necessary until he had readjusted to civilian life and his spirit was healed.

Sun/Saturn mutual reception — The reception, which dispels the harshness of the square, ensures that the adjustment occurred and that father and daughter developed a good and fulfilling relationship. The value of this reception will figure again later in seventh house matters.

A further observation regarding Saturn is worth making here. During the absence of her father, Lavinia developed a strong relationship with her paternal grandfather. By our reckoning, the way of calculating the house of the paternal grandfather is: *the tenth for the father, the tenth from the tenth for his father* — which brings us to the seventh of the chart, where Saturn is found.

Marriage and Violence

Inevitably Lavinia eventually fell in love, married and went to live in a mobile home in a nearby village. Life was not easy, but no worse than for most young people of her background, age and time. She produced a son on 15 August 1963, and a daughter on 17 May 1966. Lavinia carried with her into her own marriage that conception of marital bliss she had observed in her family home. This ideal received a severe jolt a few months later when her husband struck her. Unfortunately this first strike was not a one-off, but merely an introduction to a catalogue of violence and brutality encompassing five years.

The goat has a great capacity to survive harsh conditions, and is able to squeeze a living from the most barren landscape. Similarly, Capricorn above all signs can endure hardship and privation; indeed, sometimes the challenge of endurance provokes a strange kind of exhilaration. Yet even a goat has a breaking point, and in Lavinia's case 'the final straw' occurred on 19 January 1967.

Lavinia recalls the high points of violence in her marriage, so we reproduce the sad list here as she gave it:

August 1963   Pushed her to the floor while she was heavily pregnant.

October 1963   Hit her in the stomach with a bottle.

Winter 1963/64	Husband admitted affairs with two other women.
June 1964	Really went mad, hit her across the face and head, tore off her dress, held scissors to her throat.
August 1964	Struck her in the face.
December 1964	Struck her in the face, twisted her arm, tore at her hair.
September 1965	Threatened to kick her stomach in if she was pregnant.
September 1965	Tried to strangle her. When she was found to be pregnant, said he hated the baby and didn't want it (although the pregnancy was planned).
November 1965	Threw a fire-guard at her and injured her arm. *From then on into 1966, continual nagging . . . accusing her of having affairs with 'anything in trousers'; brutally beat son on several occasions. When arguing usually pulled her hair or twisted her nose around ('sounds funny but extremely painful').*
October 1966	Went berserk, throwing things, swearing, roaring; she managed to escape from the house.
November 1966	Hit her across head while she was ironing.
November 1966	Hit her across the shoulders with a clothes hanger.
19 January 1967	The final straw: hit her across the head, chased her from one chair to another constantly hitting her (head covered with lumps and hearing affected for about a week), chased her with a carving knife in one hand, punching her about head with the other.
15 March 1967	Moved back to parents' home.

17 October 1967   Decree *nisi*.

18 January 1968   Decree absolute.

First we need to examine the nativity for clues to Lavinia's marriage experience.

In a woman's nativity, the Sun and Mars are the main significators of marriage, and the ruler of the seventh house will often describe the marriage partner.

Saturn represents a particular challenge to any native; the house he occupies indicates the area of life experience pin-pointed by fate for special treatment. In Lavinia's chart, Saturn sits firmly in the seventh house, squaring the natal New Moon. When Saturn aspects the significators of marriage by harsh aspect, it can show that the state of marriage itself is difficult, or sometimes impossible to achieve. By harmonious aspect, Saturn often causes a delayed or late marriage. In this case however, Lavinia's marriage occurred quite early, at the age of 22 years. Marriage matters were not delayed because Sun and Saturn are in mutual reception, Mars, a general significator of marriage and also ruler of the seventh house, is powerful in Aries, conjunct Jupiter, and disposes of Saturn. So there is no difficulty in achieving marriage. However, for all the mitigation, Saturn occupies the seventh house in the violent sign of Aries, so it is certainly predictable that Lavinia is destined to experience the harsh lessons of Saturn in seventh house affairs.

The ruler of the seventh house should describe the marriage partner. Mars is in Aries (the sign in which he is most powerful), conjunct Jupiter. It does not necessarily follow that Mars in Aries would produce a violent husband (although he is square to Mercury), for he is in the sign of his dignity. Nevertheless, if Mars is going to manifest in a violent manner, his potential for violence is maximized through Aries, and further increased by the influence of Jupiter. In this case the key consideration appears to rest with the *progression* of Mars, because he will gradually move towards a square with the Sun, through which he invokes the Sun–Moon–Saturn square.

Secondary Progressions

Figure 10.2 shows the secondary progressions covering four major events during the years of marriage: marriage itself, the birth of a

Event	0	1	2	3	4	5	6	7	8	9	10	11	12	13	14	15	16	17	18	19	20	21	22	23	24	25	26	27	28	29	30
NATAL			♇		♂	☿													♅	♀			⊗	☽		♆					
			2		4	5													18	19			22	23		25					
			♌		♈	♏													♍	♒			♎	♉		♏					
			4		6	35													6	28			48	47		28					
			♃															A	☉				M		♄						
			2															17	18				22		24						
			♈															♎	♉				♋		♈						
			19															39	38				54		34						
MARRIAGE 6 OCTOBER 1962		♇					♃						☿					♀ ♅		♂						♆ ♄					
		1					6						12					17 17		19						25 25					
		♌					♈						♒					♓ ♈		♈						♍ ♈					
		33					6						28					21 59		35						10 34					
					A							☉					M														
					4							11					16														
					♏							♒					♌														
					30							46					2														
SON 15 AUGUST 1963		♇					♃							☿					♅		♂					♆ ♄					
		1					6							13					18		20					25 25					
		♌					♈							♒					♍		♈					♍ ♈					
		32					15							58					0		10					9 37					
						A							☉				M		♀												
						5							12				16		18												
						♏							♒				♌		♓												
						7							38				55		23												
DAUGHTER 15 MAY 1966		♇					♃												♅ ☿				♂			♆ ♄					
		1					6												18 18				22			25 25					
		♌					♈												♍ ♒				♈			♍ ♈					
		28					47												1 49				3			6 48					
								A								☉				M		♀									
								7								15				19		21									
								♏								♒				♌		♓									
								4								25				42		43									
ESCAPE 15 MARCH 1967		♇					♃												♅		☿		♂			♆ ♄					
		1					6												18		20		22			25 25					
		♌					♈												♍		♒		♈			♍ ♈					
		27					57												1		18		37			5 52					
								A									☉				M										
								7									16				20										
								♏									♒				♌										
								39									16				33										

Fig. 10.2

son, the birth of a daughter, and the escape from the violent marriage.

It is true to say that no important life experience will befall a native that is not symbolized by an aspect from the progressed angles (Midheaven or Ascendant) or the Sun to a radical or progressed planet, or from a progressed planet to the radical Sun or angles. So important are the Sun and the angles in prediction that we call them *Life Indicators.* To be effective, the angles need to be within a degree of exact aspect, and the Sun within a degree-and-a-half, of any significator.

The speculum given here shows the following angular and solar contacts:

Marriage:	progressed Ascendant quincunx radical Mars (ruler of the seventh house).
Birth of son:	progressed Venus (from the fifth house) sextile radical Sun.
Birth of daughter:	progressed Midheaven in opposition to radical Venus (in the fourth house).
Escape:	progressed Mars (ruler of the seventh house) square radical Midheaven, and in opposition to radical Fortuna.

The pattern also reveals how Mars, symbol of the husband, having entered the seventh house when he came into Lavinia's life a couple of years before marriage, moved from a square of the Sun and a sextile of Venus through to the square of the Midheaven during the five years. In Aries he is a forceful presence, and in the seventh house, hastening towards Saturn, he is dangerous and potentially violent. Another sign of possible violence comes from the progressed Ascendant. If, as we have already suggested, the radical conjunction of Mars–Jupiter holds the potential of violence, it is possible to see the manifestation of that experience in the way the progressed Ascendant moves between the radical Mars and the progressed Jupiter throughout the difficult years, so that it is finally separating from aspect as Lavinia escapes from her seventh house ordeal.

It is most important to realize that progressions cannot provoke into manifestation experiences that are not promised within the nativity. In this case, the progressed Ascendant coming to the quincunx of Mars, the seventh house ruler, would not indicate marriage unless marriage was judged possible and likely from the radical chart. We have already justified marriage for Lavinia. She did produce two children within the marriage, and it cannot be said that her chart is remarkable for signs of fertility. The Moon is weak in Capricorn (although not necessarily infertile); Venus in the fourth house occupies Aquarius which tends towards barrenness; Saturn, ruler of the fourth and fifth houses, is weak in Aries. There is some mitigation perhaps in the mutual reception between Sun and Saturn, but the most positive promise of offspring comes from another mutual reception, between Venus and Uranus. Not only is Venus always important in matters of childbirth, Uranus is joint ruler of the fifth house of children. So the natal promise of children is present, and the speculum shows that Venus was invoked at the birth of each child.

A progressed aspect is usually potent for at least a year in a nativity. So if we had said that Lavinia was likely to marry when one of the Life Indicators made an aspect by secondary progression to Mars (ruler of the seventh house), and that the only Indicator capable of doing so at a time reasonable for marriage was the Ascendant, we must have settled for 1962/63, when the progressed Ascendant perfected a quincunx with radical Mars. We might have said that marriage was likely to occur in 1962/63, but could we have got closer with timing? New and Full Moons are often excellent timers. When a radical pattern is made potent by progression, promising the manifestation of an important life event within the year, it is frequently the case that a New or Full Moon falling in sharp angular relationship (conjunction, square, or opposition) to that pattern will isolate the month during which the event takes place. Figure 10.3 illustrates how this happened in Lavinia's case.

Marriage — The New Moon before the marriage fell at 5° Libra, in opposition to radical Mars.

Birth of Son — A lunar eclipse five weeks before the event fell conjunct the Sun.

Birth of Daughter — the Full Moon before the event fell square Midheaven—Venus.

One can allow an orb of 5°–6° for New and Full Moons falling in relation to a potent pattern. It is worth noting that the Ascendant of a chart drawn for the moment of marriage fell upon the same degree as the progressed Ascendant for that date, and that a transit of Venus and Saturn (coming to opposition) fell across the radical Venus when Lavinia's son was born.

There is much evidence that New and Full Moons often act as timers to events presaged by progressed aspects. In fact, we have found them more reliable than transits, and we shall further address this point in the following two chapters. Meanwhile, using Lavinia and her marriage experience, we bring to your attention a kind of minefield effect.

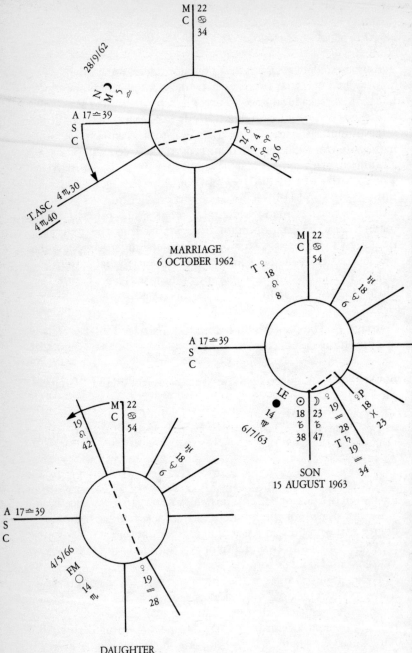

MARRIAGE
6 OCTOBER 1962

SON
15 AUGUST 1963

DAUGHTER
Fig. 10.3   15 MAY 1966

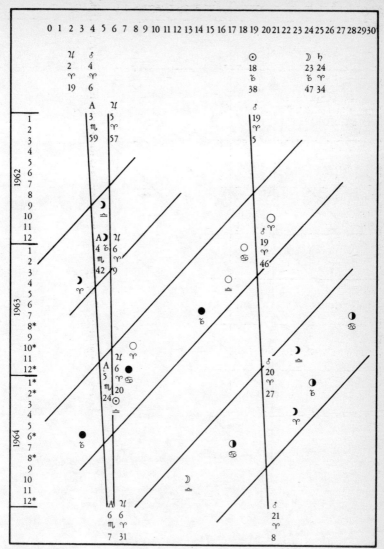

Fig. 10.4(a)

The Minefield Effect

We have shown how Lavinia's nativity held promise of marriage and
of offspring. We have indicated the planets and aspects which suggest
that her marriage experience will be harsh and probably violent.
Figures 10.4(a) and (b) isolate the two main progressed patterns which

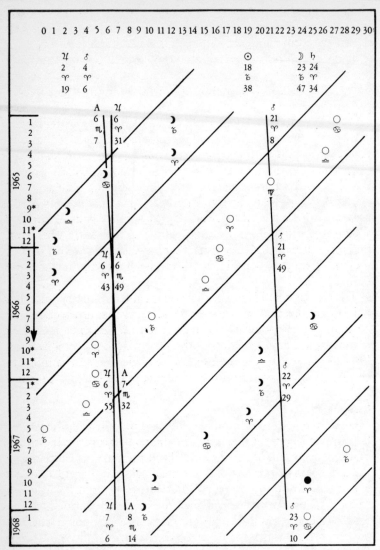

Fig. 10.4(b)

contain potential for violence, and their movement during the years she cohabited with her husband: first, the progressed Ascendant quincunx radical Mars in 1962 (the year of marriage), gradually perfecting a quincunx with progressed Jupiter by 1966, then separating slowly until the orb of half-a-degree is passed by March 1967 when she escapes, and the orb of 1° is passed by divorce (decree absolute) in January 1968; second, progressed Mars, in square aspect with the radical Sun in 1962, moving between the radical Sun–Moon during those difficult years, so that Mars is within a degree of a perfect square to the Moon when cohabitation ceased. So two clear lines of promise show the development of Lavinia's sad experience. The potential is there throughout and from time to time the violence will erupt.

As well as all the solar and lunar eclipses, we have also included in these diagrams all the New and Full Moons falling in sharp angular relationship with the two potent progressed patterns. We have also starred the months which Lavinia recalled as particularly violent, but it should be remembered that in a relationship such as this, if violence did not manifest continually, the fear of violence was ever present. It looks for all the world as though the gods of fate laid a series of minefields through which progressed Ascendant, progressed Jupiter and progressed Mars must pass. However carefully they tread, they are bound to trip and trigger an explosion now and then.

The New and Full Moons are important and effective because they fall in relationship with progressed patterns that are potent. The New and Full Moons are not evil in themselves; they blast into manifestation events related to the potential of the progressions. If the progressed patterns were indicative of pleasant and harmonious events, the Moons would bring these into operation just the same.

Escape

Lavinia lived within eight miles of her parents and a large extended family with whom she had frequent and regular contact. Incredible as it may seem, no one had a clue about the state of her marriage; she suffered in silence. Shortly after 'the final straw' her elder brother was visiting from another part of the country. He took his sister out to dinner, and during the course of the meal she confided in him. The brother had a word with his father, who thereupon rescued his daughter and grandchildren, taking them to the family home where they remained for a year.

The value of the radical Sun–Saturn mutual reception can now be appreciated. It provided an escape route (reception) through the father (Saturn) from a difficult seventh house situation.

Divorce

We have hardly, so far, distinguished between simple New and Full Moons and eclipses. In a similar manner to mundane astrology, eclipses applied to a nativity can have a delayed effect. An eclipse (solar or lunar) falling on a sensitive part of a natal chart, particularly when also allied with potent progressions, may herald an event which will occur within *six months*. Frequently a New or Full Moon falling in sharp angular relationship to the eclipse will indicate the manifestation of the event often within a few days, and usually no longer than two weeks.

We have identified the planetary influences responsible for Lavinia's harsh marriage experience, and we have also seen how she had an escape route though her father. Nevertheless, the astrologer will want to see specific signs of divorce in the nativity. The signs are there and they are classic. Uranus, by his very nature, is the planet of divorce. If he occurs in the seventh house, especially when afflicted by his condition or by aspects from other planets, divorce is almost certain. He has a similar effect in the eighth house, for this house shows what comes from marriage. Jupiter or Venus in this house often

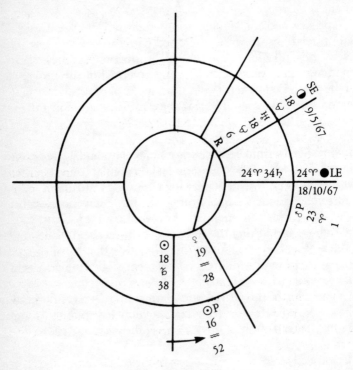

Fig. 10.5(a)   DECREE *NISI*,
17 OCTOBER 1967

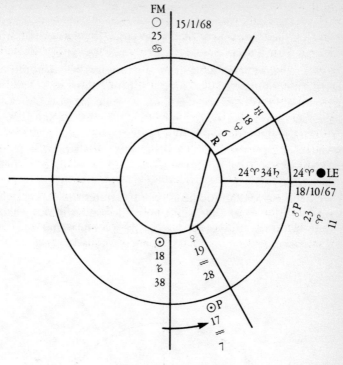

Fig. 10.5(b)
DECREE ABSOLUTE,
18 JANUARY 1968

points to gain through marriage, while Uranus suggests its break-up. The promise of divorce through eighth house Uranus in Lavinia's chart is assured by that planet's square aspect to Aquarian Venus, the natural planet of relationships; the mutual reception also gives an escape route.

Figures 10.5(a) and (b) describe how the radical Venus–Uranus square was being invoked by the progressed Sun when the divorce proceedings were under way. At the time of the decree *nisi*, the progressed Sun was applying by just over one degree to a square of Uranus, thus activating the radical square. At the time of the decree Absolute, the progressed Sun was applying to Uranus by 59 minutes of arc. (It will be remembered that the progressed Sun has an effective orb of 1½°).

You will see how, just over five months before the decree *nisi*, a solar eclipse fell right upon Uranus. Furthermore, the day after the decree *nisi*, a lunar eclipse fell right upon radical Saturn, and four

months later, just three days before the decree absolute, a Full Moon
fell at 25° Cancer at the Midheaven, squaring Saturn and the lunar
eclipse. Meanwhile, progressed Mars is getting closer to radical Saturn
all the time, and we might well wonder why he has still more than
a degree to move before perfecting the conjunction. It would have
been far more satisfying astrologically if the conjunction had been
exact at the time of divorce. Certainly it would have been pleasing,
but in fact Lavinia's aggravation from her former husband did not
end with the divorce. She, and her parents, suffered his attentions
for well over a year, until he finally moved away from the area. In
short, the aggrevation passed when Mars had passed his conjunction
with Saturn.

We believe this example neatly demonstrates the delayed effect
of eclipses in a natal chart, and it is worth mentioning that no
meaningful transits were involved in the potent patterns.

11.

PAT'S BABIES

Michael and Patricia married on 15 August 1959 in East London, and thus began a journey together that was to end in divorce some 20 years later. During their years of marriage the couple produced five children, but the first baby was still-born. The main purpose of this particular study is to show how lunations and pleniluna figured in the births of the children. During the course of this chapter we shall examine in detail the following events:

1	Marriage	15 Aug 1959	about 15.30 GMT
2	Still-born girl	2 Aug 1960	no time — noon taken
3	Healthy son	9 Jan 1962	about 06.40 GMT
4	Healthy girl	25 Feb 1963	about 09.30 GMT
5	Healthy son	20 July 1964	about 05.50 GMT
6	Healthy son	22 May 1967	about 05.55 GMT
7	Crisis	6 May 1977	No time (the day identified as the beginning of the end of the marriage)

Before delving into the business of progressions, transits, and so on, it will be both interesting and useful to take a look at the nativity of each partner to discover the natal promise in respect of marriage and children.

Michael

Indications of marriage
A boy is usually brought up by his mother. She teaches him how to survive and is his first experience of women. The quality of the influence a mother exercises upon a *boy* describes the kind of female influence with which the *man* will feel most comfortable. When

the time comes to find a wife, the man will very often seek to repeat that maternal influence. The Moon sign will also describe the *initial reaction* of the native to any crisis or new contact.

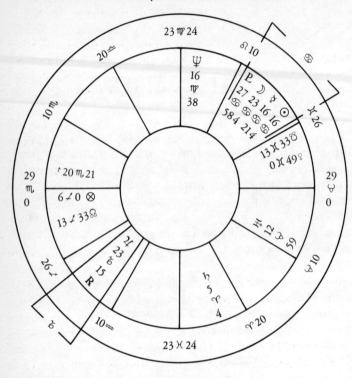

Fig. 11.1

MICHAEL,
8 JULY 1937,
16.31 GMT, 51°32′ N, 0°0′ W

In any birth chart the Moon is the significator of the mother. If the astrologer wishes to discover the kind of woman a man will marry he must look to the Moon of the nativity, and also to the ruler of the seventh house. The Moon is what he seeks; the ruler of the seventh house is what he gets! In Michael's chart (Fig. 11.1), the Moon is in Cancer with three aspects: trine Mars, opposition Jupiter, conjunction Pluto. So Michael's mother was strongly maternal (Cancer), deeply emotional (Scorpio), and a loving, caring and cherishing mother. From her he learned to trust his feelings and instincts, and throughout his life he will respond to people and situations principally through these qualities. He is a deeply emotional man and somewhat secretive.

The Moon–Pluto contact is open to varying interpretation. Some might say that it could indicate the death of the mother, or the removal of her influence from the child for some reason. Pluto *transforms* situations quite drastically and can often symbolize disappearance. This has not been our experience unless the Moon has been otherwise seriously afflicted (which is not so in this case). We have found that this contact often indicates an obsessive mother, and that is what we believe it means here; an exceptionally possessive mother who sought to exercise power over her son.

The general condition of the marriage significators is favourable. Venus is in Gemini, but she is angular and therefore strong; she is the ruler of the seventh house and posited in the seventh house. The Moon is strong in Cancer and well aspected by a dignified Mars (a most powerful contact); she is in opposition to Jupiter and conjunct Pluto, but neither of these aspects can interfere with the basic strength of the significators — marriage is assured!

The Moon's opposition to Jupiter in Capricorn in the second house shows that Jupiter is a problem, opposing as it does the whole planetary grouping in the eighth. It spells out money problems and promises that financial crises will be experienced during the course of the life. How does the mother figure in these matters? You will see that the opposition is pretty well exact, so she is drawn into the picture. She was a good mother, as we have seen, but obsessively so. The boy would have wanted for nothing; he was spoilt in a financial sense, was never taught to conserve his resources, being always able to rely upon his mother. Thus the seeds of future financial problems were planted.

We know what kind of woman he will look for. Caring and emotional, maternal and sensitive, that is his ideal. Venus, ruler of the seventh house, should describe what he actually gets. Venus in Gemini does not sound too sentimental; she is somewhat cooler than the Moon, more reasoning and logical, yet she is loving and not badly aspected. The Moon in this chart can be doting and devotional, whereas Venus looks for a good and sensible two-way relationship. The sextile aspect of Venus with Saturn shows that the wife will be blessed with practicality and common sense. The condition of Venus suggests that Michael's wife will be strongly influenced by Venus, lively and witty, sensible and practical, one who will take her role seriously.

Will the relationship succeed and survive? On the surface, yes, it should do, because there is no affliction to Venus in the seventh house. Yet the eighth house of a chart does show what comes from the marriage relationship, and the astrologer must therefore be suspicious of the Moon's conjunction with Pluto and her opposition to Jupiter.

Indications of children

Two houses immediately command our attention when investigating a nativity for the possibility of offspring: the fourth, and the fifth. The fifth house is traditionally the house of children, and the fourth must be considered because it has to do with the family, but it may be more important in a woman's chart than a man's. One should never ignore the eleventh house, for it is the fifth from the seventh, or the house of the partner's children as represented in the native's horoscope.

The ruler of the fifth house in Michael's chart is Mars, a planet strong in Scorpio and quite close to the Ascendant of which he is also traditional ruler. The strong Mars links with four planets in the family-orientated sign of Cancer by beneficial trine aspect, and the Cancer stellium falls in the eighth house of sexual power. There is little doubt that Michael has the power and inclination to produce children. A final additional piece of supporting evidence is the presence of Venus, ruler of the eleventh house, angular in the seventh house.

Pat

Indications of marriage

In a woman's chart, we look to the Sun and Venus for indications of marriage. Other significators are the ruler of the seventh house and any planets in the seventh, but we have found that the position and condition of Mars is a crucial consideration when investigating marriage in a woman's nativity. In Pat's chart (Fig. 11.2), Mars occupies the eleventh house (very close to the cusp of the twelfth) and the sign of Gemini, and that is not a strong position by house or sign. However, he is not badly aspected for he is conjunct Venus, the natural ruler of relationships, and sextile Saturn, ruler of the seventh house.

We look at a woman's chart rather differently from a man's when investigating marriage. Mars shows the power and inclination to marry. Marriage for a woman marks her move towards independence. Upon the vehicle of marriage she leaves the family home to set up on her own, and in due course she will found her own family.

We fully realize that we might be treading upon delicate ground

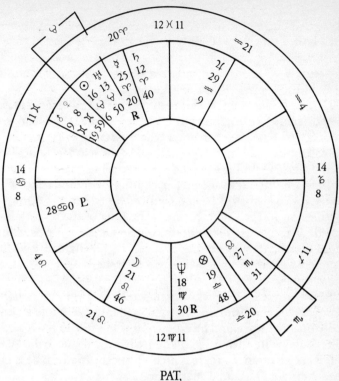

PAT,
7 May 1938,
Fig. 11.2   7.56 GMT, 51°32′ N, 0°5′ E

here, and we have no wish to deflect from our main theme into
arguments and considerations of feminism. We speak from a
traditional standpoint, and consider this approach entirely valid for
the great majority of people. We accept that others might see the
whole matter from a different angle, but we are convinced that careful
study of astrological influences will show the great power exercised
by Mars in driving a woman towards demonstrating her independence
through marriage.

In the same way as the ruler of the seventh house describes the
wife in a man's chart, so will it delineate the husband in a woman's
nativity. It has been said that the Sun in a woman's chart represents
her husband, but we cannot accept that. Such a view springs from
the days when, at marriage, a woman's destiny became entirely bound
up with that of her husband, even to the extent that the man
became owner of the woman's property. In these days it is frequently

the case that a married couple pursue independent careers and different interests, and many of the legal restrictions attending divorce have been swept away. Clearly a woman may be said to have her own destiny. Yet it is worth reflecting that these developments are comparatively recent, and we are really still within the transition stage of the 'Relationships Revolution'.

It is also traditional that Saturn in the chart of a woman represents the father and Saturn for a girl is as important as the Moon in the chart of a man because her father is her first experience of men, and she will measure the men in her life against the standard of her father. Why Saturn? Astrologically it does make sense. Cancer is the sign of the mother and the Moon is her significator; it is therefore logical that Capricorn should be the sign of the father and Saturn his significator. In Pat's chart Saturn is the ruler of the seventh house as well as the general significator of the father. Perhaps it is not unreasonable to suggest that Saturn, in the chart of a woman, represents the male influence with which she is likely to feel most comfortable.

Saturn then is in Aries, a sign which is basic, no-nonsense, masculine — the obvious archetypal man. Michael's role is clear as husband and father, and he expects his wife's role to be clear as his spouse, and as mother to his children. Saturn is sextile to the Mars—Venus conjunction. So there is no bad aspect to Saturn; he is given good humour, wit and a sharp mind.

Notice that the Sun and Moon are in square aspect. We have found that the relationship between the Lights in any chart symbolizes the parental relationship as seen and experienced by the child. With a square between the lights, that relationship may have been seen as strenous by the native when she was a child.

Pat's horoscope is very interesting in view of the conjunction of Sun–Uranus in the eleventh house. This is about as Aquarian as you can get without the Sun actually being in Aquarius. Sun in Taurus is hardly a rebel; rebellion takes too much effort, and in any case Taureans do not like upheavels which destabilize their environment. Yet the Uranian–Aquarian influence gives a great need to establish and demonstrate one's own individuality, so there is quite a contrast here: Taurus Pat, a creature of the herd, with a need to express her independence of the herd. The conjunction is intercepted in the eleventh house, so its power is not immediately obvious, but at some time in the life it will be powerfully activated and the astrologer might wonder how it would manifest.

If it is normal practice in the society of the native for a woman to marry in her late teens or early twenties, there is nothing in this chart to suggest that this native will not follow that practice. So marriage is not denied or delayed because Mars is in good aspect to Saturn, the ruler of the seventh house. Saturn in Aries sextile Mars-Venus in Gemini describes the kind of man she is likely to marry, or the kind of man with whom she would feel most at ease. Well, you can see the chart of the man she actually married, and you may ask yourself whether there is some discrepancy between what she expected and what she actually got, and you may ask the same question from Michael's point of view.

Indications of children

Pat experienced childbirth five times; the first pregnancy resulted in a still-birth but the rest were successful. By modern standards her family is larger than average.

Sepharial said that the Moon was important in these matters because she shows the *inclination in the male* and the *power in the female*. It has been generally held that when the Moon occupies a fruitful sign (Cancer–Scorpio–Pisces) then she is inclined to produce children. The Moon in Leo is supposed to indicate barrenness. Why? Leo, after all, is the fifth sign and by nature creative. The Moon in this chart is in Leo. She is squared by Uranus and the Sun, and this would be normally regarded as most unpromising for the production of offspring. Pat's experience defies these indications. We have an explanation of the still-birth from the square of the Moon to Uranus, and conjunction of Venus (ruler of the fifth house) with Mars (Mars is often destructive), but how do we explain *four healthy children*?

Although the negative interpretation of Venus–Mars might be the destruction of children, Mars, none the less would give considerable force to the desire to produce children. Also, despite the violence commonly found in Martian nature, Gemini is not associated with such unpleasantness. The Venus–Mars conjunction in this chart shows the coming together of Pat's fifth house ruler and her partner's fifth house ruler in the dual sign of Gemini. However, the Sun in Taurus (and Taurus is without doubt a most fruitful sign), enjoys a mutual reception with the Moon in Leo. The Moon occupies the sign of the Sun's dignity and the Sun the sign of the Moon's exaltation. This reception may be judged as fortunate, despite the fact that the aspect is traditionally a strenuous one. It allows the mutual exchange of planetary qualities, and this reception therefore augurs well for children.

The final consideration in this area of life, as in any other, is whether the native is likely to experience abnormal conditions. It is quite normal to produce children, the usual result of love and marriage. This is the natural response to the deep instincts which motivate most individuals, and therefore if a soul is to be denied the experience of children the astrologer will expect very clear indications to that effect in the nativity. In this case, with the ruler of the fifth house conjunct Mars, the ability (Venus) is activated by the desire (Mars), and with a reception between the Lights, a full eleventh house (fifth from seventh), and Fortuna on the fifth cusp, there is no reason to suppose that the native will be childless. However, one would recognize danger from the Moon–Uranus square.

Having reviewed the natal promise in respect of marriage and children in each case, our next task is to demonstrate how the astrologer might have been able to determine *when* the events of marriage and childbirth would occur.

Progressions

We have found that secondary progressions, allied with lunations, pleniluna and sometimes transits also, can be a most effective way of divining future events. We have already established that Pat was married at the age of 21 which is normal, and therefore nothing in the chart should suggest that she would marry late in life, or that marriage would be denied.

If at birth we had been asked to predict the year in which the subject would marry, would we have been able to do so? First, we would have isolated the pattern in the nativity which suggests marriage; then we would have calculated when one of the Life Indicators made a meaningful aspect to that pattern. We describe the Sun and the angles as Life Indicators, as they progress on the basis of a-day-for-a-year. It does not matter which Life Indicator makes contact with the natal pattern (the Indicators themselves are neutral); it is the radical and progressed planets, and the planetary patterns that they activate which are important. Figures 11.3(a) and (b) show all the secondary progressions for the material dates.

In this case we would probably have got it wrong! We can see that none of the Life Indicators will make an aspect to Saturn, ruler of the seventh house, before the age of 27 when the progressed Sun comes to sextile, and that is too late. Having abandoned Saturn as a possible marriage significator we must turn to Mars and the Sun. The Sun does not work because the progressed Midheaven will not make an aspect until the age of 36. Mars is a likely candidate, by

	0	1	2	3	4	5	6	7	8	9	10	11	12	13	14	15	16	17	18	19	20	21	22	23	24	25	26	27	28	29	30
NATAL									♂				M	♄	♅		☉		Ψ		⊗	☽				☿			♇	♃	
									9				12	12	13		16		18		19	21				25			28	29	
									♓				♓	♈	♑		♑		♍		♎	♌				♈			♋	♒	
									19				11	40	50		6		30		48	46				20			0	9	
									♀					A																	
									8					14																	
									♓					♋																	
									59					8																	
MARRIAGE 15 AUGUST 1959	A	♃				♀	☉							☿		♅			Ψ			☽		♂					♇		
	0	1				4	6							13		15			18			22		23					28		
	♌	♓				♋	♓							♑		♑			♍			♑		♓					♋		
	1	20				46	36							12		2			21			59		42					19		
						M									♄																
						5									14																
						♈									♈																
						6									52																
STILL—BORN GIRL 2 AUGUST 1960	♃					♀	☽	☉						☿	♅				Ψ						♂				♇		
	1					5	7	7						14	15				18						24				28		
	♓					♋	♓	♓						♑	♑				♍						♓				♋		
	25					56	21	31						34	6				21						21				20		
	A						M								♄																
	0						6								14																
	♌						♈								♈																
	43						10								57																
SON 9 JANUARY 1962		♃				♀	☉							♅	☿	Ψ								♂					♇	☽	
		1				7	8							15	16	18								25					28	28	
		♓				♋	♓							♑	♑	♍								♓					♋	♑	
		31				40	54							10	40	21								18					22	56	
		A					M									♄															
		1					7									15															
		♌					♈									♈															
		46					46									5															
DAUGHTER 25 FEBURARY 1963		♃	A					♀	☉					♅	☽	Ψ									♂				♇		
		1	2					9	9					15	15	18									26				28		
		♓	♌					♋	♓					♑	♋	♍									♓				♋		
		35	36					1	59					14	56	21									4				23		
										M						♄			☿												
										9						15			18												
										♈						♈			♅												
										1						11			23												

Fig. 11.3(a)

nature and through his conjunction with Venus, the planet of relationships. The progressed Sun comes within acceptable orbs of that conjunction between the ages of 22 and 23, and that is the aspect we would have plumped for. Yet Pat married at 21! This sort of thing is most frustrating for the astrologer, and immediately throws doubt on the accuracy of the birth time. So, back we go to the native to further enquire into the reliability of the birth moment she has given. When she tells you that her mother confidently affirmed that

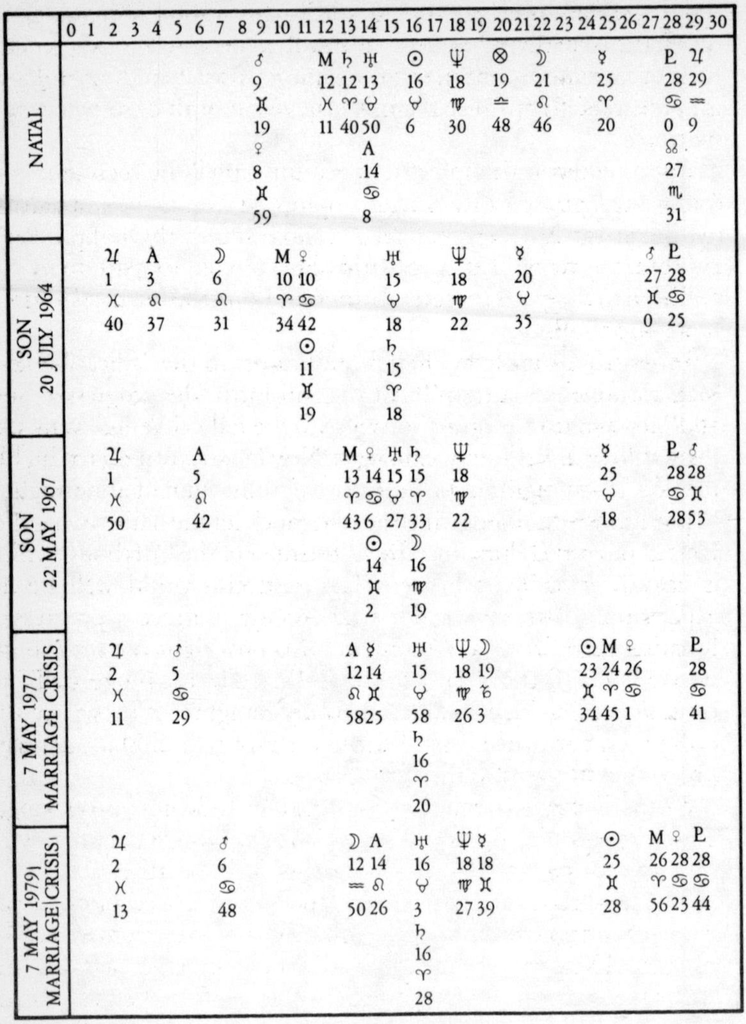

	0 1 2 3 4 5 6 7 8 9 10 11 12 13 14 15 16 17 18 19 20 21 22 23 24 25 26 27 28 29 30
NATAL	♂ M ♄ ♅ ☉ Ψ ⊗ ☽ ♀ ♇ ♃ 9 12 12 13 16 18 19 21 25 28 29 ♓ ♈ ♈ ♈ ♈ ♏ ≏ ♌ ♈ ♋ ♒ 19 11 40 50 6 30 48 46 20 0 9 ♀ A ♌ 8 14 27 ♓ ♋ ♏ 59 8 31
SON 20 JULY 1964	♃ A ☽ M ♀ ♅ Ψ ♀ ♂ ♇ 1 3 6 10 10 15 18 20 27 28 ♓ ♌ ♌ ♈ ♋ ♈ ♏ ♈ ♓ ♋ 40 37 31 34 42 18 22 35 0 25 ☉ ♄ 11 15 ♓ ♈ 19 18
SON 22 MAY 1967	♃ A M ♀ ♅ ♄ Ψ ♀ ♇ ♂ 1 5 13 14 15 15 18 25 28 28 ♓ ♌ ♈ ♋ ♈ ♈ ♏ ♈ ♋ ♓ 50 42 43 6 27 33 22 18 28 53 ☉ ☽ 14 16 ♓ ♏ 2 19
7 MAY 1977 MARRIAGE CRISIS	♃ ♂ A ♀ ♅ Ψ ☽ ☉ M ♀ ♇ 2 5 12 14 15 18 19 23 24 26 28 ♓ ♋ ♌ ♓ ♈ ♏ ♂ ♓ ♈ ♋ ♋ 11 29 58 25 58 26 3 34 45 1 41 ♄ 16 ♈ 20
7 MAY 1979 MARRIAGE CRISIS	♃ ♂ ☽ A ♅ Ψ ♀ ☉ M ♀ ♇ 2 6 12 14 16 18 18 25 26 28 28 ♓ ♋ ≏ ♌ ♈ ♏ ♓ ♓ ♈ ♋ ♋ 13 48 50 26 3 27 39 28 56 23 44 ♄ 16 ♈ 28

Fig. 11.3(b)

her daughter was born 'just in time for school, a few minutes before 9 a.m.' (BST), you have no option but to accept it. When further tests and investigation reveal that at the very moment of marriage the Moon was transiting the radical seventh cusp, and that at the birth of the final child the progressed Venus (ruler of the fifth house) was exactly on the radical Ascendant, one tends to give up disputing the birth data and return to the drawing board.

In the year of marriage the progressed MC was square the

progressed Venus. This is not an ideal signification of marriage in this particular nativity, but it can be justified because Venus is general ruler of relationships. It makes even more sense when the astrologer is made aware that Pat had a miscarriage a month or so before her marriage.

Running down through the speculum, it will be seen that this contact (progressed MC square progressed Venus) was operative (within an orb of 1°) for many years, and certainly throughout Pat's childbearing years. Let us call this line of contact pattern **A**. In addition to this pattern, several others indicate the birth of children more specifically.

Let us call contacts by the Life Indicators to the radical Venus–Mars conjunction pattern **B**. At the still-birth, the progressed Sun and Moon were in conjunction close to the radical Venus. Why was this a still-birth? In horary astrology a New Moon is considered highly malefic; it is thought to be indicative of some kind of abnormality, or producing conditions which are too much for the native to handle. Here, a progressed lunation afflicts the ruler of the fifth house which is already radically conjunct Mars, and this could well be an explanation of the event, for whatever significance a progressed lunation might have as a moment in its own right, we may count it here as an affliction. The first son is shown by the progressed Sun conjunct radical Venus–Mars; the only daughter is shown by the progressed Sun which is still within orbs of radical Mars, and the progressed MC sextile the conjunction.

With half of Pat's family complete, the Life Indicators can no longer make contact with the radical Venus–Mars, although the progressed MC square progressed Venus contact is still operative.

We mentioned the radical Sun/Moon mutual reception as the strongest indication of children. Now consider the movement of the progressed Mercury, ruler of the fourth house, in respect of that natal square between the lights (pattern **C**). He confirms the misfortune of the still-birth by a conjunction with destructive Uranus. Between the birth of the first son and the second son, he is moving within that radical square.

Now, with the Life Indicators out of contact with radical Venus–Mars, Mercury beyond the radical Sun–Moon, and three children clinging to her skirts, we rather suspect Pat fancied her family complete. But no, another little one in the shape of progressed Venus is approaching her radical Ascendant, and when she is within two minutes or arc, a further son arrives to augment her brood. As will be seen, this contact properly belongs to pattern **A**.

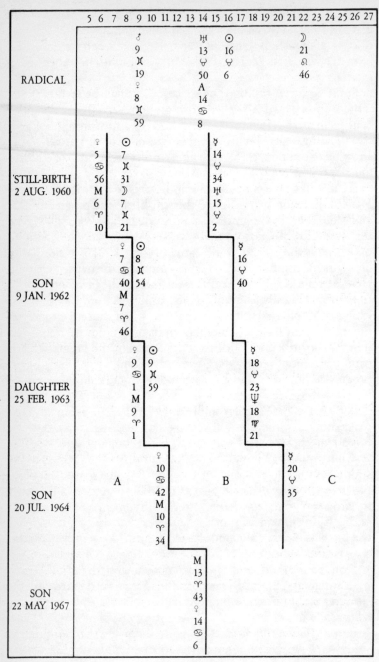

Fig. 11.4

Figure 11.4 illustrates these various channels of contact identified as **A, B, C**.

Eclipses

When a year has been isolated during which some important development has been judged likely to occur, we have found that it is often possible to get closer to the timing of the event by drawing upon eclipses, and New and Full Moons. It is frequently the case that when a radical pattern which holds the promise of a certain life experience is activated by an aspect from one of the Life Indicators, an eclipse (solar or lunar), falling in angular relationship (usually conjunction, square, or opposition), to the activated pattern, indicates the manifestation of that experience within six months. Figure 11.5 shows how eclipses fell in relation to the radical and progressed patterns which promise children:

The still-birth — a solar eclipse at 7° Aries emphasizes the progressed MC square the progressed Venus just over four months before the event.

First son — A lunar eclipse at 3° Pisces fell square to the progressed Sun about four and a half months before the birth; and a solar eclipse fell conjunct the radical moon some five months before.

Daughter — No eclipses emphasize the patterns.

Second son — The New Moon and Full Moon before the event were both eclipses falling in signs opposed to each other. If one takes the middle point between the eclipse degrees, one arrives at 10½° Cancer/Capricorn, conjunct the progressed Venus and square the progressed MC.

Third son — No eclipse allied itself with the progressed patterns, but just over six months before the event a solar eclipse fell square to the radical Moon, and the New Moon before the event, which was also a solar eclipse, fell conjunct the radical Sun. In this way the radical mutual reception between the Lights was activated by two eclipses.

Eclipses falling in close relationship to progressed patterns, or sensitive parts of a nativity, appear to be effective within a range of about six months.

	4	5	6	7	8	9	10	11	12	13	14	15	16	17
RADICAL					♀ 8 ♊ 59	♂ 9 ♊ 19					A 14 ♋ 8			
STILL—BIRTH 2 AUG. 1960		♀ 5 ♋ 56	M 6 ♈ 10	◑ 27.3.60 7 ♈ 0										8.7.60 ○ 17 ♑ 0
SON 9 JAN. 1962				♀ 7 ♋ 40	M 7 ♈ 46								6.1.62 ☽ 16 ♑ 0	
DAUGHTER 25 FEB. 1963						♀ 9 ♋ 1 M 9 ♈ 1								
SON 20 JULY 1964	● 25.6.64 4 ♍ 0						M 10 ♈ 34	♀ 10 ♋ 42						9.7.64 ◑ 17 ♋ 0
SON 22 MAY 1967										M 13 ♈ 43	♀ 14 ♋ 6			

	3	4	5	6	7	8	9	10	11	12
RADICAL						♀ 8 ♊ 59	♂ 9 ♊ 19			
STILL—BIRTH 2 AUG. 1960					☽ 7 ♊ 21	☉ 7 ♊ 31				
SON 9 JAN. 1962	● 26.8.61 3 ♓ 0						☉ 8 ♊ 54			
DAUGHTER 25 FEB. 1963								☉ 9 ♊ 59		
SON 20 JULY 1964										
SON 22 MAY 1967										

	12	13	14	15	16	17	18	19	20	21	22	23	24	25
RADICAL					☉ 16 ♉ 6						☽ 21 ♌ 46			
STILL—BIRTH 2 AUG. 1960			☿ 14 ♉ 34	♅ 15 ♉ 2										
SON 9 JAN. 1962						☿ 16 ♉ 40		◑ 11.8.61 19 ♌ 0						
DAUGHTER 25 FEB. 1963							♆ 18 ♍ 21	☿ 18 ♉ 23	○ 8.2.63 19 ♌ 0					
SON 20 JULY 1964														
SON 22 MAY 1967						9.5.67 ◑ 18 ♉ 0		12.11.66 ◑ 20 ♏ 0	☿ 20 ♉ 35					

Fig. 11.5

Preceding New and Full Moons

We have also found that when such a radical pattern has been activated by a Life Indicator, and when an eclipse has fallen in relationship to that activated pattern, it is often the case that a New or Full Moon falling sharp in relationship with the whole pattern, or a related part of the nativity, indicates the manifestation of the event before the Moon becomes New or Full again, i.e normally within two weeks, sometimes within a month. In other words, the New or Full Moon preceding the event can provide a further indication of an event.

With the still-birth the preceding Full Moon, and with the first son the preceding New Moon, fell in opposition to the Cancer Ascendant. In the case of the daughter the preceding Full Moon fell square to progressed Mercury and conjunct the radical Moon. The two eclipses already mentioned in respect of the second son were in fact the preceding New and Full Moons. With the third son the solar eclipse falling conjunct the radical Sun was also the preceding New Moon.

It is worth noting how syzygies related either to the Cancer Ascendant or the Sun/Moon reception in every experience of childbirth.

Transits

We have often remarked that we are not over-impressed with transits as indicators of events. It is certainly not possible to make predictions through transits alone, and any astrologer who attempts to time experiences using transits is likely to come to grief.

As an example, consider Pluto. At the marriage he occupied the third house of Pat's chart at the fourth degree of Virgo. Pluto first entered the house in 1951 and would leave it in 1963 with such a slow movement that one could not argue that he would be responsible for any dramatic events, but he might be responsible for the gradual unfolding of a certain potential within the chart. Pat identified 6 May 1977 as the day which started the chain of events which led to the break-up of her marriage. During 1976/78 Pluto was transiting the opposition points of the radical and progressed Saturn (ruler of the marriage house), and also transiting square the seventh cusp. Throughout that period events were in progress that would transform the native from a married woman into a divorcee.

People tend to remember the great events of their lives — marriage, children, serious illness, deaths, etc. — but the flavour of everyday life and the hundreds of minor events are soon lost to memory. There must be a case for suggesting that secondary progressions mark life's great events while transits are more related to minor joys and aggravations of everyday living.

The debate about the comparative power of transits and progressions continues, but we agree with Ron Davison, author of *The Technique of Prediction*, and state that *nothing of great import can befall the native unless indicated by secondary progressions involving progressed or radical Sun and angles.*

Normally we would not make much of the transits of the inner planets (Sun, Moon, Mercury, Venus, Mars), but a most interesting pattern arises in this case. At the time of marriage Venus was retrograde and moving only a few minutes a day. On the day before the wedding, Venus made an exact conjunction with the then forward-moving Mars. That conjunction occurred at a point trine the radical Sun, thus creating a *Grand Trine in Earth Signs*. It was a unique pattern because at no other time could the Moon aspect everything else from the cusp of the seventh.

At the time of the still-birth, Uranus was at 20°41′ Leo and Venus at 21°24′ Leo, in close proximity to the radical Moon. It must be important that at the time of the still-birth Uranus (20°41′ Leo) was transiting the radical Moon. It is true to say that Uranus held this conjunction within a degree for a whole year, but the day of the event was emphasized by a transit of Venus (21°24′ Leo) moving across Uranus, thus making the conjunction special to that day. Here once again is a valuable indication from a transit.

On the day of the birth of the second son, Mercury (19°33′ Leo) was transiting the radical Moon. Sometimes transits are around at the right time and sometimes not, and they cannot really be taken on their own without reference to secondary progressions, eclipses, and New or Full Moons.

12.

A WHITE MAN'S BURDEN

On 18 May 1982, I replied to a letter from South Africa on behalf

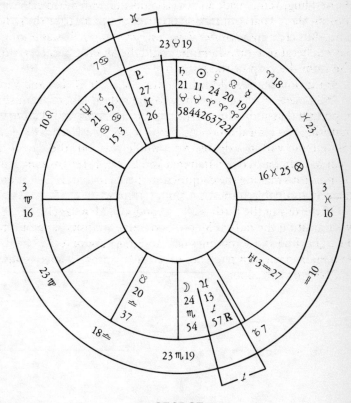

GEORGE
2 MAY 1912,
12.52 GMT, OLDHAM,
53°33′ N, 2°8′ W

Fig. 12.1

of the Astrological Lodge of London. Thus began a correspondence with George, which has continued on a casual basis ever since. During our astrological discussions, George told me about his experiences in Africa. He would be the first to agree that he is no latter-day Rhodes or Livingstone, just an ordinary working man who settled in a far corner of the British Empire a decade or so before its dissolution really got under way. His personal life became caught up in a web of political events over which he had no control. He was obliged to fight his own mini-battle for survival on the sidelines of a greater battlefield.

His story is strangely moving, and we decided to make it the subject of our final chapter. In relating the chronology of events, we often use George's own words, and they appear with his kind permission.

DEREK APPLEBY

Scale across top: 0 1 2 3 4 5 6 7 8 9 10 11 12 13 14 15 16 17 18 19 20 21 22 23 24 25 26 27 28 29 30

Event	Planetary positions (degree · sign · minute)
RADIX	♅ 3° ♒ 27'; A 3° ♍ 16'; ☉ 11° ♑ 44'; ♃ 13° ♐ 51'; ♂ 15° ♋ 3'; ☊ 19° ♈ 22'; ♆ 21° ♋ 15'; ♄ 21° ♀ 58'; M 23° ♀ 19'; ♀ 24° ♈ 26'; ☽ 24° ♏ 54'; ♇ 27° ♓ 26'
MARRIAGE 9 JAN. 1932	☉ 0° ♓ 45'; ♅ 3° ♒ 23'; ☿ 6° ♀ 48'; ♃ 11° ♐ 49'; ☽ 12° ♌ 40'; M 11° ♓ 44'; A 16° ♍ 26'; ♀ 18° ♆ 35'; ♆ 21° ♋ 41'; ♄ 24° ♀ 30'; ♂ 26° ♋ 25'; ♇ 27° ♓ 50'
SON 15 JUN. 1933	☉ 2° ♓ 7'; ♅ 3° ♒ 22'; ☽ 2° ♍ 58'; ☿ 8° ♀ 49'; ♃ 11° ♐ 38'; M 13° ♐ 5'; A 17° ♍ 25'; ♀ 20° ♋ 20'; ♆ 21° ♋ 43'; ♄ 24° ♀ 41'; ♂ 27° ♋ 15'; ♇ 27° ♓ 52'
DAUGHTER 3 AUG. 1936	♅ 3° ♒ 19'; ☉ 5° ♓ 8'; ♃ 11° ♐ 15'; ☊ 13° ♀ 31'; ☽ 15° ♎ 34'; M 16° ♓ 1'; A 19° ♍ 35'; ♆ 21° ♋ 48'; ♀ 24° ♋ 10'; ♄ 25° ♋ 5'; ♇ 27° ♓ 52'; ♂ 29° ♋ 6'
SAILING 27 JULY 1939	♂ 0° ♌ 51'; ♅ 3° ♒ 16'; ☉ 7° ♓ 59'; ♃ 10° ♐ 52'; ☊ 18° ♀ 21'; M 18° ♐ 49'; A 21° ♍ 39'; ☽ 24° ♏ 1'; ♄ 25° ♀ 28'; ♀ 27° ♀ 50'; ♆ 21° ♋ 53'; ♇ 28° ♓ 0'

Fig. 12.2   GEORGE, PROGRESSIONS

Nativity

Oldham, 2 May 1912 at 12.52 GMT, a man-child hails the world
for the first time, and is named George. Solid Taurus presided at
his birth, but from the East the Virgin brings her gift Mercurial,
so the mind is sharpened and the spirit made restless for adventure.
Old Saturn, at the southern gate, tightly holds the key to worldly
fame, and will not easily give it up. Each small success must be hardly
won, and every lesson harshly learned. Yet he is the best of fathers,
and wisdom comes with age. Scorpionic Moon protects the family
in the north with intense devotion, ever struggling with Saturn's
stony heart. But from his secret hiding place Jupiter sends his blessings

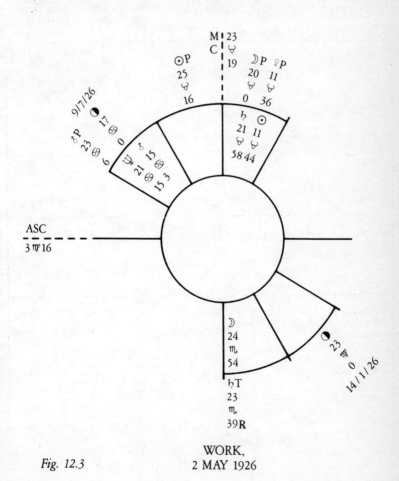

Fig. 12.3

WORK,
2 MAY 1926

out to deflect, from time to time, the hammer-blows of fate.

Figure 12.2 sets out the speculum of planetary contacts covering several important events until George sailed away from his homeland at the age of 27, but we will now look at these moments in detail.

Work — (See Fig. 12.3.) Times were hard in Lancashire between the wars. Boys quickly donned the caps of men, 14 years was age enough, and as the Sun progressed across the Midheaven to oppose the Moon, George passed through the factory gate. Confirmation comes from Mars, who by his very nature casts the fledgling from the nest to forage for himself. Here he moves neatly to sextile the Midheaven, and is brought to full potency by the solar eclipses of the year.

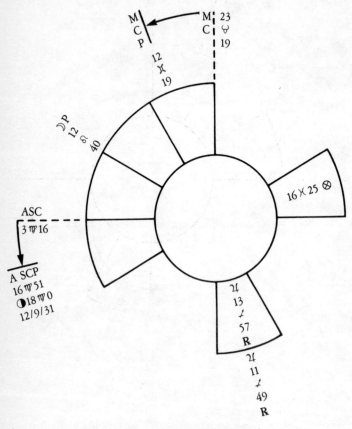

Fig. 12.4

MARRIAGE,
9 JANUARY 1932

Marriage — (See Fig. 12.4.) Sun passed into Gemini, but Midheaven was way ahead — in argument with Jupiter. The powerful Lord of Marriage brooked no delay, for, as he said: 'If 14 years produce a man, then 20 years can easy see him wed.' Scorpio was near at hand, as she had always been, on the nadir of his chart — and so they wed, George and his childhood sweetheart. Quite properly, when men are wed, the Moon illuminates the chart, for from her Leonian throne she draws the opposition happily to herself. The seventh house Fortuna atracts progressed Ascendant, already sensitized by the preceding eclipse.

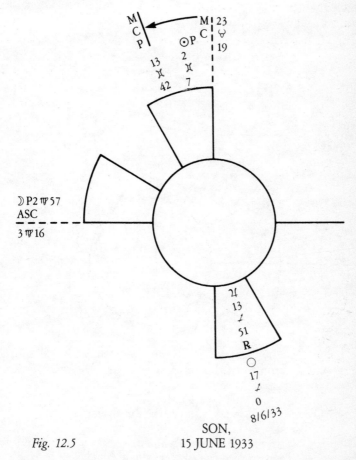

Fig. 12.5   SON,
                                          15 JUNE 1933

Children — (See Figs. 12.5 and 12.6.) Saturn from his lofty seat declares fatherhood his natural right, but Jupiter performed the miracle of birth when winged Gemini brought Geoffrey down to

earth, within a week of the Full Moon. Barbara chose the moment
when sweet Venus from the Midheaven stood opposite the Moon,
for Leo when she comes upon the stage demands attention from
the first. No syzygy attended this nativity, but Venus snuggled close
to Saturn, governor of the fifth.

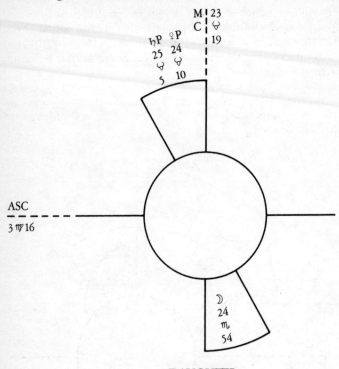

Fig. 12.6

DAUGHTER,
3 AUGUST 1936
Emmigration

Take up the White Man's Burden —
Send forth the best ye breed —
Go, bind your sons to exile
To serve your captive's need . . .
The White Man's Burden — RUDYARD KIPLING

10 February 1939; I don't know why this date sticks in my mind, I
am not good at dates, Read an adertisement in a trade journal, and
feeling guilty about looking for another job. Three situations — Isle
of Wight, Shrewsbury, RHODESIA! I said to myself 'that's where
I'm going'. Intuition?

Sailing 4 p.m., 27 July 1939. It was not a happy moment, more like in a daze — Neptunian events had overtaken my life. Little money in my pocket, wife and two children aged 6 and 3. A person like myself who had suffered harsh and adverse working conditions — for 10 years, six days a week — does not respond readily to fairyland conditions, especially being an introvert, shy and timid.

I didn't know the people I was to work for except they had a sound reputation and I was met at Cape Town Head Office 10 August 1939. They were very nice, naturally, because I was going into 'Darkest Africa' to look after their little empire, as well as Empire Building for good King George.

Arrived in Bulawayo 7 a.m., 12 August 1939, 10 shillings in my pocket, and nowhere to live. Nevertheless we found a boarding house by 6 p.m. — one room, two beds, wash-basin, and my wife in tears. That's pioneering!

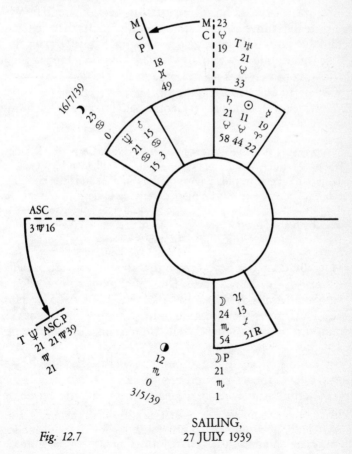

Fig. 12.7

SAILING,
27 JULY 1939

Sailing — (See Fig. 12.7.) Left to himself, Taurus is usually content
to fence and cultivate his private field, but this bull has a buzzing
in his brain. Arian Mercury, impatient to be off, allies himself with
optimistic Jupiter, and they through Neptune tempt with dreams
of gold and happiness in other lands. Where to go? England for
centuries has pushed her children out to every corner of the globe,
half the world is coloured red in deference to the Motherland, and
the Sun finds no rest on his imperial patrol. Go where you will!
Mercury says Rhodesia, settlers are needed there.

In May, the Scorpionic eclipse sent a charge of energy to ninth
house Sun, a reminder of his destiny. With Moon returning to her
natal place, Midheaven caressing Arian Mercury with a sextile touch,
and Uranus in transit of Saturn, George and his family embarked
upon their ship of fate. Neptune too was all about, bobbing on a
Cancer sea since birth; he now transits progressed Ascendant which
by sextile bids him raise his sail. A New Moon lifts the anchor and,
before she waxes full, the voyage had begun. Saturn, dozing on his
Midheaven throne, woke annoyed when Ascendant tapped him on
the foot, and there was no welcome in Bulawayo, he saw to that.
It was not an auspicious beginning.

A few weeks after his arrival George paid homage to the founder
of his new country:

> 3 September 1939: We were visiting the grave of Cecil John Rhodes
> about 25 miles from Bulawayo, Matapos Hill (World View), a
> panorama of granite hills as far as the eye could see and little knowing
> what was ahead and a little pioneer helping to develop the British
> Empire — what a laugh — what tragedy 40 years later, good Queen
> Elizabeth and 'Maggie' (Margaret Thatcher) signed it all away and
> *most* important, left its own kith and kin to rot — *Kismet?*

How could George have known that the die was cast in Belfast,
when he was but 10 years old? The actual moment was when the
Senate voted itself out of the Irish Free State (3.28 p.m., 5 December
1922), for that was the inception of the United Kingdom of Great
Britain and Northern Ireland. (The United Kingdom chart appears
in Chapter 5, Fig. 5.2.)

See how Pluto sits in the second house of possessions, how the
Moon (ruler of the second house) separates from Pluto by 13°, and
how powerful Saturn (ruler of the eighth, ninth, tenth, and eleventh
houses) squares the Pluto/Moon midpoint. Here is the promise of
massive loss of possessions, the forewarning of the dissolution of the
British Empire, and a radical transformation of national status and

	4	5	6	7	8	9	10	11	12	13	14	15	16	17	18	19	20	21	22	23	24	25	26	27
UK RADICAL PATTERN						♅ 9 ♓ 49	♇ 10 ♋ 39							♄ 17 ♎ 44						☽ 23 ♋ 13				
INDIA 14 AUG. 1947	A 4 ♋ 49					☉ 9 ♑ 54	♇ ♅ 10 10 ♋ ♓ 10 26									♄ 19 ♎ 24								
1 JAN. 1948 CEYLON 4 FEB.		A 5 ♋ 9					♇ ☉ ♅ 10 10 10 ♋ ♑ ♓ 9 17 27									♄ 19 ♎ 25								
1 JAN. 1957 GOLD COAST 6 MAR. MALAYA 31 AUG.						♇ 9 ♋ 58	♅ 10 ♓ 47		A 12 ♋ 21							☉ ♄ 19 19 ♑ ♎ 28 47								
1. JAN. 1960 CYPRUS 16 AUG. NIGERIA 1 OCT.						♇ 9 ♋ 54	♅ 10 ♓ 55				A 14 ♋ 38					♄ 19 ♎ 53			☉ 22 ♑ 31					
1 JAN. 1961 SIERRA LEONE 27 APR.						♇ 9 ♋ 53	♅ 10 ♓ 57					A 15 ♋ 23				♄ 19 ♎ 55				☉ 23 ♑ 32				
1 JAN. 1962 WESTERN SAMOA 1 JAN. JAMAICA 6 AUG. TRINIDAD & TOBAGO 31 AUG. UGANDA 9 OCT. TANGANYIKA 9 DEC.						♇ 9 ♋ 52		♅ 11 ♓ 0					A 16 ♋ 7			♄ 19 ♎ 56					☉ 24 ♑ 33			
1 JAN. 1963 KENYA 12 DEC.						♇ 9 ♋ 51		♅ 11 ♓ 3					A 16 ♋ 51			♄ 19 ♍ 58						☉ 25 ♑ 34		
1. JAN. 1964 MALTA 21 SEPT. N. RHODESIA 24 OCT.						♇ 9 ♋ 50		♅ 11' ♓ 5						A 17 ♋ 35		♄ 19 ♎ 59								
1 JAN. 1965 THE GAMBIA 18 FEB. RHODESIA UDI 11 NOV.						♇ 9 ♋ 48		♅ 11 ♓ 8							A 18 ♋ 8		♄ 20 ♎ 0							

Fig. 12.8

		4 5 6 7 8 9 10 11 12 13 14 15 16 17 18 19 20 21 22 23 24 25 26 2
UK RADICAL PATTERN		♅ ♇ ♄ ☽ 9 10 17 23 ♓ ♋ ♎ ♋ 49 39 44 13
1 JAN. 1966 BRITISH GUYANA 26 MAY NYASALAND 6 JUL. BECHUANALAND 30 SEPT. BASUTOLAND 4 OCT. BARBADOS 30 NOV.		♇ ♅ A ♄ 9 11 19 20 ♋ ♓ ♋ ♎ 47 11 2 1
1 JAN. 1968 MAURITIUS 12 MAR. SWAZILAND 6 SEPT.		♇ ♅ ♄ A 9 11 20 20 ♋ ♓ ♎ ♋ 45 16 3 27
1 JAN. 1970 TONGA 7 JUNE FIJI 10 OCT.		♇ ♅ ♄ A 9 11 20 21 ♋ ♓ ♎ ♋ 43 22 5 52
1 JAN. 1973 BAHAMAS 10 JULY		♇ ♅ ♄ A 9 11 20 23 ♋ ♓ ♎ ♋ 39 31 6 58
1 JAN. 1974 GRENADA 1 FEB.		♇ ♅ ♄ A 9 11 20 24 ♋ ♓ ♎ ♋ 38 34 7 39
1 JAN. 1975 PAPUA NEW GUINEA 16 SEPT.		♇ ♅ ♄ A 9 11 20 25 ♋ ♓ ♎ ♋ 37 37 7 20
1 JAN. 1976 SEYCHELLES 28 JUNE		☽ ♇ ♅ ♄ A 7 9 11 20 26 ♋ ♋ ♓ ♎ ♋ 33 36 40 7 2

Fig. 12.8

influence. That it was achieved through voluntary withdrawal is due to the nature of Pluto; that it was carried out peacefully, for the most part, is due to Jupiter trine Pluto and Venus trine Moon; that the British Empire was transformed into an international brotherhood known as the Commonwealth is due to an eleventh house Uranus trine Pluto.

Turn to Fig. 12.8 and see how well the winding-up of the Empire is symbolized by secondary progressions. The progressed planetary positions are given for the exact day in the case of India, and for the first day of the year in all other cases.

As the progressed Sun made opposition contact with Pluto and a sextile with Uranus, the unbelievable happened; Britain plucked the brightest jewel from its Imperial Crown and surrendered India to the Indians. Six months later it was the turn of Ceylon.In 1931,

Winston Churchill had said in a speech to the House of Commons: 'The loss of India would be final and fatal to us. It could not fail to be part of a process that would reduce us to the scale of a minor power.' Now the process had begun. It appears to have taken nine years for Britain to recover from the shock of India, but in 1957 the Gold Coast (Ghana) headed the long list of colonial possessions to be given independence over the next 20 years. The progressed Sun moved in opposition between radical Pluto and radical Moon, to be followed by the progressed Ascendant moving from conjunction to conjunction, and on their journey both points squared radical and progressed Saturn.

George was not privy to these heavenly signs when he sailed into the sunset of the Empire in 1939, nor probably was anyone else, certainly not the Ulstermen who unwittingly precipitated the moment. Nor could George have been aware that his own Mars–Neptune conjunction in Cancer, in his house of hopes and wishes, was intimately connected with the radical pattern of the United Kingdom chart responsible for the dissolution of the Empire. However, let us return to Bulawayo and George in 1939.

Some astrologers believe that when a person moves from their birth place to live somewhere else, their natal chart should be adjusted to the new location, and the aspects produced by progressing the adjusted angles will give a better symbolism of life events. It is also held that whatever adjustments are made the original birth chart will faithfully symbolize the life of the native and the unfolding of his or her destiny. If you wish to relocate a birth chart, all that is necessary is to set the birth moment for the coordinates of the new place of residence, after ensuring that you have converted the birth time to GMT. Obviously the positions of the planets will remain the same, but the Ascendant, Midheaven and other house cusps will change. Apart from the possibility of planets changing houses, which might provoke some reassessment of the natal promise, aspects formed by the progressed angles to natal and progressed planets will be different. Quite often, particularly in a small country, moves from town to town will not result in much of a variation, but we are dealing here with a man who not only changed continents but moved from the Northern to the Southern Hemisphere. George presents us with an ideal opportunity to consider the angular secondary progressions both for the birth place and relocated to Africa.

Figure 12.9 shows the nativity relocation to Bulawayo. It will be seen that the Moon–Saturn opposition has moved away from the MC/IC axis, Sun–Saturn are now in the eighth house, and the

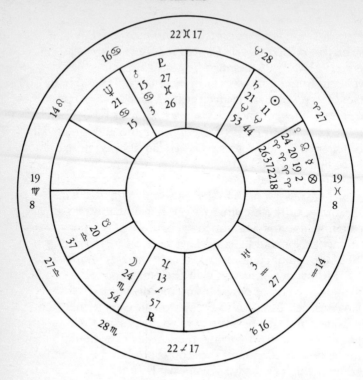

GEORGE, NATAL CHART
RELOCATED TO
Fig. 12.9   BULAWAYO

previously empty seventh house has become well tenanted. Initial
experiments tend to favour the view that the progressed relocated
chart angles give a more reasonable explanation of life events, so
we will work with them, but when examining crucial dates in detail
we shall illustrate both charts. Figure 12.10 picks out the notable
contacts of the relocated chart for the arrival at Bulawayo, and marks
the starting point for progressions in Africa. Figure 12.11 gives
progressed positions for the relocated chart for every two years from
1943 until 1951.

Between 1939 and 1940 George gradually established himself and
eventually found a house for his family.

But wait, we are preparing for war, and Southern Rhodesia —
Northern Rhodesia — Nyasaland are good forward bases. Southern
Rhodesia was the first country in the British Empire to start the Empire
Air Training Scheme, first week of May 1940 — beat Canada by a

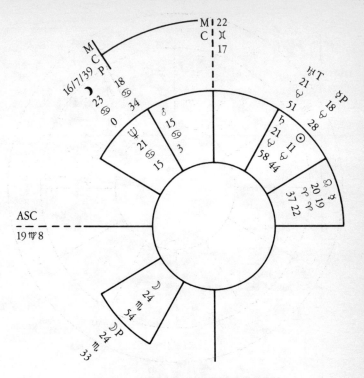

ARRIVAL IN BULAWAYO,
12 AUGUST 1939,
Fig. 12.10   RELOCATED CHART

week. The Rhodesian war effort is another story.

Arian Mercury, ever hasty with a pen, wrote to give advice to the Finance Ministry upon the state of government transport. George was summoned to the army by return! Sickness freed him in a year, but then he stood without a home, without possessions, he and his family in a boarding house. At last, Jupiter awakened, and he was given a new house for ex-servicemen; he had his base.

Now come years of struggle and crisis, fighting to survive, drifting from one unhappy crisis to another. Family sickness, doctors' bills, marital tension. In retrospect, George aptly blames Mercury–Venus square Neptune and Mars in Cancer.

George joined the army in September 1942 and, as he did so, progressed Mars was moving to oppose Uranus, while the progressed Midheaven was in conjunction with Neptune as well as sextile Saturn. Also progressed Mercury, the chart ruler, was conjunct progressed

	0 1 2 3 4 5 6 7 8 9 10 11 12 13 14 15 16 17 18 19 20 21 22 23 24 25 26 27 28 29 30
RADIX RELOCATED TO BULAWAYO	⊗ ♅ ... ⊙ ♃ ♂ ... ♉ ☊ ♆ ♄ ... ♀ ☽ ♇ 2 3 ... 11 13 15 ... 19 20 21 21 ... 24 24 27 ♈ ♒ ... ♍ ♐ ♋ ... ♈ ♈ ♋ ♍ ... ♈ ♏ ♓ 18 27 ... 44 57 3 ... 22 37 15 58 ... 26 54 26 A M 19 22 ♍ ♓ 8 17
2 MAY 1943	A ♀ ♅ ... ♃ ⊙ ... ♆ ... ♂ ♄ ♇ 0 2 3 ... 10 11 ... 22 ... 24 25 28 ♏ ♓ ♒ ... ♐ ♓ ... ♋ ... ♋ ♋ ♓ 19 26 12 ... 23 35 ... 0 ... 58 57 5 ♂ ... ☽ ... M M* A* 3 ... 10 ... 22 22 24 ♌ ... ♍ ... ♋ ♓ ♍ 4 ... 21 ... 8 22 18
2 MAY 1945	♅ ♂ ♀ ... ♃ ⊙ ... ♆ M ♄ ♇ ♂ 3 4 4 ... 10 13 ... 22 24 26 28 28 ♒ ♌ ♓ ... ♐ ♓ ... ♋ ♋ ♋ ♓ ♋ 10 15 54 ... 8 30 ... 3 3 12 8 42 A ☽ ... M* A* 2 4 ... 24 25 ♏ ♒ ... ♓ ♍ 47 14 ... 15 42
2 MAY 1947	♅ ♂ ♀ ♃ ... ⊙ ... ♆ ... ♄ A* ♇ 3 5 7 9 ... 15 ... 22 ... 26 27 28 ♒ ♌ ♓ ♐ ... ♓ ... ♋ ... ♋ ♍ ♓ 7 26 21 53 ... 25 ... 7 ... 27 7 11 ☿ A ... M M* ☽ 2 5 ... 25 26 27 ♓ ♏ ... ♋ ♓ ♒ 36 12 ... 58 9 ·58
2 MAY 1949	♅ ♂ A ♃ ... ⊙ ... ♆ ... ♄ ♇ M* 3 6 7 9 ... 17 ... 22 ... 26 28 28 ♒ ♌ ♏ ♐ ... ♓ ... ♋ ... ♋ ♓ ♓ 4 38 34 38 ... 20 ... 11 ... 42 13 2 ☿ ♀ ... ☽ ... M A* 6 9 ... 22 ... 27 28 ♓ ♓ ... ♓ ... ♋ ♍ 38 48 ... 10 ... 52 32
2 MAY 1951	♅ ... ♂ ♃ A ☿ ♀ ... ☽ ⊙ ♆ ... ♄ ♇ M M* 3 ... 7 9 9 10 12 ... 17 19 22 ... 26 28 28 29 ♒ ... ♌ ♐ ♏ ♓ ♓ ... ♈ ♓ ♋ ... ♋ ♓ ♋ ♓ 1 ... 49 23 55 48 15 ... 23 15 15 ... 57 16 47 56 A* 29 ♍ 57

Fig. 12.11

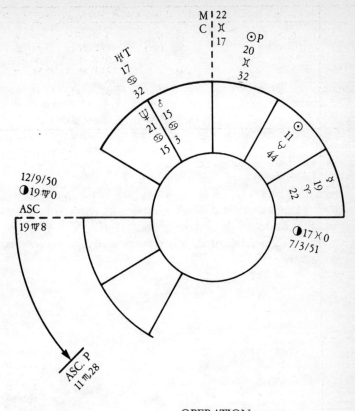

Fig. 12.12(a)

OPERATION,
6 SEPTEMBER 1952

Saturn. The sickness which freed George from uniform is well
symbolized by the Mercury–Saturn contact, Mercury ruling the body
and Saturn joint ruler of the sixth house.

The Ascendant, now progressed into Scorpio, must square Uranus
and progressed Mars, both strenuous aspects, and both in their own
way indicating a struggle to survive; that aspect was not cleared until
1949/50. Between 1944/46 the progressed Sun was opposing Jupiter,
doubtless producing problems with the marriage, for Jupiter rules
the seventh house. This opposition also indicates a struggle to achieve
a degree of prosperity, and it is not assisted by Venus (ruler of the
second house), having to oppose progressed and radical Jupiter
between 1948 and 1952. We have entered the progressed angles for
the original birth chart set for Oldham (marked with an asterisk in

each case), to see if they better reflect these difficult years, but we
do not think they do so. For several years they are both involved in
contacts with Pluto, which does not seem relevant to the flavour of
the period.

> Eventually it all caught up with me — middle 1951 first signs of ulcer,
> 6 September 1952, operation for duodenal ulcer and I am left with
> a fifth of a stomach. By December 1952 I am down to 100 lbs from
> 128 lbs. Life doesn't mean much and in fact wish I was dead. I only
> made a livable recovery after 3—5 years, with the help of a spiritual
> healer who I visited every week for a year.

From Fig. 12.12(a) it can be seen how, when George's chart is
relocated to Bulawayo, the Ascendant aspects Mercury (chart ruler)
by an exact quincunx, while Mercury himself is square Mars–Neptune
in Cancer. The quincunx, among other things, is an aspect concerned

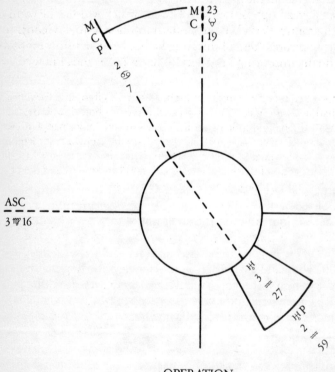

Fig. 12.12(b)   OPERATION,
                       6 SEPTEMBER 1952

with health. Here it links the Ascendant with the ruler of the Ascendant. Mercury in Aries causes fret and worry, and the effects of that worry go straight along the line of the square to Mars–Neptune in Cancer to attack the stomach; small wonder we have an ulcer! When the problem first became apparent in mid-1951, the progressed Sun was exactly square the Ascendant and thus activated the whole pattern. The eclipse of late 1950 and early 1951 doubtless lent their force to the eruption, and Uranus transiting between Mars–Neptune assisted in the attack. The chart is set for the actual operation, and the progressed Ascendant was opposing the Sun in the eighth house of surgery.

Figure 12.12(b), shows the only aspect of note in the original chart. It makes some sense that the progressed Midheaven is quincunx the ruler of the sixth house, but this chart has nothing like the finesse of the former.

It will take the progressed Ascendant about 18 months or so to disengage from the Sun, and the progressed Midheaven now in Leo must pass an opposition with Uranus which will not be complete until around 1955. We can understand how it took George some years to recover. Yet, all this time he has been gainfully employed, gradually improving his position, let us move ahead now to 1960.

> October 1960; A significant event, Mother (Virgo) arrives whom I had not seen since 1939 — Wife (Scorpio) — how do you describe Sun/Moon opposition twice? R.C. Davison says: 'Not a happy augury for domestic bliss; (in a male horoscope) trouble involving womenfolk, especially wife and mother.' My mother being accustomed to the bright lights of Blackpool left for UK — February 1961 and died the same month, leaving me a legacy of £4,000.

At the time of writing, £4,000 would be a handy sum to come one's way. It might possibly replace the windows in a house, pay for a couple of good holidays, or a reasonable second-hand car. In 1960 in England, £4,000 would have bought two respectable houses, and represented at least five years' salary for most working people. George had come into a tidy sum! He spent the summer on holiday in England, left some money in London but invested half of his legacy in Durban.

> There was a certain significance in this — particularly the £2,000 invested in Durban saved me from the poorhouse today. My chart does not significantly show legacy, and the second house is empty,

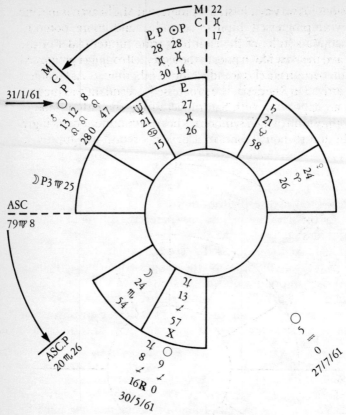

LEGACY, ETC.,

Fig. 12.13(a) CALCULATED FOR 1 OCTOBER 1960

which in my opinion fits nicely. I have worked hard, earned average money, but never been able to save.

In the relocated chart progressed, shown in Fig. 12.13(a), which was calculated for 1 October 1960, the progressed Sun was in contact with Pluto in the tenth house; a major transformation had occurred in George's life. Pluto transforms for good or ill, and the inheritance was part of the positive manifestation. George says that his nativity does not show legacy, which is an eighth house matter. True enough, the original natal chart has no planets in the second or eighth houses, but Jupiter is ruler of the eighth, and is powerful in the house of the mother. However, the relocated chart has Sun–Saturn in the eighth, while Jupiter is in the third but is ruler of the fourth. This fortune came from Jupiter. It shows up quite strongly in the progressions in two ways. First, the progressed Midheaven is in trine aspect with progressed Jupiter; secondly, and more potently, progressed Mars (ruler of the eighth) is trine Jupiter (ruler of the fourth), and the New Moon prior to the legacy fell conjunct progressed Mars. This pattern is a classic indication of inheritance. As George's mother arrived in Rhodesia, the progressed Ascendant was moving towards an opposition with Saturn, activating the radical Moon–Saturn opposition, which symbolizes her death quite convincingly. Since the fourth house controls a person's roots, and Jupiter in

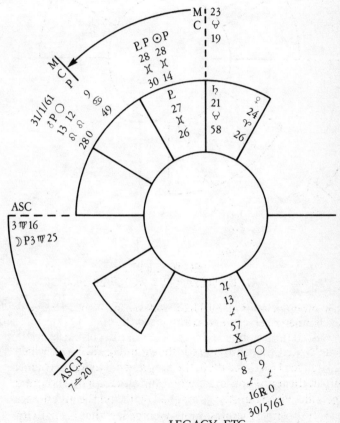

Fig. 12.13(b)   LEGACY, ETC.,
CALCULATED FOR 1 OCTOBER 1960

Sagittarius speaks of long voyages, it is not surprising that George returned to England during the influence of this aspect, and it is entirely appropriate that the Full Moon before the trip fell conjunct progressed Jupiter, and that the Full Moon preceding his return to

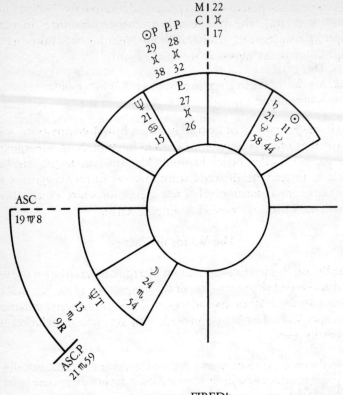

M │ 22
C │ ♓
  │ 17

⊙P ℞ P
29   28
♓   ♓
38   32

℞
27
♓
26

♄
21
♋ ♋
58 44

♃P
21
♋
15

⊙
11
♋
44

ASC
19 ♍ 8

☽
24
♏
54

♀T
13
♏

℞
9℞
♏

ASC.P
21 ♏ 59

Fig. 12.14(a)

FIRED!
22 MARCH 1962

Rhodesia opposed the progressed Midheaven.

The original radical chart progressed (Fig. 12.13(b)), calculated for 1 October 1960, also shows the legacy through progressed Mars trine radical Jupiter, but in this case Mars is ruler of the fourth house and Jupiter is ruler of the eighth. The progressed Ascendant was approaching a sextile with progressed Jupiter, which explains the general good fortune and the visit to England, but the mother's death is not so apparent. It is striking, however, that in the very month when the Virgo mother appears in person after 21 years of separation, progressed Virgo Moon slips over the Ascendant of the Oldham chart. If nothing else, it is a remarkable testimony to the accuracy of the birth-moment.

Now it is not in the nature of this nativity that George should be allowed to receive a substantial benefit and enjoy himself in England without being required to pay a price. While the above aspects were still potent, Saturn presented his account. As illustrated in Fig. 12.14(a), the progressed Ascendant was then in exact opposition to Saturn, and transiting Neptune was hovering in opposition aspect between Sun and Saturn:

> 22 March 1962: Fired after 23 years service — Why? Oh! they wanted a change.

He was actually fired by the chairman from Johannesburg, who in the next breath offered him a job in Johannesburg. George did not accept the offer; he felt he would have died on the job if he had done so. Instead, he allowed Saturn to wreak further vengeance for his earlier good fortune. This was a time of white exodus from Rhodesia, for things were changing in Africa.

The Winds of Change

The British Prime Minister, Harold Macmillan, was well on the way to disposing of the remainder of the Empire. In 1960, Macmillan, during a tour of Africa, had addressed the South African parliament at Cape Town. His long and wide-ranging speech included the following words:

> In the twentieth century, and especially since the end of the war, the processes which gave birth to the nation states of Europe have been repeated all over the world. We have seen the awakening of national consciousness in people who for centuries lived in dependence upon some other power. Fifteen years ago this movement spread through Asia. Many countries there of different races and civilizations pressed their claim to independent national life. Today the same thing is happening in Africa, and the most striking of all impressions I have formed since I left London a month ago is of the strength of this African national consciousness. In different places it takes different forms, but it is happening everywhere. The wind of change is blowing through this continent, and, whether we like it or not, this growth of national consciousness is a political fact. We must all accept it as a fact, and our national policies must take account of it.
>
> [From an Address by Harold Macmillan to members of both houses of parliament of the Union of South Africa, Cape Town, 3 February 1960]

Macmillan was giving notice to the white colonists of the continent. The following month the infamous Sharpeville disaster occurred, and a year later, on 31 May 1961, South Africa left the Commonwealth and declared itself a republic. In Northern Rhodesia and Nyasaland, and Southern Rhodesia, black politicians made their play for power, while white politicians sought to stem the tide. Eventually, unable to achieve independence on acceptable terms, the whites of Southern Rhodesia made their Unilateral Declaration of Independence (UDI) on 11 November 1965, and attained the interesting status of a Colony in Rebellion.

Meanwhile, George, at 50 years of age, and without a job, decided to go into chickens:

1962: Over the past 4/5 years I had built a nice house on four acres nine miles from town. Decided to go into poultry farming, which after thorough investigation with government poultry experts was sound. It took me six months to realize the government experts didn't have to make a living, by which time I was in up to my neck. Within two years I was the largest poultry keeper around Bulawayo (20,000 birds) — little realizing (like many) that the 'winds of change' were blowing up, deviously fanned by the London Foreign Office . . . we were expendible, and betrayed by 'perfidious Albion'. UDI 11 November 1965: The result of this was within nine months I was financially crippled, and it was only because I was a loyal Rhodesian and Taurus obstinacy that kept me going, September 1967: Moment of decision: expand business (more debt) or phase out? Decided to run down business (it took two years) at great loss. Got a job as a representative, and Jan./Feb. 1968 went to night school to learn work study and O and M for one year.

George's situation paralleled that of Rhodesia itself; he had decided to go it alone. His first attempt failed, and at an age when most men think of retirement, he retrains himself for a new career and tries again. It doesn't work, and at last he accepts defeat

Opened my own office Jan./Feb. 1969 and carried on over the next 10 years — feast and famine — but slowly bleeding to death in keeping with the Rhodesian situation and thousands of other Rhodesians. By now the terrorist war is hotting up. Imagine me at 65 in the Reserve Police dashing around the bush at night with a .303 rifle looking for terrorists — but so were thousands of other men. By now I had sold all equipment on the farm at great loss. 1 March 1979: Back to a flat after 20 years — sold house to keep financially viable — heartbreaking for wife; but apart from money, it was getting dangerous to live out of town. The 'barbarians' were knocking at the gates and Britain was cheering on the sidelines. By now my thoughts were turning to Britain or taking a chance in South Africa.

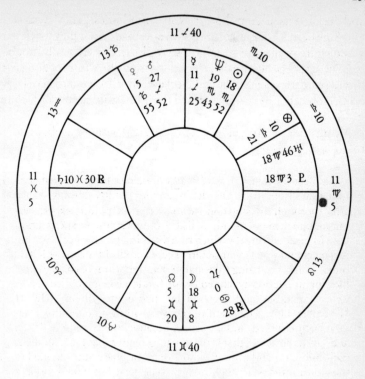

Fig. 12.15

RHODESIA — UDI,
11 NOVEMBER 1965,
11.15 GMT, 17°50' S, 31°0' E

Unilateral Declaration of Independence

Given the nature of the times, it is obvious in retrospect that the
Rhodesian colonists were doomed. The 'wind of change' blowing
through Africa had become a force 10 gale, impossible to withstand.
Yet the astrologer cannot help but wonder whether, if independence
had been declared at a moment elected to harmonize with the
heavens, matters may have developed differently. The Rhodesian
Prime Minister, Ian Smith, who had distinguished himself as a fighter
pilot in the Second World War, may have deliberately selected the
eleventh day of the eleventh month (and the eleventh hour in
London), for its emotive association with Rememberance Day.
Whatever the reason, it was not a happy moment astrologically. Figure
12.15 the chart for UDI, set for Salisbury, Rhodesia, has a retrograde
Saturn at the Ascendant as part of a mutable angular Grand Cross

ECLIPSES

UK CHART RADICAL PATTERN	♅ 9 ♓ 49	♇ 10 ♋ 39	♄ 17 ♎ 44	☽ 23 ♋ 13
UK CHART PROGRESSED TO UDI	♇ 9 ♋ 50	♅ 11 ♓ 5	A 17 ♋ 35	♄ 19 ♎ 59
UDI CHART 11 NOV. 1965 SALISBURY	♄ 10 ♓ 30	A 11 ♓ 5	♇ 18 ♍ 3	♅ 18 ♍ 46
GEORGE RELOCATED ASCENDANT			A 19 ♍ 8	
SOLAR ECLIPSE 30 MAY 1965	◑ 9 ♓			

Fig. 12.16

involving Mercury, the Moon, and the Uranus–Pluto conjunction. The Sun–Neptune conjunction on the evil degree of Serpentis (19° Scorpio) in quincunx with the fourth house Moon poisons foreign relations and trade, and Rhodesia was subjected to damaging sanctions from the first. But how could she prevail against the great Uranus–Pluto conjunction in the seventh house, which itself (through another line of astrological reasoning) symbolized the break-up of the great European colonial Empires? It is rather like a 'mini' attempting to impeded the passage of a Sherman tank.

From Fig. 12.16, it can be seen how this moment linked in with the United Kingdom chart, for the UDI Ascendant–Saturn, the focal

	0	1	2	3	4	5	6	7	8	9	10	11	12	13	14	15	16	17	18	19	20	21	22	23	24	25	26	27	28	29	30
RADIX RELOCATED TO BULAWAYO			⊗ 2 ♈ 18	♅ 3 ♒ 27								☉ 11 ♉ 44		♃ 13 ♐ 57		♂ 15 ♋ 3				☿ 19 ♈ 22; A 19 ♍ 8	☊ 20 ♈ 37	♆ 21 ♋ 15; ♄ 21 ♉ 58	M 22 ♊ 17		♀ 24 ♈ 26; ☽ 24 ♏ 54			♇ 27 ♊ 26			
2 MAY 1963	☉ 0 ♋ 42							♃ 7 ♐ 58				M 11 ♌ 15				♂ 15 ♌ 1							♆ 22 ♋ 39	A 23 ♏ 10					♄ 28 ♉ 23		
11 NOV. 1965 UDI				☉ 3 ♋ 7				♃ 7 ♐ 42						M 13 ♌ 39			♂ 16 ♌ 33									A 25 ♏ 47			♄ 28 ♉ 40		
1 FEB. 1969							☉ 6 ♋ 11	♃ 7 ♐ 23									M 16 ♌ 44		♂ 18 ♌ 30											A 29 ♏ 2; ♄ 29 ♉ 2	
2 MAY 1975						A 5 ♐ 7	♃ 6 ♐ 49						☉ 12 ♋ 8										♂ 22 ♌ 18; M 22 ♌ 41								
2 MAY 1977							♃ 6 ♐ 39	A 7 ♐ 0							☉ 14 ♋ 3									♂ 23 ♌ 31	M 24 ♌ 35						
1 MAR. 1979 SALE OF HOUSE							♃ 6 ♐ 30		A 8 ♐ 42							☉ 15 ♋ 48	♀ 16 ♋ 26							♆ 23 ♋ 13; ☽ 23 ♈ 38	♂ 24 ♌ 38						

Fig. 12.17

point of the Grand Cross, was conjunct the UK Uranus — part of the radical pattern promising the dissolution of the Empire. Even poor old George did not escape this stellar bombardment, for his relocated Ascendant was flattened by the great conjunction.

Rhodesia struggled on for 14 years, living on its wits, ostracized by the international community, fighting an internal war funded and supplied from abroad. Then Margaret Thatcher entered the world stage and set about solving the 'Rhodesia Crisis'. The Lancaster House Conference opened on 10 September 1979; a ceasefire

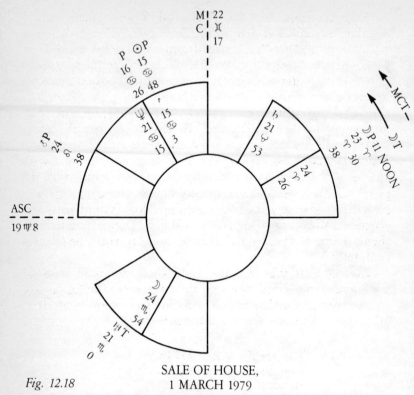

Fig. 12.18
SALE OF HOUSE,
1 MARCH 1979

agreement was signed on 21 December; Robert Mugabe formed a
government on 4 March 1980; Zimbabwe became independent on
18 April 1980.

We refer now to Fig. 12.17. By 1963 George was into chickens.
The progressed Midheaven, which had been in trine aspect with
progressed Jupiter when he came into his legacy, was on its way towards
a trine with radical Jupiter. The rapid expansion of his business fits
in very nicely with the Jupiter contact, but once the Midheaven had
separated, his prosperity was at an end. Jupiter was not the only potent
planet at this time. The progressed Ascendant was moving between
an opposition of radical and progressed Saturn. It made a conjunction
with the radical Moon on the way (UDI), and by 1969, when George
opened his office and began a new project, the progressed Ascendant
and Saturn were in exact opposition. All this time the progressed
Midheaven was struggling to capture progressed Mars, and as they
came to conjunction George found himself running around the bush
with a rifle (1974/75).

Dogged and persistent Sun-Taurus had weathered many storms, and determined Moon-Scorpio had finally got the better of Saturn when she fulfilled her Neptunian dream and built her house. Now Mars, tetchy and spiteful, gave vent to his spleen. As the progressed Sun made a conjunction, George was forced to sell his house in order to survive. Venus (ruler of the second house) demanded money, and she had nowhere else to go. Figure 12.18 shows the progressed Sun and progressed Venus activating the radical Mars square Venus contacts, and also the progressed Mars square radical Moon, and Uranus now transiting opposition radical Saturn and moving towards the Moon. No syzygies attended this event, but, remarkably, the progressed Moon was conjunct radical Venus, thus invoking the whole pattern, on the very day the transiting Moon would pass over progressed Moon somewhere around midnight. During the afternoon the transiting Midheaven did likewise, possibly when the sale was completed.

After 40 years this was the end. Rhodesia would soon be transformed into Zimbabwe, and there was no future for George in the country he had helped to build and had fought to preserve. What now? Where to live? How to make a living?

> Take up the White Man's burden,
> And reap his old reward —
> The blame of those ye better
> The hate of those ye guard
> The cry of hosts ye humour
> (Ah slowly)! toward the light:
> Why brought ye us from bondage,
> Our loved Egyptian night?

The White Man's Burden — RUDYARD KIPLING

The Republic

1 April 1980: Spent two weeks in South Africa looking around and me agitating with my wife to move — no go! Of course moving without a job would be risky, even if the South African government would allow us to settle which at our age with little money would be doubtful. 19 May 1980: Visiting one of my clients — a furniture factory whom I had dealt with for six years (and known for 30 years), asked me to open a furniture shop for them in Johannesburg. After much preparation and planning by the three directors I now had an empty shop and cheque book in South Africa.

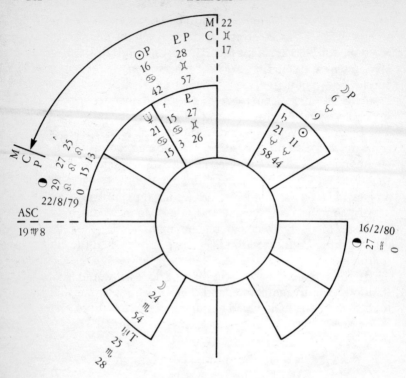

Fig. 12.19   TO SOUTH AFRICA,
                          FEBRUARY 1980

George now became involved in some dubious transfer of goods
between Rhodesia and South Africa, but the enterprise did not
prosper and George became very ill. Eventually he parted company
with the businessmen, and took his chance in South Africa.

Leave in February 1981. No work — illegal — nowhere to live and
very little money, living out of a suitcase and my wife still in Bulawayo.
After a month I get a small job at a computer company, after which
I move to a big cable company 1 August 1981 which allows me to
get established. Fired from the cable co. 1 March 1984.

We do not have the exact date of leaving Rhodesia for the Republic
of South Africa. We know it was in February 1981, so let us take the
middle of the month — 14 February — and look at the detail. Figure
12.19 shows the progressed Sun leaving the conjunction with Mars,
and in less than five years he will conjunction Neptune. Progressed
Midheaven is appropriately sextile Pluto, showing the complete

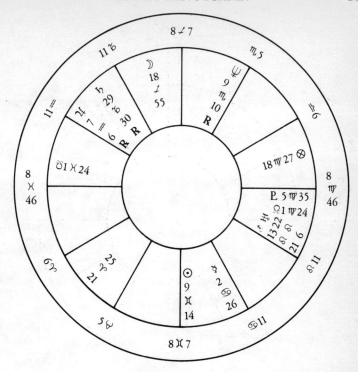

Fig. 12.20

SOUTH AFRICA — REPUBLIC
30 MAY 1961,
22.00 GMT, PRETORIA

transformation George is about to experience. Progressed Mars is square the Moon, forcing a change of home, ably assisted by a transit of Uranus. The eclipse at 29° Leo, falling six months before the move, was neatly confirmed by another eclipse falling opposite in the middle of February. Once again the potential of the progressed patterns is energized by a pair of eclipses. If George left on 9 February, the transiting Moon would have been conjunct radical the Moon and transiting Uranus', if he left on 22 February, the transiting Moon would have been in opposition to these positions.

The Union of South Africa came into being on 30 May 1910, at 00.00 hrs LT, Cape Town. When she left the Commonwealth and declared herself a Republic, South Africa aquired a new map. The chart for the Republic has been generally accepted as 30 May 1961, at 00.00 hrs, Pretoria; this is the data given in *Mundane Astrology* (Baigent, Campion and Harvey). However, George researched this matter in South Africa and gave the following information: 'After

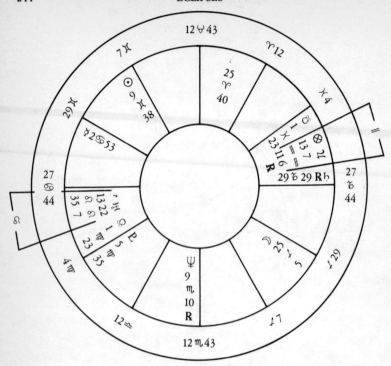

SOUTH AFRICA — REPUBLIC,
31 MAY 1961,
Fig. 12.21   08.14 GMT. PRETORIA

leaving the Commonwealth it [the Republic] was announced and
made law in parliament — Pretoria, 10.14 a.m., 31 May 1961.' We
give both maps here (Fig. 12.20 and 12.21). Tempting though it is,
we must not deviate from our subject so far as to conduct an
investigation into these charts in this book. It is enough for our
purposes to remark that George found refuge in South Africa and
was able to establish himself there in his latter years; his radical Sun
is within a degree of South Africa's Midheaven, and his radical Venus
is within a degree of her Venus.

As has been related above, George found employment and
was able to continue working until he was almost 72 years of
age. Then, finally, he was fired, or forced to retire. From Fig. 12.22
(which has been relocated to Johannesburg) you will see how the
progressed Sun had arrived at Neptune (a perfect symbol of
retirement), the progressed Midheaven was square progressed Saturn,
and the Full Moon before the event fell conjunct the progressed

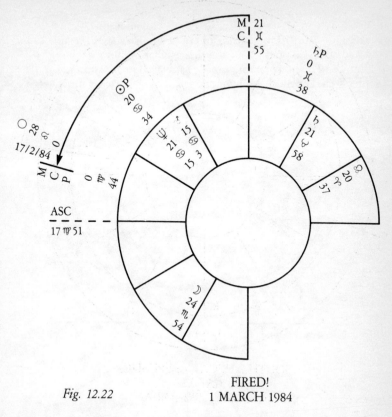

Fig. 12.22

FIRED!
1 MARCH 1984

Midheaven. Saturn ceased his demands and allowed George to retire to Durban.

The sting in the tail

It must be apparent by now, if we didn't already know it, that a Taurean Saturn is an exceedingly hard task-master, relentlessley driving his victim into each experience, but when aided by a Scorpionic Mars his heavy blows are laced with sheer spite. Not content to leave George sitting quietly in well-earned retirement, in 1986 they combined for a particularly nasty double assault. They could no longer strike at his career, so they turned their full venom on his body. George invokes his powerful Jupiter to tell the tale with a touch of humour.

The Moon is approaching conjunction to progressed MC — semi-sextile natal Descendant and opposition Uranus. On 21 February

1986: Slight discomfort left side of bowels (no problem, have had discomfort for 30 years), 22 February, a little tender but no cause for alarm, 23 February, on getting out of bed to get dressed unable to bend left leg to put sock on and managed only after a struggle. By 9 a.m. and no sign of improvement I am taken to local hospital and after X-rays and much prodding and poking — blockage of the bowels

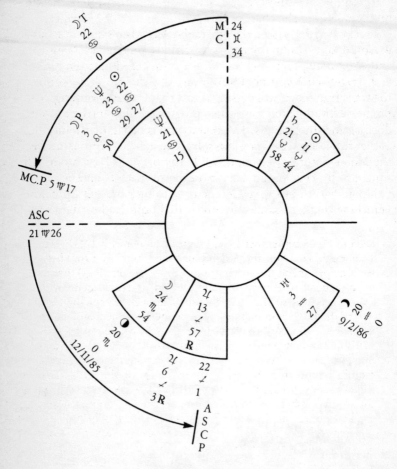

A 'DIETARY BLOCKAGE',
Fig. 12.23   21 FEBRUARY 1986

— which is surprising when I go to the toilet 3/4 times a day. I was fortunate in getting a top-rate doctor (which perhaps shows somewhere in the chart) who after listening to the history of my belly concluded it was not the normal bowel blockage but a dietary blockage. Treatment — starvation! Ten days plus drip treatment, antibiotics, drain my stomach for three days, light diet, more X-rays and internal examination on the video, and blown up like a balloon and stagger out of hospital after two weeks and lost 7kg, now 40kg and takes me three months to recover 7kg.

The quincunx aspect, as we have said, often indicates a health problem, and in the chart of this event (see Fig. 12.23) which has been relocated to Durban, the progressed Ascendant stands quincunx to radical Saturn (joint ruler of the sixth house) and radical Neptune, and also to the progressed Sun which is squeezed between radical and progressed Neptune. On the very day the problem erupted, the transiting Moon was passing across that Cancer grouping. The progressed Midheaven was square progressed Jupiter (the top-rate doctor), and the progressed Moon was opposing Uranus (joint ruler of the sixth house). The previous solar eclipse at 20° Scorpio invoked the Moon–Saturn opposition, while the previous New Moon fell square to it. This was an assault on the stomach (Cancer).

Moon–Saturn just gave George time to pick himself up before launching another assault, this time with Scorpio leading the attack.

Refer to 17–23 September 1986. Progressed Moon is at 12°32′ Leo, T-square to natal Sun and Moon plus trine Jupiter (not that I can see it helped me in this instance but I count my blessings). I went to hospital out-patients for economic reasons and convenience with a severe head cold such as I had not experienced for years on the 17th. After a thorough examination . . . prescribed treatment and return in three days. On second day my right ear was discharging and slightly bleeding from my punctured ear-drum which I was born with and never had any trouble in 74 years. My foreskin starts to swell like an old bicycle tube which also hasn't given me any trouble in 74 years. Right, back to the hospital and see a different lady doctor and explain my trouble. After examination, stop treatment, urine test and antibiotic injection. See the specialist on 23 D–Day! The urologist on examination (a little brutal) says Circumcision — When! — Now — Right! Into next room, strip, on to table, three local injections and in 15 minutes I am no longer a gentile. Joked with Sister, who was more dithery than I was. Told to return daily for dressing. Home, uncomfortable, but not as bad as having a tooth out. Return next day at 10 a.m., wait till 11.50, personal attention of senior Sister who discovers I have been bound up with ordinary sticking tape with no dressing and severely adhered to flesh — it will not come off. After half an hour battle senior Sister retires more upset than me — except I keep going into shock with pain. Another comes to try and lasts

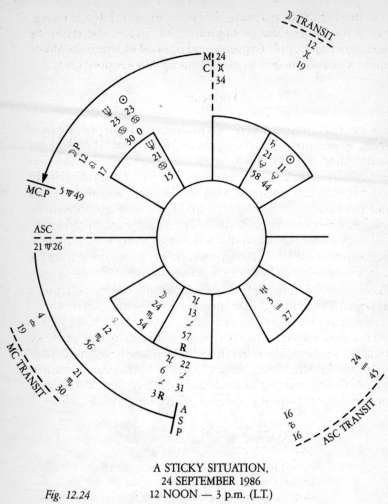

A STICKY SITUATION,
24 SEPTEMBER 1986

Fig. 12.24   12 NOON — 3 p.m. (L.T.)

only 15 minutes. Finally Sister from operating theatre arrives with
a determined manner, announces she will take it off! And she did!
Fall from table at 3 p.m. after three hours — punch drunk. After
a cup of tea, suggested to staff that the case should be put in Medical
Journal as 'The man who came in with a headcold and staggered
out circumsized'!

There is not a great deal of difference between the previous chart
and that shown in Fig. 12.24, apart from the progressed Moon, but
in this case we have the approximate times of the ordeal. When the

procedure began, the transiting Midheaven was at 4° Libra; as George fell off the table it was in opposition to Saturn; the transiting Ascendant began at 16° Capricorn and finished square to the Moon. Jupiter was also invoked by the transiting Moon opposition.

Epilogue

Now into his 77th year, George sits in Durban and, in philosophical mood, reflects upon his adventures in Africa. What if he had not gone to Rhodesia? 'If I had not taken the opportunity, I would have been subjected to the same events on a different stage and no doubt would have always wondered what would have happened if I had gone to Rhodesia.' If he had gone to the Isle of Wight instead, he wonders whether it would have declared UDI from Britain!

George's story has shown that it is no easy thing to be burdened with Saturn at the Midheaven, particularly when opposed from the IC by a Scorpio Moon. But surely Saturn must have had some positive manifestation? Saturn after all, is sextile Fortuna and Mars–Neptune in Cancer. So what was the compensation? 'My wife and I produced a boy and a girl, who in turn produced a boy and girl, and two boys and two girls, respectively, making six grandchildren. One grandson is still not married. The other five grandchildren have produced 12 great-grandchildren — six boys and six girls.' So that was the purpose of it all? George was destined to found a dynasty! Sun, Moon, Mars, Jupiter, Saturn, Neptune, Fortuna, all in 'signes prolificall'.

> Take up the White Man's burden!
> Have done with childish days —
> The lightly proferred laurel,
> The easy ungrudged praise:
> Comes now, to search your manhood
> Through all the thankless years,
> Cold, edged with dear bought wisdom,
> The Judgement of your peers.

The White Man's Burden — RUDYARD KIPLING

CONCLUSION

Broadly, eclipses have three main areas of application in astrology. First, when an eclipse is set as a mundane chart for a specific place, it may reflect the nature of future events affecting the human, animal and natural worlds within that area during a given time. Secondly, the degree of the eclipse represents a point of energy, which can stay dormant in the cosmos for two to three years. When radical or progressed patterns of various foundations or inception charts configurate with these eclipse degrees, events symbolized by those radical or progressed patterns may be brought to manifestation within six months. Thirdly, eclipses may act in a similar manner in respect of human nativities, the dormant period is being usually confined to six months. In all cases, syzygies falling in sharp angular relationship with the eclipse degree may bring the promised event to pass within two weeks, and sometimes transits (particularly conjunctions and oppositions) will isolate the very day.

The effects of eclipses upon human nativities has been demonstrated in the preceding three chapters and the optimum potency range of six months seems reasonable. It is also apparent that they act principally as timers when configured with secondary progressions activating radical patterns. It further emerged that when eclipses are around they act strongly, but if they are not, the heavens will latch on to anything (progressed Moon, transits, ordinary New and Full Moons) in order to trigger the energy of progressed patterns. As a by-product of our natal examples, it was also established in 'A White Man's Burden' that the nativity relocated to a new place of residence, and when progressed gives a more telling symbolism of events than the chart set for the birth place.

We set out to investigate whether an eclipse chart could be judged as a mundane map, in a similar manner to the quarterly ingress figures. Lilly's exposition of the 'Black Munday' chart, gave a remarkable example of the skill of our forefathers. Some convincing evidence emerged, particularly from the 'Three Kings' and 'Two Disasters'. However, the key consideration is whether events could reasonably have been predicted in advance, for astrologers can always find the appropriate symbolism with the benefit of hindsight. It seems that if one is in close touch with political and social developments in the area for which the figure is set, judgements may be made with the assistance of the chart. However, it would be dangerous to leap too far ahead and attempt prediction in isolation from the temper of the times.

We also looked at the validity of Ptolemy's rather intricate rules for finding the most likely time of manifestation for the radical promise. Again, there is some evidence to show that the immediate effects of an eclipse may be determined from the angle nearest to which it fell, but not invariably so. As to the matter of the long-term delayed effects, where the effects of an eclipse may extend over any third part of a three-to-four year period, we remain to be convinced that Ptolemy's opinion holds good. Yet in fairness we cannot dismiss it on the basis of a mini-study; the whole matter requires a detailed and deep-ranging investigation. What did emerge was that the eclipse degree retains power for between two to three years in mundane judgments, and sensitizes an area of a radical chart well in advance of events. The power of eclipse/Transit combinations was seen in 'The Battle of Britain', and of secondary progressions/ eclipse/transit in 'Nigeria' and 'Europe Ablaze'. While it may be the case that an eclipse acts with greater power in those areas of the world where it is visible, lack of visibility does not appear to preclude judgement.

The relocation of an inception chart to related areas of activity, the progressing of the relocated chart, and the relevance of eclipses to the end result was clearly demonstrated in 'Kitty Hawk Progressed'.

The year 1987 was heavily marred by tragedy. The *Herald of Free Enterprise* ferry disaster and the Kings Cross Underground fire immediately spring to mind, as well as the Remembrance Day massacre at Enniskillen. Readers may like to relate these happenings to the solar and lunar eclipses for the year.

In conclusion we direct your attention to 'Black Monday', 19 October 1987, the day when world stock markets crashed. Share prices on Wall Street plunged by 25 per cent in one day, almost double that of the great crash of 1929; the London FT SE Index fell 250 points (10.6%).

Figure 13.1 shows the previous solar eclipse set for London, and

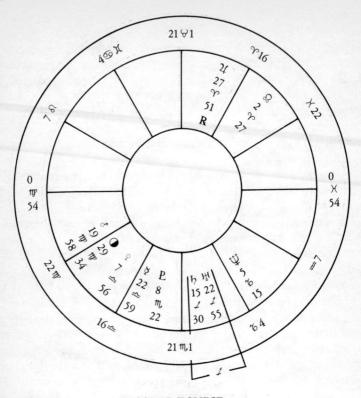

SOLAR ECLIPSE,
23 SEPTEMBER 1987
Fig. 13.1   03.09 GMT, LONDON

it takes little imagination to relate the happenings of 'Black Monday'
to the position of the eclipse in the second house in opposition to
the degree of the malefic Fixed Star Scheat, but planetary positions
at noon on the fatal day do not reveal any obvious transits to activate
the eclipse degree. Figure 13.2 gives the same eclipse set for New
York where it fell in the fourth house, which is not as descriptive
as the London chart. However, the Sun and Moon are rulers of the
Second House.

Just three days before 'Black Monday', Britain was devastated by
a great storm such as had not been experienced since 1703.
The previous lunar eclipse occurred on 7 October at 4.13 a.m.
(see Fig. 13.3). In the chart set for London, the Saturn–Uranus
conjunction in Sagittarius fell astride the fourth cusp. Sagittarius
will produce great winds, and the fourth house does control the

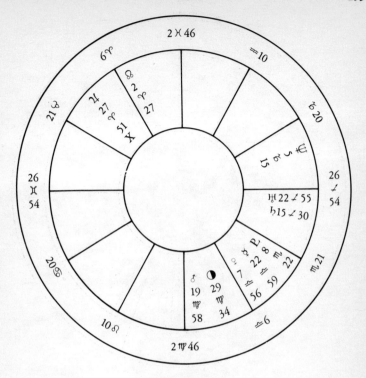

SOLAR ECLIPSE
23 SEPTEMBER 1987,
Fig. 13.2   03.09 GMT, NEW YORK

weather, so the disruptive and destructive combination is
appropriately placed. Again, no obvious transits triggered the eclipse
chart on the day of the storm, but the following declinations will
be of interest:

	Eclipse Declination	Storm Declination
Saturn	21°29'S	21°35'S
Neptune	22°20'S	22°20'S
Uranus	22°20'S	23°26'S
Moon	6°11'N	
8 Oct Noon	14°29'N	
9 Oct Noon	19°49'N	
10 Oct Noon	24°02'N	
11 Oct Noon	26°58'N	

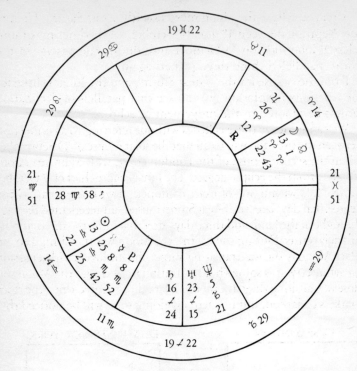

Fig. 13.3

LUNAR ECLIPSE,
7 OCTOBER 1987,
4.13 GMT, LONDON

	Eclipse Declination	**Storm Declination**
12 Oct Noon	28°28′N	
13 Oct Noon	28°33′N	
14 Oct Noon	27°16′N	
15 Oct Noon	24°46′N	
16 Oct Midnight	23°07′N	The storm struck
1 a.m.	22°58′N	the far west at
2 a.m.	22°49′N	around midnight
3 a.m.	22°40′N	and roared and
4 a.m.	22°30′N	smashed its way
5 a.m.	22°21′N	across southern
6 a.m.	22°21′N	England, reach-
7 a.m.	22°02′N	ing London by
Noon	21°13′N	about 6 a.m.
17 Oct Noon	16°49′N	

After the eclipse the Moon moved swiftly across Saturn, Uranus and Neptune between 10 and 11 October, reached her maximum celestial longitude on 13 October and, during the passage of the storm, paralleled those three planets again.

From the eclipse for the 'Great Storm', and the lunar eclipse for the Chernobyl explosion, we can see that parallels of declination cannot be ignored in the judgement of eclipses.

We cannot leave these eclipses without referring to a connection between the two. You will recall that the solar eclipse of 23 September fell in the second house of the London chart, with Mars just about 10° away from the eclipse degree. The lunar eclipse chart of 7 October shows Mars within 36′ of exact conjunction with the solar eclipse degree. Ten days later the Great Storm caused unprecedented damage throughout the land, and three days after that came the international financial crisis. During the Storm, the Moon was transiting Leo; on Black Monday she was transiting Virgo. To astrologers with a passion for symmetry, it is somewhat frustrating to find that the Moon was close to transiting directly over the solar eclipse degree when the stock markets collapsed, but not actually doing so. It will be noticed that

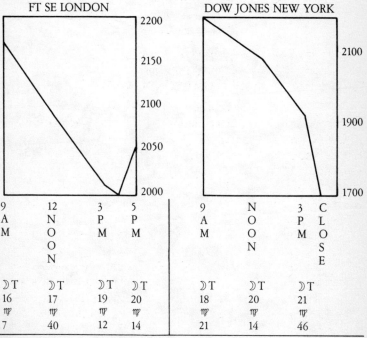

Fig. 13.4

she was in fact passing over the eclipse Mars, and also moving between a square of eclipse Saturn and Uranus. Figure 13.4 gives a rough picture of the share price movement in London and New York and the Moon's longitude at critical times. From this example, and that of the Great Storm, the Lord of the Eclipse would appear to have been Mars.

The limitations of this work are obvious, for we have given you the broadest of introduction to a subject which involves all branches of astrology, but if we have kindled your interest we are content. Take our examples as a starting point and develop your own special spheres of interest. Eclipses, the power-points of astrology, have not been accorded the respect which is their due in modern times, and they badly need your attention!

APPENDIX 1

AN EASIE
AND FAMILIAR
METHOD

WHEREBY TO

Iudge the effects depending

ON

ECLIPSES,

Either of the Sun or Moon.

By WILLIAM LILLY *Student*
in Astrologie.

Non nobis nati sumus ; partim patria, partim amici
vendicant.

LONDON,
Printed for the Company of Stationers, and
H. Blunden, at the Castle in Corn-
Hill, 1652.

To the reader

I intended in 1648 to have printed this small discourse for judging of Eclipses, (for so long time it hath layn by me;) how or by what means it was not then done, I doe not know remember; such as it is, I here present unto the young students, intending by the blessing of Almighty God, one day or other to inlarge it, and of Ptolemy's own method, though somewhat more harsh, which I have also taken care to be printed together with mine. Several persons, and men of great learning have treated of Eclipses, but as yet I cannot well approve of their method or wayes, being their Doctrines are full of intricacies, too much to puzzle any younger brother. I will endeavour with Captain Wharton or Master . . . , to frame some Tables, and print them in their next labours, whereby without any prolixity, thou mayst find either the day when the effect shall begin, or the continuance of them.

W. LILLY.

A Short Method How To Judge The Effects Of Eclipses And What Events May Be Expected From Them

An Eclipse is no other thing than an interception or privation of the light of the luminaries, viz. of the Sun and Moon, a lunar Eclipse, or of the Moon, is privation of light in the Moon, occasioned by the interposition of the Earth between the Sun and the Moon; a solar Eclipse is an interception or obscuration of the light of the Sun, caused by interposition of the Moons body between the Sun and our sight.

Of these Eclipses, some are total, others but in part; we may call an Eclipse total, in respect of the obscuration of the whole body of light, so far as it occupies the whole body of the luminary, distinguished into twelve digits by the wisdome of Astronomers; a partial Eclipse, or but in part, is when those twelve digits or parts of the luminar body are not all of them darkened: So then we say, an Eclipse of the Sun is ever the New Moon or Change, an Eclipse of the Moon is always upon her opposition to the Sun or upon the Full Moon, which is all one. In every Eclipse there are four things considerable, after you have erected the Scheme and reduced the planets to the meridian desired.

1. Unto what region, Kingdom, City or people the effects of the Eclipse shall appertain.
2. The time to be enquired, viz. either when the effect shall begin, or how long time the effects of an Eclipse shall continue.

3. What events may be expected from the Eclipse.

4. The quality or species of them, whether they intend war or famine, etc., whether plenty or dearth, etc., or who, or what people shall doe best if they signify war, etc.

To know what Kingdom or City the effects shall belong

In every great Eclipse of the Sun and Moon, you must observe the place of the zodiac, that is, in which of the Twelve Signs the defect is in, and consider the Kingdoms, Cities, or Countries subject unto that sign, according to their several distributions.

You must also observe the Ascendant or Midheaven at the time of the building of any City, and the place or signs wherein either the Sun or Moon were at that time, and see if the sign werein the Eclipse is, be in any of those signs yea or no! You are also to take notice of the Midheaven, viz., or sign culminating of the King or principal Governor of that Kingdom, Metropolitan City or Country, viz., if the sign wherein the Eclipse is; be his, viz., the King's or Governor's Midheaven, or if at his birth either of the lights were near the degree eclipsed, or where the present defect is. For you shall usually find, that where the Ascendant or Midheaven of those Cities or Men doe concur with the place of Heaven eclipsed or defective, that in great measure the effects shall appear and manifest themselves upon those Men, Kings, or Rulers, Kingdoms or Cities, especially if the Eclipse be above the Earth, for all Eclipses are held to extend their effects most forcibly when above the Earth, weakly and not so vigourously when under the Earth; but that they have also then some manifest operation greater or lesser, I could manifest by many examples of Eclipses in this age, and confirm my own judgement by the opinion of several learned men; I shall instance only CARDAN SEG. 7 APH081. Eclipses in the Fourth House of Heaven, are more forcible than those in the Eighth or Eleventh, those in the First more strong than they in the Ninth or Twelfth, and it must be acknowledged that although Eclipses in the First House cannot be visible, yet we are by no author prohibited to judge them, nay Leovitius the most painful man that ever wrote in Astrology and of Eclipses, doth deliver many judgements and predictions upon Eclipses falling in the Ascendant itself, and that I may not proceed to former times, let us consider that in JUNE 1648, 10th DAY, 12th HOUR, 38' PM, AN ECLIPSE OF THE SUN WAS IN 0D.3M. OF CANCER NEAR THE CUSP OF THE FOURTH HOUSE. Cancer is the Ascendant of Scotland, then did tht people raise their malignant army, which in AUGUST 1648 plundered our Northern

Countries. Because I would leave no scruple in the minds of young students, I shall by example explain this chapter more fully. In the ECLIPSE of 19 NOVEMBER 1648 you see the SUN was in the 8D.44' of GEMINI. If the Astrologer knew any man, who had in the radix of his nativity either SUN or MOON in that degree, or in the degree opposite, or in the like degrees of VIRGO/PISCES, or if the degree culminating in any mans nativity was either 9 GEMINI/SAGITTARIUS/VIRGO/PISCES, or if the degree Ascending was in those degrees, or within one degree thereof, the native did suffer more or less by the influence of this Eclipse; according to the signification of the House of Heaven, wherein the Sun or Moon, was in at the birth, and was either well fortified or aspected of the benevolent planets, or ill-aspected, or afflicted of the malevolents. If you have the Ascendant of a City, Town, or Corporation, or if you have the Radix or positure of heaven of a family, or any new or old Inception etc., do therein as formerly directed: ever observing that the more Digits Eclipsed, the greater the Eclipse is, and by how much more near to an Angle the Eclipse falls, the more strong and forcible will the Effecs demonstrate themselves. London is subject to the sign Gemini, ergo, much trouble did it produce there, as also to Spain subject to SAGITTARIUS, and Portugal, also in Paris France. Charles, late King of England, had the Sun in 8°3' of SAGITTARIUS: and this Eclipse 19 NOV 1648 of the Moon was celebrated the day of the Revolution of his Birth, she being in 8°44' in direct opposition on to the place of the Sun; who also hastened unto an opposition of Saturn. We know how suddenly after he was beheaded.

Of the time when events shall appear

You are to observe in every Region where the Eclipse is visible, that so many hours as an Eclipse of the Sun continues, so many years the effects or Events of a Solar Defect shall continue, and so parts of hours, shall signifie parts of the year proportionable to the minutes of the hour; but in an Eclipse of the Moon, so many hours as she is defective or suffers an Eclipse, so many moneths the Events thereby signified shall continue; As the Lunar Eclipse 1649 continuing from the beginning to the end 3 HOURS and 33 MINUTES, the effects of it did operate three whole months and a half, and two dayes etc., wherein you must observe, that in the Duration of all Eclipses, the length of the hour is according to the Equall hour, or 60 minutes for one hour, and not the Artificiall or Astronomicall hour, being more or less unequall by reason of the motion of the Sun, and length or shortness of the day.

The beginning, the increase, and determination of the effects are known, by that place or part of the Scheme of heaven wherein the Eclipse is, having relation to the Angles of the figures.

For when the place Eclipse, or the Eclipse itself, shall be in the Ascendant, the effects shall then begin in the 1, 2, 3, and 4 months next after the appearance of the Eclipse, but its greatest vigour, and most material accidents designed from the Eclipse, shall show themselves in the first third part of time allotted to the universal duration thereof.

But if the place defective, of Eclipse itself, be in the Midheaven, or near it, the effects shall begin in the 5, 6, 7, and 8 months, taking place from the beginning of the Eclipse, and shall operate most forcibly in the second division of time allotted to the whole continuance; but if the Eclipse be in the Angle of the West, or Seventh House, the first apparation of the effects shall be in the 9, 10, 11, and 12 last months after the Eclipse, and the most vehement effects in the Third Triene or part of time assigned for continuance of the Eclipsar effects. These last lines require an easy explanation, and some perfect method, else we shall not benefit either the more Ancient or Modern Scholar in these Astrological well-wishes. This method you must understand, and constantly follow, viz. if an Eclipse be in the Ascendant, or near unto it, and doth signify either War, Famine, Plague, Tumults, Murders, etc., its then intended, that such like things shall begin their operation, and to appear, within the first four months, after the day of the Eclipse; and whereas we mention, that it shall most forcibly operate in the third part of time allotted unto the whole duration of its effects, which Ptolemy calls PRIMA TRIENS, the true meaning of our words and his are these, viz. that if a Solar Eclipse be of one hour and one half hour continuance, and be near the Ascendant, or in it, then in the four first months next succeeding the day of the Eclipse, the effects thereof, or of the Eclipse, shall begin, and shall operate most forcibly by the space of six months succeeding next after those four months, and shall after by little and little decrease and vanish for 18 months, being the whole time limited for the continuance of the effects, the middle six months are the second TRIENT, as Ptolemy calls it, and the last six months are the third TRIENT, or third part of time. Again if the Eclipse be in or near the Midheaven, then the matter or thing designed by that Eclipse shall apparently declare itself, betwixt the fourth and eighth months from the hour of the Eclipse; and for the next six months immediately succeeding, that is during the ninth, tenth, eleventh, twelfth, thirteenth and fourteenth months from the time or day of the Eclipse, the Plague or matter signified shall begin to appear, and to increase moderately; but in the fifteenth, sixteenth, seventeenth, eighteenth, nineteenth, twentieth months from the hour of the Eclipse, the thing or business designed, shall most effectively operate, and the last six months begin to lessen and decline etc. Again, let the Eclipse be near the cusp of the Seventh House, or in that House, then the effects depending thereon, shall begin to be active and take place from the eighth month until the twelfth, to be accounted from the day of the Eclipse and then for twelve whole months next after, the effects thereof shall operate very sensibly and to purpose, but in the last six months of that whole time assigned for its continuance, the Plague, Pestilence, or Famine signified thereby, shall be in its greatest force, and do most mischief. From hence it appears, an Eclipse according to the Doctrine of Ptolemy shall begin to declare its effects within one year next after the day of its being; nor can the effects of a Solar Eclipse continue, or be extended, above three years and one half, or of a Lunar Eclipse above six months etc., so that Haly and those adhering unto him were much deceived.

But if you will judge when particular remissions, or more hasty intensions, shall be, or in more plain language, if you will know when the effects will work with great force, when more slowly, you must take notice thereof from the several Conjunctions, Oppositions, or Quadratures which shall be made either in that part, viz. degree of the sign wherein the Eclipse was, or in such part of the zodiac, viz. in such degrees of the signs which behold that place so Eclipsed, as also from the several Quadratures and Oppositions of other Planets as well as of the Sun and Moon, or their arising, or first appearance above the Horizon, together with either of the Lights in that place of the zodiac, and which have signification in determining the Events of that Eclipse you do Astrologically judge of, and these especially, when either in the Ascendant or Seventh House, or in their Stations, or in their Vespertine rising viz. When they first appear upon the Suns setting, they aspect the signs and degrees where the Eclipse was. The rising of the planets and their stations in those places or parts where the Eclipse was, declare the increase and greatness of the Events which are to succeed. But when those stars or planets are either under the Suns beams, or in their Vespertine rising, they intend a more remissness, and not so strong events to succeed. By Station is intended, when a planet comes to be Stationary, or to stand still, and to move very little in any degree of the zodiac, either in the degree Eclipsed, or opposition thereof, or in dexter or sinister Quadrate unto it. Its believed by many, and found true by experience, that when a planet is stationary, he is then by reason of his standing still, firm and able to settle and impression; but when a planet is under the Sun beams, he resembles a man limited, and one who hath none or little power of himself, or a masculine planet having power in the said places when he first rises above the earth after the Sun set is conceived to produce very small, or but weak effects in any Eclipse, or Conjunction of Superiour planets.

Of The Kind Or Quality Of Events

That this be artificially, and with judgement performed; first, you must erect the scheme of heaven for the middle time of the Eclipse, and reduce the motion of the Sun, Moon, and other planets to your own Meridian or that place of the World, for which you intend to erect the figure, and thereupon to give judgement, and then seriously considering the degree of the sign wherein the Eclipse is, (the sign I mean wherein the Sun is, if it be a Solar Eclipse, the sign wherein the Moon is, if it be a Lunar Defect.) Consider also to place, Asterism, Sign and Degree of the Zodiac, in the Angle next following the Eclipse, as if the Eclipse be in the ninth, eighth or seventh, you are to consider which planet hath most power and dignities in the tenth house, for that is the angle succeeding them; but if the Eclipse be in the tenth, eleventh, or twelfth, then you must see to the fortitude of that planet who hath most dignities essential in the Ascendant, that being the Angle subsequent to the Eclipse, being in the 10, 11, 12 House. Herein you must reckon no dignities unto any planet, but what that planet hath either by house, exaltation, triplicity, term or face, accidental fortitudes or dignities in this judgement are not admitted. For that planet who hath most dignities in the place, viz. in the sign and degree either culminating or ascending he shall be Lord of the Eclipse, or principal Ruler; but if it happen that one planet alone have not most dominion or greatest fortitudes in the place Eclipsed and Angle subsequent but that there are two which may equally challenge Prerogative, he shall be preferred who is Lord of the place, or sign Eclipsed, and the other planet shall be joined to him in signification who agreeth to either place and shall be called Partner in judgement. But if many planets hath dignity in the aforesaid places, and do also behold both the place Eclipsed, and succeeding Angles, we mean not the whole sign, but the degree, that planet shall be preferred who is in Situation or Position nearest to an Angle, or more powerful in signification, or more agreeable

in quality, that is in nature, or by triplicity. Concerning the Fixed
Star or Stars that shall participate in judgement, this is generally
observed, to take that Fixed Star which at the time of the Eclipse
doth precede the place Eclipsed in an Angle, and is of great or
eminent magnitude, viz. of the first or second, and hath little latitude,
but is seated near the ecliptic line, or which at that instant time of
the Defect doth arise or culminate, following the place Eclipsed, the
preceding words are thus to be understood, viz. that if an Eclipse
be between the Seventh House and Midheaven, most consideration
is to be had unto that Fixed Star which possesseth the Angle of the
Seventh, for that star precedes; next who are in the Tenth House,
for they follow; but if the Eclipse be between the Midheaven and
Ascendant, those Fixed Stars in the Midheaven are preferred before
those in the Ascendant.

Other notable considerations

The Asterism also or Constellation in which the Eclipse is, as also
the principal ruler or rulers of the Eclipse, are most to be considered,
as also the sign wherin the Eclipse itself is, for such signs in the
zodiac and constellations which have human shape or form, have
signification of men, and things humane; Terrestial signs signify
according to the forms and shapes thereof; Signs that signify the
milder creatures or beasts, show loss and damage to such like beasts
as are useful for man, according to the reason of the singular shapes,
forms and figures thereof, whether they be horses, oxen etc.
Septentrional Constellations, show sudden Earthquakes, Meridional,
declare unexpected and great showers. When the Ecliptical place
is either in Virgo or Sagittarius, damage follows to such fowl as
men feed on, but if it be in watery Signs or Constellations, much
of the event shall appear in the waters, at sea, and in fish, or fishing,
and to men Navigating; yet if it fall out in Aquarius or Pisces,
men receive great loss by overflow of rivers, and swellings of
fountains.

When the Eclipse is in Tropical or Equinoctial signs, viz. ARIES,
CANCER, LIBRA, CAPRICORN, commonly the Eclipse is
prejudicial to the air and the present season. In the Spring it destroys
the growth of such herbs as spring out of the earth, and the budding
and blossoming of trees. In the Summer solstice, it hurts the corn,
and lessens the burden of fruit; in the Autumnal equinox it
prejudiceth the seed; in the Winter it gives too much moisture. When
the Eclipse is also in Aries or Libra, there follows controversies in
Religion, or some change or alteration; in Tropics viz. CANCER or

CAPRICORN, alteration of air, and of offices or places or Governments.

Fixed signs, as TAURUS, LEO, AQUARIUS, SCORPIO, show much ado about buildings, double-bodied signs, as GEMINI, VIRGO, SAGITTARIUS, PISCES, threaten matter to Kings, Princes, or principal Magistrates.

Those defects which happen in the First House, have relation to fruits, or to youth, or matter newly begun; in the Midheaven, to Kingdoms, Cities, or Countries, Kings, Princes, or Nobles, or persons of quality, or men of middle age; in the West or 7th House, the change and mutation of laws, customs, contentions, law-suits, quarrels, wars, the death of aged men, for the most part some slaughter or bloodshed.

The greater the defect is, and the stronger the principal ruler or rulers of the Eclipse is or are, so much more famous and eminent are the effects of the Eclipse. All effects are diminished when the Eclipse of the Sun is near his setting, or of the Moon to her Matutine rising, but when any Eclipse of the Sun is in the morning or Matutine, or of the Moon Vespertine or towards sun-setting, the evils signified thereby are increased, and the effects operate most vigorously. Leovitius doth deliver a method for finding the time when the effects of an Eclipse shall begin, in his book fol. De ecliptibus, but because the operations is troublesome, and doth nothing conduce for enlarging the students judgement, and also because it would make our book swell too much, I leave further discourse thereof.

What manner of events shall happen, and whether they shall be good or ill

This doctrine being most necessary and profitable, is naturally thus deduced, viz. from the nature of the predominating planets in the principal places of the figure, viz, in that sign of the Eclipse and sign of the Angle subsequent, their commixion one with another, and with those places or houses of the Zodiac in which they are posited; in this signification you must not collect the dignities of the Sun or Moon, or make them significators of the kinds or qualities of the events; for they being Governors of other planets, and the principal causes of events, commanding the power of other stars, do either confirm or destroy the virtues of the predominant planets.

The consideration of those planets, who have most right, and greater fortitude in their commixions, doth declare the quality and kind of the events which may ensue after the Eclipse, or of which the Eclipse is precursor. But let us begin with the planets in their several kinds, and the first of Saturn when he is principal ruler of, or Lord of the Eclipse, or when any fixed star of his nature doth most principally manifest the effects of the Eclipse.

When Saturn is Lord of the Eclipse
He is generally the cause of corruptions by reason of cold, more properly he declares continued diseases in the bodies of men, as wasting of the body, or a consumption which hath its original from some deflux of Reume, he denotes disturbance of the radical humours, fluxes, quartane agues, banishments, poverty. Misery, lamentation, vain fears, mortality of old men especially. A scarcity of such cattle as are useful for mankind, afflicting such cattle which escape death with diseases, so that men are infected that use those cattle, or after the cattle's death feed upon them. In the air, he stirs up most horrible colds, frosty and icy weather, cloudy and pestilent, the air oftentimes molested; long continued frosts, thick clouds, misty foggy weather, much darkness, abundant snows nothing profitable but destructive, from whose corruptions many poisonous and hurtful creatures proceed. In rivers and the sea he stirs up most bitter tempests, sudden and manifold shipwrecks, difficult and dangerous voyages and passages, and a dearth of fish and waterfowl. Generally in the sea peculiar recesses or backslidings of the sea from its former bounds and banks, leaving thereby its former channels. In rivers there are great overflowings, violent inundations and corruption of waters; upon earth there follows scarcity of grain, fruit and corn, all things very dear, all manner of provisions scanty and rarely to be had, such especially which conduce to the preservation of mans life; destruction of fruits by caterpillars, worms, locusts etc. Of grass and hay by floods, by immoderate showers, or by sudden hailstorms, and furious tempests, so that men perish by famine and such like casualties, and beasts by the unseasonable getting in of Winter provisions, and the unnatural nourishment of that food they eat. Old men die more plentifully, or more aboundance of them perish than in other years; much rancour and malice, and stiff law-suits do rage amongst the vulgar clowns or country people.

Of Jupiter when he alone is ruler of the Eclipse
When Jupiter alone have chiefest dominion in an Eclipse, generally he produceth an increase of all things; and when the event appertains unto men, he signifies glory, fertility, tranquility and peace; every man thrives and becomes rich, each man signified by him enjoys health and quiet of mind, he promiseth gifts and favours from Kings, he adorns Governors or Magistrates with fame and estimation, and

to speak truly, he is the cause of all good things. He multiplies all living creatures which are behooseful to man, and portends destruction to such animals that are hurtful unto man. In the air he declares a good and wholesome temperature, windy, moist, or inclining to showers; nourishing all living creatures procreated from, or feeding on the fruits of the earth. Sailors and merchants sail without danger, and make good voyages; the rivers swell with no immoderate floods; plenty of all manner of fruit appears; religious men increase in the church, many whereof attain to very high preferments, or have great honours conferred on them; ministers grow proud and haughty, (an easy sin in that generation). The laws are executed, and upright judges are employed by the States; New customs or privileges are conferred on the people; New Corporations, new Honours etc.

Of Mars when Lord of the Eclipse

When Mars alone shall obtain the Government of an Eclipse, he generally is the cause of corruption in regard of his too much dryness, and this especially when he is in a fiery sign. When the events appertain unto men, he stirs up wars, seditions, intestine risings, and tumults, imprisonments, banishments, besieging and taking of towns or cities, popular tumults, frowns of Princes on several of their subjects, divers principal men suddenly arraigned, condemned and beheaded; moreover he pertains tertian fevers, acute diseases, corruption of blood, or infirmities by breaking or stretching of veins, violent, untimely, and the sudden deaths of young men; he inclines Kings and Princes unto tyranny, violence, injuries, and injustice; the soldier to firing of houses, to manslaughters, rapines, thefts, robberies on highways, lawsuits, duels. In the air he stirs up extraordinary soultry blasts and great heat, hot pestilent winds, pestiferous and infectious, thunder, lightening, whirl-winds, immeasurable droughts. In the sea he occasions impetuous storms, and denotes sudden and violent shipwrecks by reason of inordinate blasts etc. In rivers he lessens or drys up the streams, and drains the fountains dry, corrupting all waters, causing putrefaction in them. He occasions or more naturally signifies scarcity of grain, and of all such things as are produced or grow out of the earth, either causing untimely heats whereby nourishment sufficient cannot come to maintain the root, or destroying the tender grain by unseasonable dry blasts of wind ere it be mature, and by mildews etc. Usually he excites mens minds to great rashness and fool-hardiness, provoking to duels, to all manner of evils, as thefts, murders etc. Great dissension amongst kindred, much undutifulness in children, yet many times it foreshews amongst mechanical men, some rare or admirable men produced to light.

Venus — when she only rules the effects of an Eclipse

Venus generally in all things is like unto Jupiter, and produceth such like effects, with a certain kind of gracefulness; peculiarly she gives renown unto men, honour, cheerfulness; plentiful years in the fruits of the earth, or great increase of all harmless living creatures, delightful marriages, numerous issues, firm friendships, constant leagues, increase of mens estates, cleanliness in diet and manner of living, reverence, obedience and conformity in religion, mens bodies are sound and lusty, little need physick, much unity and good correspondency betwixt the King and his Subjects, a perfect understanding betwixt the Magistrate and the vulgar people. In the air he stirs up temperate blasts of wind, moist and fructifying, no unpleasing weather, or troublesome tempests, serene fair seasons in all part of the year, very pleasing moistening showers; successful navigations, gainful and advantageous to the merchant, safe for his own person, wholesome for the mariners. In rivers, it denotes their gentle inundation, and pretty swellings without harming any thing, not destructive or violently breaking forth, plenty of all manner of working cattle, and abundance of all sorts of fruit growing forth and out of the earth, great store of wine, oil and figs; in general, its the forerunner of a quite peacable time upon earth, I mean in those countries where the Eclipse is visible.

When Mercury is sole ruler of the Eclipse

When Mercury of himself is Lord and principal ruler of the Eclipse, he generally assumes unto himself part of the nature of the planet with whom he is in aspect, or is corporally joined unto, however he is the author of quick and violent motion; he declares in humane affairs celerity, industry, craft, subtilty, in performing what is then upon the stage of the world. He shows the highways obstructed with thieves, and the seas with pirates; he causes men to be short breathed, and to fetch their wind difficulty, and when he is joined with the infortunes, he signifies dry diseases, quortidian fevers, the ptisick, consumptions, alteration in ceremonies, heresies and schisms in religion, detriment in the revenues of Kings, and of the Nobles and Gentry of the Kingdom; great controversy in the customs, laws and privileges of the people, and all thing according to the nature of the planet with whom he hath familiarity. In the air (himself being dry and swift, and always in motion near unto the Sun) he produces inordinate high winds, sudden tempests quick changing, thunders, lightenings, opening of the earth, and earthquakes; in regard of these properties his influence or effects are destructive unto plants and living creatures. When he is occidental he lessens the growth of increase of rivers, when oriental he increaseth their streams, causing aboundance of waters.

This is the nature of every planet by himself, but being mixed with others, they have signification of other events, and effects, by reason of the variety of aspects and signs, and their position to the Sun and so conveniently do change the actions which they soley of themselves did signify, but this commixion is left to the discretion of every Astrologer, being impossible to give such particular rules as in every positure of heaven would hold good.

Who participate in Eclipses

In general it is held for an assured maxim, that as unto mens and womens nativities, every Eclipse of the Sun and Moon chancing in that very degree of the sign, wherein either of them both were at the birth of any one, shall in one way or another be very fatal, or signify somewhat very material unto that native. I have found by experience that much affliction and trouble do accompany those persons, who casually in the course of their lives have an Eclipse in either of the signs and degrees, where either of the luminaries were, or in the opposite degree, at the time of their birth, but I have not yet found that death did ensue, although either the Sun and Moon was at the birth the only and principal HYLEG or APHETA (except in King Charles). I do attribute nothing unto the colours of the Eclipse, yet would wish every man in his nature to follow what he hath found true by experience.

There are some who do much adhere unto the Arabic Doctrine in Astrology, having added what they thought fit for illustration of this learning concerning Eclipses, and do say, Eclipses of the Sun or Moon in the FIERY TRIPLICITY, do declare the death of herds both of great and small cattle, the banishment of some great King, Prince, or eminent man, or his imprisonment or beheading. Amongst the vulgar people, or men of somewhat better quality, it excites emnity, jarring one with another, much dissembling with each other, the motion of some great Army or Company of men, horrible Wars, slaughter of men, thefts, murders, many towns or places depopulated, woman suffering by abortions, sharp fevers, strange apparations in the air, epidemical diseases by reason of scorching heat; scarcity of fruit, especially in those Countries which are subject to the sign

Eclipsed, admirable mutation in many things.

When an Eclipse happens in the EARTHLY TRIPLICITY, there follows scarcity of corn, especially of fruit, and all such things as are annually sown, or put into the earth.

An Eclipse of either of the Lights in the AIRY TRIPLICITY shows famine, most violent and fierce sicknesses, pestilent diseases, stormy high-winds, very prejudicial to mankind, and blowing down trees by the roots, and very many houses.

An Eclipse of the Sun or Moon in the WATERY TRIPLICITY presages rot or consumption of the vulgar sort of people, rumours, seditions, and expectation of Wars, destruction of water fowl, great inundations and overflowings of the sea-banks.

Again they affirm if an Eclipse appear in ARIES, it produceth great alteration in fruits, as in tender vines, corruption in fig trees.

In TAURUS, LEO, SCORPIO, or AQUARIUS, many ancient buildings are ruinated or pulled down, the divisions of the Clergy are high, they hate each other obstinately, and stir up tumults: a thing very frequent with them in all ages.

In CANCER, an Eclipse procures a rottenness or corruption in the fruit when its gathered, occasioning surfeits, and sicknesses unto such as eat them; sea fights, long and dangerous navigations.

In GEMINI or SAGITTARIUS, an Eclipse threatens destruction to flying fowls, unto such especially, which men eat or feed upon, whereby many men come to sudden death.

In VIRGO or PISCES, it signifies much harm to vegetable plants, and to such creatures as live in the water or of the water it shows that very many fountains shall be corrupt and grow impure, and the river waters not wholesome.

In CAPRICORN it denotes olives to be devoured by locusts, or worms, many ships drowned, alteration in mens manners and conditions, peculiarly in those Cities or Countries subject unto the sign wherein the Eclipse is.

Of the Sun Eclipsed in any decanate of the 12 signs

Aries
When the Sun is Eclipsed in the first ten degrees of ARIES, it portends the frequent Motions of Armies, and rumours of Wars, continual expeditions, assaults, and batteries, yea, and Wars, with much noise and tumult; Seditions, Controversies, and intemperacy of the air verging principally unto dryness.

When in the Second Decanate, or from 10 to 20 degrees it brings some King, Prince, or eminent officer to Prison or restraint of Liberty, it adds sorrow and danger of Death unto him, destruction of the bearing fruit-trees, and it portends the rottenness or putrification of such things as the earth produces, whereby both men and beasts are afflicted.

When in the last 10 degrees of Aries, its the forerunner of lamentation, woes, and mourning, unto mortal men, or most sorts of men, and the death of some Noble woman; unto these I may add, that it designs destruction unto the lesser cattle, as sheep, conies, goats, hares etc.

Taurus

An Eclipse of either of the Lights in the first ten degrees of Taurus, afflicts such as Negotiators, Solicitors, Agents, or are generally employed in mens affairs, or in the public; it compels men to undertake unnecessary business it brings to nought, and confounds all factions undertaken by the former sort of men, and is sufficiently hurtful to corn.

In the Second Decanate, it shows innumerable difficulties, and many discommodities to Travellers, and to such as bear children many abortions, and births not natural, or monsters are produced.

In the Third Face or Decanate, it signifies both Plague and Famine, Mortality in an amongst Oxen, Cows and Horses.

Gemini

Eclipses in the ten first degrees of Gemini, stir up dissensions, strifes, seditions amongst those we call Priests, and all manner of Merchants and Mechanics of every order, or any qulity that is amongst them. Deadly hatred, contempt of Laws, neglect of piety and holy duties doth also follow, so also breach of covenants.

In the second Decanate or Face, much Piracy at Sea, and Murders, many fruitless treaties, many turbulent Petitions presented by the people to their Superiours.

In the last Face of Gemini, when any Eclipse happens, the Death of some King or great person follows; various and sundry losses unto the State public, much actions to no purpose in the Managing of the Civil affairs of the Commonwealth; many simple Consultations and no Conclusions; Superiour men grant Commissions, which inferiour Officers never regard; much prattling, no action.

Cancer

In the first ten degrees of Cancer, it disturbs the air, and stirs up strange weather, and variety of it, inclines men unto arms, and to violate National Leagues, deceitfully under the species of Religion.

In the Second Decanate, it drys up rivers and fountains, and intends much inconstancy in men and women, and petulancy, or ill offices amongst mortal men, viz. one cunningly thrusting another out of his place.

In the last decanate it emits the Pox (I conceive the French Pox) amongst the men of that Country subject unto Cancer, many diseases, and seditions or risings of the people, the vulgar man afflicted generally with the Dropsy, or such malevolent matter in his stomach as brings him to a consumption.

Leo

In the first Face or Decanate of Leo, it premonstrates the Death of some certain famous Prince as also a great scarcity of corn and grain; if the Prince miss death, he avoids not the occasion of many misfortunes and consumption of Treasure.

In the second Decanate it threatens great tribulation and many damages unto Kings, Peers, and Prime of the Nobility; what is meant of persons of quality, must have relation to all Magistrates.

In the third Decanate, its presages Captivities, besieging of Towns, Plunderings, Profanation of holy places, a scarcity of Horses, or a destructive Murrain amongst them.

Virgo

In the first Decanate of Virgo, it argues the lamentable death, or pitiful end of some certain Prince or Nobleman, and a general ruin or slaughter of men, scarcity of corn and all manner of sustanance fit for men.

In the second Decanate, it designs Famine, Plague, and seditions of mortal men, great drought, and thereby no plentiful crops for Summer corn.

In the third Decanate it pours down vengeance on poor Poets, Painters, or Limners, and men Mercurial, who flourish with excellent understandings, nothing thrives with them, nor are their purses full, it produces Murders, Banishment etc., it imposeth on the vulgar Writers of those times, harsh conceptions, and no esteem of their rude Poems.

Libra

In the first Decanate of Libra, it corrupts the air, begets the Plague, inclines youth to much wantoness, yet straightens provisions, and makes them dear.

In the seond Decanate, it portends the Death of some eminent Prince or Kings, or Nobleman, and for breach of Customs, stirs up Seditions, and designs a Famine.

In the third Decanate, it premonishes of high Controversies amongst the Nobility, and great deteriment in their estates, much prodigality amongst them, and the extirpation of some one family.

Scorpio

In the first Decanate of Scorpio, it moves and raises warlike tumults, murders, dissentions, captivities, and cherishes underhand practices, or plots of Treasons.

In the second Decanate, it argues destruction of some certain King, or person of worth, and declares his mind averse to Armies or wars.

In the third Decanate, it portends the coming of some stranger tyrant, and the drowsy dullness and slothfulness of the former King odious unto all men; sometimes it portends a deposing of the then present Governor or King, or great dislike with him.

Sagittarius

An Eclipse in the first Decanate of Sagittarius, doth manifest most dangerous seditions amongst men, and renders mens minds averse to all manner of accommodations, or Treaties; each man fearing deceit in the man he deals with, or one Prince fearing another will delude him.

In the second Decanate, it portends the Death, or much destruction unto such cattle as naturally bray, and of the bigger sort of any such beasts as are useful for man.

In the last Decanate, it afflicts severall manner of ways Horses, and prejudiceth such Armies as then are on foot, all things and matters go hardly on with the Nobility, who willingly and foolishly undo themselves to no purpose.

Capricorn

In the first Decanate of Capricorn, it imports the unhappy chances attending Great men, and strange casualties unto such; the transmigration, or oft shifting of places of some King, Prince, or person of eminent rank and quality, and it implies the revolt or rebellion of Nobles, and others of meaner quality, viz, of the common people; it imports a covetous Prince or Magistrate, by reason of his oppression, shall cause insurrections.

In the second Decanate, it stirs up the spirits of sworn soldiers against their Commanders in Chief, or against their Emperor, King or Prince, it renders all their endeavours fruitless, and the events thereof unprosperous; it is the forerunner of scarcity of corn, and that many will die for want thereof.

In the third Decanate, it implies the tumultary motion of a King, and induces famine, and shows great poverty unto the Husbandman, bad crops, little hay or grass.

Aquarius

In the first Decante of Aquarius, it affords matter of public sorrow and mourning unto Gentlemen, but comfort to the Country man,

In the second Decanate, Thefts publically countenanced, Robberies, Rapines, Earthquakes, Famine, Monopolies, pilling and poling the people.

In the third Decanate, it tells the death of field cattle and such creatures, it shows great inundations to succeed the Eclipse.

Pisces

In the first Decanate of Pisces, it drains the rivers of their waters, infortunates the sea coasts, and drives fishes far from shore.

In the second Decanate, it designs the death of a famous and excellent man, destruction and waste of fish near the Sea Towns, it imports and Earthquake, some great Churchman questioned and called to account for his knavery.

In the third Decanate, it presages sedition, cruelty, bitterness of spirits, and the inhumanity of soldiers, and also much Controversy amongst Divines, and Lawyers.

The affects of lunar Eclipses when they happen in the several decanates of every sign

Aries

If an Eclipse of the Moon be in the first ten degrees of Aries, she portends that fevers shall be frequent, many houses fired, woods destroyed or cut down and burned, as also a general dryness of air, many caterpillars and destructive vermin appear.

In the second Decanate, a pestilence, and fatality in most diseases, few falling sick that escape.

Taurus

In the first Decanate of Taurus, household cattle are tormented with several unusual diseases i.e. the oxen and horses of the ploughman fall sick and die, and general disease reigns amongst cattle.

In the second Decanate, it points out the death of some Queen, as also a dearth of such seeds as are usually sown, it signifies barreness of the earth to continue during the time the affects of the Eclipses influence.

In the third Decanate, it implies a plague amongst creeping and noxious creatures; and also amongst rats and mice, and such vermin as do most devour the Countrymans grain or corn.

Gemini

In the first ten degrees of Gemini, it threatens incursions and rapines of Enemies; fraudulent Negotiations, many Treaties, violent Petitions, many Missives, and much employment for Scribes and Secretaries.

In the second Decanate, the sudden motion of Armies, and declares mens solicitations and cares, both of private and public affairs; and that Judges will be careful executing Justice.

In the third Decanate, it foretells the death of some famous man, for the most part this man happens to be a Scholar, viz. either a Lawyer or Divine,

Cancer

In the first Decanate of Cancer, it wholly excites mens minds unto War, Treachery, and Apostacy.

In the second Decanate, most bitter and sharp exactions, intolerable assessments, and such like burdens oppress the Commonalty; vulgar tumuks, much harm at sea.

In the third Decanate, it foretells diseases to the female sex, and also sudden, miserable and unexpected deaths unto many; and they of ignoble births, or of the meaner sort of people.

Leo

In the first Decanate of Leo, it denotes a present and unlooked for infirmity to befall unto some great Prince, or the Death of some very much noted Person, usually of the blood of Princes.

In the second Decante, some journey to be undetaken by a King, with a strange mutation and catastrophe in mundane affairs.

In the third Decanate, it swells and animates the dispositions both of the people and the soldiery, so that they run after novelties, desiring new Laws and new Governors.

Virgo

In the first Decanate of Virgo, it declares sicknesses unto Kings, manifold discords and dissentions universally raging amongst men.

In the second Decanate, it prepares destruction and calamities, informs matter against Counsellors, Lawyers, Secretaries, and such like men, for their oppression, bribery, and indirect dealings.

In the third Decanate, it afflicts mankind with many diseases, and intimates scarcity of bread, and all sorts of grain.

Libra
In the first Decanate of Libra, hail, storms, ill weather, turbulent winds, violent tempests, very harmful.

In the second Decanate, a rot amongst pettyfoggers, informers, and such like cattle, they whipped and stripped to purpose.

In the third Decanate, some eminent and noted person dies; the Religious swell in every country, and raise seditions in the Courts of Princes.

Scorpio
In the first Decanate of Scorpio, terrible Thunders, terrible Lightenings, many times Earthquakes, aboundance of destructive creatures in the waters.

In the second Decanate, hot and sharp fevers afflict men, ficcity destroys the Olives, and infects the air.

In the third Decanate, many seditions, murders, and all manner of wretchedness succeeds, mankind oppressed with abundance of obnoxious diseases, and these general.

Sagittarius
In the first Decanate of Sagittarius, many Thiefts and Rapines.

In the second Decanate, Diseases rage against and amongst Horses, Mules etc, the seas troubled with pirates.

In the third Decanate, a Plague follows, and great evils afflict all mankind, consumptions more than ordinary.

Capricorn
In the first Decanate of Capricorn, it moves many slanders and false aspersions against very many men, and declares an untimely death unto some person of worth.

In the second Decanate, uproars very frequent in the Soldiery, oft incursions into neighbour-countries, captivities, plunderings.

In the third Decanate, the death of a King, conspiracies in the People, or Mutinies.

Aquarius
In the first Decanate of Aquarius, it shows averse health to a certain king.

In the second Decanate, it hinders the seed-time.

In the third Decanate, a wonderful change in all affairs.

Pisces

In the first Decanate of Pisces, sorrow to men of religion, and to religious houses.

In the second Decanate, death of some great and illustrious person.

In the third Decanate, threatens robberies and promiscuous assaults and rapines, both on land and on sea.

APPENDIX 2

ECLIPSE LIST FOR THE TWENTIETH CENTURY

The following list shows solar eclipses (SE) in the left-hand column and lunar eclipses (LE) in the right-hand column, given to the nearest degree of longitude in Greenwich Mean Time.

Date	Class	Degree	GMT	Date	Class	Degree	GMT
28.05.1900	SE	07°Gem.	14.50	13.06.1900	LE	22°Sag.	03.39
22.11.1900	SE	30°Sco.	07.18				
18.05.1901	SE	27°Tau.	05.38				
11.11.1901	SE	18°Sco.	07.35	27.10.1901	LE	04°Tau.	15.08
08.04.1902	SE	18°Ari.	13.51	22.04.1902	LE	02°Sco.	18.50
31.10.1902	SE	07°Sco.	08.14	17.10.1902	LE	23°Ari.	06.02
29.03.1903	SE	07°Ari.	01.27	12.04.1903	LE	21°Lib.	00.19
21.09.1903	SE	27°Vir.	04.31	06.10.1903	LE	12°Ari.	15.24
17.03.1904	SE	26°Pis.	05.40				
09.09.1904	SE	17°Vir.	20.44				
06.03.1905	SE	15°Pis.	05.20	19.02.1905	LE	01°Vir.	18.52
30.08.1905	SE	06°Vir.	13.14	15.08.1905	LE	22°Aqu.	03.33
23.03.1906	SE	04°Pis.	07.58	09.02.1906	LE	20°Leo	07.47
21.07.1906	SE	28°Can.	13.00	04.08.1906	LE	11°Aqu.	13.00
20.08.1906	SE	26°Leo	01.28				
14.01.1907	SE	23°Cap.	05.57	29.01.1907	LE	09°Leo	13.46
10.07.1907	SE	17°Can.	15.17	25.07.1907	LE	01°Aqu.	04.30
03.01.1908	SE	12°Cap.	21.44				
28.06.1908	SE	07°Can.	16.32				
23.12.1908	SE	01°Cap.	11.50				
17.06.1909	SE	26°Gem.	23.29	04.06.1909	LE	13°Sag.	01.25

Date	Class	Degree	GMT	Date	Class	Degree	GMT
12.12.1909	SE	20°Sag.	19.59	27.11.1909	LE	04°Gem.	08.52
09.05.1910	SE	18°Tau.	05.33	24.05.1910	LE	02°Sag.	05.39
02.11.1910	SE	09°Sco.	01.57	17.11.1910	LE	24°Tau.	00.26
28.04.1911	SE	07°Tau.	22.25				
22.10.1911	SE	28°Lib.	04.10				
17.04.1912	SE	27°Ari.	11.41	01.04.1912	LE	12°Lib.	22.05
10.10.1912	SE	17°Lib.	13.41	26.09.1912	LE	03°Ari.	11.35
06.04.1913	SE	16°Ari.	17.49	22.03.1913	LE	01°Lib.	11.56
31.08.1913	SE	08°Vir.	20.39	15.09.1913	LE	22°Pis.	12.47
30.09.1913	SE	06°Lib.	04.57				
25.02.1914	SE	06°Pis.	00.03	12.03.1914	LE	21°Vir.	04.19
21.08.1914	SE	28°Leo	12.27	04.09.1914	LE	11°Pis.	14.02
14.02.1915	SE	24°Aqu.	04.32				
10.08.1915	SE	17°Leo	22.53				
03.02.1916	SE	14°Aqu.	16.06	20.01.1916	LE	29°Can.	08.30
30.07.1916	SE	07°Leo	02.16	15.07.1916	LE	22°Cap.	04.41
24.12.1916	SE	03°Cap.	20.32				
23.01.1917	SE	03°Aqu.	07.40	08.01.1917	LE	17°Can.	07.42
19.06.1917	SE	28°Gem.	13.03	04.07.1917	LE	12°Cap.	21.41
19.07.1917	SE	26°Can.	03.01	28.12.1917	LE	06°Can.	09.52
14.12.1917	SE	22°Sag.	09.18				
08.06.1918	SE	17°Gem.	22.03	24.06.1918	LE	02°Cap.	10.39
03.12.1918	SE	11°Sag.	15.20				
29.05.1919	SE	07°Gem.	13.13	07.11.1919	LE	15°Tau.	23.36
22.11.1919	SE	29°Sco.	15.20				
18.05.1920	SE	27°Tau.	06.26	03.05.1920	LE	12°Sco.	01.48
10.11.1920	SE	18°Sco.	16.06	27.10.1920	LE	04°Tau.	14.10
08.04.1921	SE	18°Ari.	09.06	22.04.1921	LE	02°Sco.	07.49
01.10.1921	SE	08°Lib.	12.27	16.10.1921	LE	23°Ari.	23.01
28.03.1922	SE	07°Ari.	13.04				
21.09.1922	SE	27°Vir.	04.39				
17.03.1923	SE	26°Pis.	12.52	03.03.1923	LE	12°Vir.	03.24
10.09.1923	SE	17°Vir.	20.54	26.08.1923	LE	02°Pic.	10.31
05.03.1924	SE	15°Pis.	15.59	20.02.1924	LE	01°Vir.	16.08
31.07.1924	SE	08°Leo	19.43	14.08.1924	LE	22°Aqu.	20.20
30.08.1924	SE	07°Vir.	08.38				
24.01.1925	SE	04°Aqu.	14.46	08.02.1925	LE	20°Leo	21.50
20.07.1925	SE	28°Can.	21.41	04.08.1925	LE	12°Aqu.	12.00
14.01.1926	SE	23°Cap.	06.36				
09.07.1926	SE	17°Can.	23.07				
03.01.1927	SE	12°Cap.	20.29	15.06.1927	LE	23°Sag.	08.20
29.06.1927	SE	07°Can.	06.33	08.12.1927	LE	16°Gem.	17.33
24.12.1927	SE	01°Cap.	04.14				
19.05.1928	SE	28°Tau.	13.15	03.06.1928	LE	13°Sag.	12.14
17.06.1928	SE	26°Gem.	20.43	27.11.1928	LE	05°Gem.	09.07

Date	Class	Degree	GMT	Date	Class	Degree	GMT
12.11.1928	SE	20°Sco.	09.36				
09.05.1929	SE	18°Tau.	06.08				
01.11.1929	SE	09°Sco.	12.02				
28.04.1930	SE	08°Tau.	19.09	13.04.1930	LE	23°Lib.	05.50
21.10.1930	SE	28°Lib.	21.49	07.10.1930	LE	14°Ari.	18.57
18.04.1931	SE	27°Ari.	01.01	02.04.1931	LE	12°Lib.	20.06
12.09.1931	SE	18°Vir.	04.27	26.09.1931	LE	03°Ari.	19.46
11.10.1931	SE	17°Lib.	13.07				
07.03.1932	SE	17°Pis.	07.45	22.03.1932	LE	02°Lib.	12.38
31.08.1932	SE	08°Vir.	19.55	14.09.1932	LE	22°Pis.	21.07
24.02.1933	SE	06°Pis.	12.45				
21.08.1933	SE	28°Leo	05.49				
14.02.1934	SE	25°Aqu.	00.44	30.01.1934	LE	10°Leo	16.32
10.08.1934	SE	17°Leo	08.47	26.07.1934	LE	03°Aqu.	12.10
05.01.1935	SE	14°Cap.	05.21	19.01.1935	LE	29°Can.	15.46
03.02.1935	SE	14°Aqu.	16.28	16.07.1935	LE	23°Cap.	05.01
30.06.1935	SE	08°Can.	19.46				
30.07.1935	SE	06°Leo	09.34				
25.12.1935	SE	03°Cap.	17.51				
19.06.1936	SE	28°Gem.	05.15	08.01.1936	LE	17°Can.	18.16
13.12.1936	SE	22°Sag.	23.26	04.07.1936	LE	13°Cap.	17.36
08.06.1937	SE	18°Gem.	20.44	18.11.1937	LE	26°Tau.	08.11
02.12.1937	SE	10°Sag.	23.12				
29.05.1938	SE	08°Gem.	14.01	14.05.1938	LE	23°Sco.	08.40
22.11.1938	SE	29°Sco.	00.06	07.11.1938	LE	15°Tau.	22.25
19.04.1939	SE	29°Ari.	16.36	03.05.1939	LE	12°Sco.	15.16
12.10.1939	SE	19°Lib.	20.31	28.10.1939	LE	04°Tau.	06.43
07.04.1940	SE	18°Ari.	20.20				
01.10.1940	SE	08°Lib.	12.42				
27.03.1941	SE	07°Ari.	20.14	13.03.1941	LE	23°Vir.	11.48
21.09.1941	SE	28°Vir.	04.39	05.09.1941	LE	13°Pis.	17.37
16.03.1942	SE	26°Pis.	23.51	03.03.1942	LE	12°Vir.	00.21
12.08.1942	SE	19°Leo	02.29	26.08.1942	LE	02°Pis.	03.47
10.09.1942	SE	17°Vir.	15.54				
04.02.1943	SE	15°Aug.	23.30	20.02.1943	LE	01°Vir.	05.46
01.08.1943	SE	08°Leo	04.08	15.08.1943	LE	22°Aqu.	19.35
25.01.1944	SE	05°Aqu.	15.25				
20.07.1944	SE	27°Can.	05.44				
14.01.1945	SE	24°Cap.	05.08	25.06.1945	LE	04°Cap.	15.09
09.07.1945	SE	17°Can.	13.36	19.12.1945	LE	27°Gem.	02.18
03.01.1946	SE	13°Cap.	12.31	14.06.1946	LE	23°Sag.	18.43
30.05.1946	SE	09°Gem.	20.51	08.12.1946	LE	16°Gem.	17.53
29.06.1946	SE	07°Can.	04.07				
23.11.1946	SE	01°Sag.	17.25				
20.05.1947	SE	29°Tau.	13.44	03.06.1947	LE	12°Sag.	19.28

Date	Class	Degree	GMT	Date	Class	Degree	GMT
12.11.1947	SE	20°Sco.	20.02				
09.05.1948	SE	18°Tau.	02.31	23.04.1948	LE	03°Sco	13.30
01.11.1948	SE	09°Sco.	06.04				
28.04.1949	SE	08°Tau.	08.03	13.04.1949	LE	23°Lib.	04.09
21.10.1949	SE	28°Lib.	21.24	07.10.1949	LE	14°Ari.	02.54
18.03.1950	SE	28°Pis.	15.21	02.04.1950	LE	13°Lib.	20.50
12.09.1950	SE	19°Vir.'	03.30	26.09.1950	LE	03°Ari.	04.22
07.03.1951	SE	16°Pis.	20.51				
01.09.1951	SE	08°Vir.	12.51				
25.02.1952	SE	06°Pis.	09.17	11.02.1952	LE	21°Leo	00.29
20.08.1952	SE	28°Leo	15.22	05.08.1952	LE	13°Aqu.	19.41
14.02.1953	SE	25°Aqu.	01.11	29.01.1953	LE	10°Leo	23.45
11.07.1953	SE	19°Can.	02.29	26.07.1953	LE	03°Aqu.	12.21
09.08.1953	SE	17°Leo	16.12				
05.01.1954	SE	14°Cap.	02.22	19.01.1954	LE	29°Can.	02.38
30.06.1954	SE	08°Can.	12.26	16.07.1954	LE	23°Cap.	00.30
27.09.1954	SE	03°Lib.	00.51				
20.06.1955	SE	28°Gem.	04.13	29.11.1955	LE	07°Gem.	16.52
14.12.1955	SE	22°Sag.	07.08				
08.06.1956	SE	18°Gem.	21.30	24.05.1956	LE	03°Sag.	15.27
02.12.1956	SE	10°Sag.	08.13	18.11.1956	LE	26°Tau.	06.45
29.04.1957	SE	09°Tau.	23.54	13.05.1957	LE	23°Sco.	22.35
23.10.1957	SE	30°Lib.	04.44	07.11.1957	LE	15°Tau.	14.33
19.04.1958	SE	29°Ari.	03.24	03.05.1958	LE	13°Sco.	12.24
12.10.1958	SE	19°Lib.	20.54				
08.04.1959	SE	18°Ari.	03.30	24.03.1959	LE	03°Lib.	20.03
02.10.1959	SE	09°Lib.	12.32				
27.03.1960	SE	07°Ari.	07.38	13.03.1960	LE	23°Vir.	08.27
20.09.1960	SE	27°Vir.	23.14	05.09.1960	LE	13°Pis.	11.19
15.02.1961	SE	27°Aqu.	08.11	02.03.1961	LE	12°Vir.	13.35
11.08.1961	SE	19°Leo	10.37	26.08.1961	LE	03°Pis.	03.14
05.02.1962	SE	16°Aqu.	00.11				
31.07.1962	SE	08°Leo	12.25				
25.01.1963	SE	05°Aqu.	13.43	06.07.1963	LE	14°Cap.	21.56
20.07.1963	SE	27°Can.	20.43	30.12.1963	LE	08°Can.	11.05
13.01.1964	SE	24°Cap.	20.45	25.06.1964	LE	04°Cap.	01.09
10.06.1964	SE	19°Gem.	04.23	19.12.1964	LE	27°Gem.	02.43
09.07.1964	SE	17°Can.	11.32				
04.12.1964	SE	12°Sag.	01.19				
30.05.1965	SE	09°Gem.	21.13	14.06.1965	LE	23°Sag.	02.01
23.11.1965	SE	01°Sag.	04.11				
20.05.1966	SE	29°Tau.	09.43				
12.11.1966	SE	20°Sco.	14.28				
09.05.1967	SE	18°Tau.	14.56	24.04.1967	LE	04°Sco.	12.05

Date	Class	Degree	GMT	Date	Class	Degree	GMT
02.11.1967	SE	09°Sco.	05.49	18.10.1967	LE	24°Ari.	10.12
28.03.1968	SE	08°Ari.	22.49	13.04.1968	LE	23°Lib.	04.53
22.09.1968	SE	30°Vir.	11.09	06.10.1968	LE	13°Ari.	11.47
18.03.1969	SE	28°Pis.	04.52				
11.09.1969	SE	19°Vir.	19.57				
07.03.1970	SE	17°Pis.	17.44	21.02.1970	LE	02°Vir.	08.20
31.08.1970	SE	08°Vir.	22.02	17.08.1970	LE	24°Aqu.	03.16
25.02.1971	SE	06°Pis.	09.49	10.02.1971	LE	21°Leo	07.42
22.07.1971	SE	29°Can.	09.16	06.08.1971	LE	14°Aqu.	19.43
20.08.1971	SE	27°Leo	22.55				
16.01.1972	SE	25°Cap.	10.53	30.01.1972	LE	10°Leo	10.59
10.07.1972	SE	19°Can.	19.40	26.07.1972	LE	03°Aqu.	07.24
04.01.1973	SE	14°Cap.	15.43	10.12.1973	LE	18°Gem.	01.36
30.06.1973	SE	09°Can.	11.40				
24.12.1973	SE	03°Cap.	15.08				
20.06.1974	SE	29°Gem.	04.56	04.06.1974	LE	14°Sag.	22.11
13.12.1974	SE	21°Sag.	16.26	29.11.1974	LE	07°Gem.	15.11
11.05.1975	SE	20°Tau.	07.06	25.05.1975	LE	03°Sag.	05.52
03.11.1975	SE	10°Sco.	13.07	18.11.1975	LE	26°Tau.	22.29
29.04.1976	SE	09°Tau.	10.21	13.05.1976	LE	23°Sco.	20.05
23.10.1976	SE	30°Lib.	05.11				
18.04.1977	SE	28°Ari.	10.36	04.04.1977	LE	14°Lib.	04.10
12.10.1977	SE	19°Lib.	20.32				
07.04.1978	SE	17°Ari.	15.16	24.03.1978	LE	04°Lib.	16.21
02.10.1978	SE	09°Lib.	06.43	16.09.1978	LE	24°Pis.	19.02
26.02.1979	SE	07°Pis.	16.46	13.03.1979	LE	23°Vir.	21.15
22.08.1979	SE	29°Leo	17.11	06.09.1979	LE	13°Pis.	11.00
16.02.1980	SE	27°Aqu.	08.53				
10.08.1980	SE	18°Leo	19.11				
04.02.1981	SE	16°Aqu.	22.15	17.07.1981	LE	25°Cap.	04.40
31.07.1981	SE	08°Leo	03.54				
25.01.1982	SE	05°Aqu.	04.57	09.01.1982	LE	20°Can.	19.54
21.06.1982	SE	30°Gem.	11.53	06.07.1982	LE	14°Cap.	07.33
20.07.1982	SE	28°Can.	18.58	30.12.1982	LE	08°Can.	11.34
15.12.1982	SE	23°Sag.	09.20				
11.06.1983	SE	20°Gem.	04.39	25.06.1983	LE	03°Cap.	08.33
04.12.1983	SE	12°Sag.	12.27				
30.05.1984	SE	09°Gem.	16.50				
22.11.1984	SE	01°Sag.	22.58				
19.05.1985	SE	29°Tau.	21.42	04.05.1985	LE	14°Sco.	19.54
12.11.1985	SE	20°Sco.	14.22	28.10.1985	LE	05°Tau.	17.39
09.04.1986	SE	19°Ari.	06.09	24.04.1986	LE	04°Sco.	12.48
03.10.1986	SE	10°Lib.	18.56	17.10.1986	LE	24°Ari.	19.23
29.03.1987	SE	08°Ari.	12.47	07.10.1987	LE	13°Ari.	04.13

Date	Class	Degree	GMT	Date	Class	Degree	GMT
23.09.1987	SE	30°Vir.	03.09				
18.03.1988	SE	28°Pis.	02.03	27.08.1988	LE	04°Pis.	10.57
11.09.1988	SE	19°Vir.	04.51				
07.03.1989	SE	17°Pis.	18.20	20.02.1989	LE	02°Vir.	15.33
31.08.1989	SE	08°Vir.	05.46	17.08.1989	LE	24°Aqu.	03.08
26.01.1990	SE	07°Aqu.	19.21	09.02.1990	LE	21°Leo	19.17
22.07.1990	SE	29°Can.	02.55	06.08.1990	LE	14°Aqu.	14.21
15.01.1991	SE	25°Cap.	23.51	21.12.1991	LE	29°Gem.	10.25
11.07.1991	SE	19°Can.	19.07				
04.01.1992	SE	14°Cap.	23.11	15.06.1992	LE	24°Sag.	04.52
30.06.1992	SE	09°Can.	12.19	09.12.1992	LE	18°Gem.	23.43
24.12.1992	SE	02°Cap.	00.44				
21.05.1993	SE	01°Gem.	14.08	04.06.1993	LE	14°Sag.	13.03
13.11.1993	SE	22°Sco.	21.36	29.11.1993	LE	07°Gem.	06.32
10.05.1994	SE	20°Tau.	17.08	25.05.1994	LE	04°Sag.	03.40
03.11.1994	SE	11°Sco.	13.38				
29.04.1995	SE	09°Tau.	17.38	15.04.1995	LE	25°Lib.	12.10
24.10.1995	SE	01°Sco.	04.38				
17.04.1996	SE	28°Ari.	22.50	04.04.1996	LE	15°Lib.	00.08
12.10.1996	SE	20°Lib.	14.16	27.09.1996	LE	04°Ari.	02.52
09.03.1997	SE	19°Pis.	01.16	24.03.1997	LE	04°Lib.	04.47
01.09.1997	SE	10°Vir.	23.53	16.09.1997	LE	24°Pis.	18.52
26.02.1998	SE	08°Pic.	17.27				
22.08.1998	SE	29°Leo	02.04				
16.02.1999	SE	27°Aqu.	06.40	28.07.1999	LE	05°Aqu.	11.26
11.08.1999	SE	18°Leo	11.11				
05.02.2000	SE	16°Aqu.	13.04	21.01.2000	LE	00°Leo	04.41
01.07.2000	SE	10°Can.	19.21	16.07.2000	LE	24°Cap.	13.58
31.07.2000	SE	08°Leo	02.27				
25.12.2000	SE	04°Cap.	17.23				

SELECT BIBLIOGRAPHY

The Encyclopedia of Military History, Jane's Publishing Co. (London,1980).

The Middle East and North Africa 1981-82, Europa Publications (London, 1986).

The Observer, The Worst Accident in the World, Pan Books (London, 1986).

Baigent, Campion and Harvey, *Mundane Astrology*, Aquarian Press (Wellingborough, 1984).

Carter, Charles, *An Introduction to Political Astrology*, L.N. Fowler & Co. (Romford, 1951).

Crowder, Michael, *The Story of Nigeria*, Faber and Faber (London, ?).

Doane, Doris Chase, *Horoscopes of the US Presidents*, Professional Astrologers Inc. (Hollywoood, 1971).

Eaton, John P., and Haas, Charles A., *Titanic — Destination Disaster*, Patrick Stephens (Wellingborough, 1987).

Forsyth, Frederick, *The Biafra Story*, Severn House (London, 1983).

Frazer, Antonia, *The Kings and Queens of England*, Weidenfeld & Nicholson (London, 1975).

Jain, Manik Chand, *Mundane Astrology*, Sangar Publications (New Delhi, 1973).

Longford, Elizabeth, *Winston Churchill*, Panther Books, Granada Publishing (London, 1978).

McCraig, Hugh, *The 200 Year Ephemeris*, Macoy Publishing Co. (Richmond, Virginia, 1949).

Ottewell, Guy, *The Astronomical Companion*, pub. by author at the Dept. of Physics, Furman University, Greenville, South Carolina (1979).

Pedler, Frederick, *Main Current of West African History 1940-1978*, Macmillian Press (London, ?).

Ptolemy, *Tetrabiblos*, W. Foulsham & Co. (London 1917)..

Robson, Vivian, *Fixed Stars and Constellations in Astrology*, Aquarian Press (Wellingborough, 1969).

Sepharial, *Eclipses in Theory and Practice*, W. Foulsham & Co. (Slough, ?).

Shirer, William, L., *The Rise and Fall of the Third Reich*, Pan Books (London, 1964).

INDEX